TRUST, DEMOCRACY, AND MULTICULTURAL CHALLENGES

TRUST, DEMOCRACY, AND MULTICULTURAL CHALLENGES

PATTI TAMARA LENARD

THE PENNSYLVANIA STATE UNIVERSITY PRESS
UNIVERSITY PARK, PENNSYLVANIA

Library of Congress Cataloging-in-Publication Data
Lenard, Patti Tamara, 1975-
Trust, democracy, and multicultural challenges / Patti
Tamara Lenard.
p.   cm.
Includes bibliographical references and index.
Summary: "Examines the potential for distrust in an
environment of ethnocultural diversity arising from
increasing rates of immigration, and its implications for a
democratic society. Incorporates democratic theory,
multiculturalism theory, and migration theory"—Provided
by publisher.
ISBN 978-0-271-05253-3 (cloth : alk. paper)
ISBN 978-0-271-05254-0 (pbk. : alk. paper)
1. Democracy—Social aspects.
2. Multiculturalism.
I. Title.

JC423.L464 2012
306.2—dc23
2011034411

CONTENTS

———————

ACKNOWLEDGMENTS

This book has its origins in two distinct incidents. One is a lecture I attended given by Dr. Charles Pentland at Queen's University on the structure of the United Nations trusteeship in Kosovo. His lecture prompted me to consider the phenomenon of trust and the institutional structures that can support trusting relations among citizens. Another is a conversation I had long ago with Angela Kaida in which we both learned that we shared a key experience as children of immigrants: a moment in which an adolescent friend pointed out something we had never before noticed, that our parents have "weird accents" in English. My intellectual preoccupations with both trust and the immigrant experience have, after many years, culminated in the arguments I make in this book.

The road from these incidents to this book is of course long, and I owe thanks to many people for friendship and intellectual stimulation of all kinds.

Although this book is a distant relative of the DPhil that preceded it, the original ideas were crafted under the careful supervision of David Miller at Nuffield College, Oxford University. Several of the individual chapters were sharpened (and one abandoned!) as a result of discussions with my thoughtful and engaged external readers, Anne Phillips and Mark Philp. Avigail Eisenberg and Mathew Festenstein attentively reviewed the original manuscript for Penn State Press and offered invaluable comments, for which I and the final manuscript are deeply appreciative.

Zofia Stemplowska and Jacob J. Krich read the near-final version of the manuscript and offered careful and incisive suggestions that improved the book immensely. Jacob is married to me, and so may have been contractually obligated to carry out this task (I can't say for sure because our marriage contract is in a language I do not speak or read), but no such contract obligated Zofia. I am beyond lucky to have benefited from her careful criticism (all trenchant), her thoughtful suggestions (all but one taken), and her friendship (valued immensely).

Avia Pasternak and Terry Macdonald, close friends with whom many of the ideas in this book have been discussed at great length and with extraordinary generosity of spirit, both stepped in at crisis moments. Avia read and immeasurably improved a chapter with her comments. Many of the ideas that form the foundation of the book were formulated over discussions with Terry in the years we were students, and flatmates, at Nuffield College. She also read the entire manuscript and offered encouragement at the precise moment that I needed someone to tell me to press on.

Others have read or commented on individual chapters, and I hope the final product shows that I have listened to them carefully: Clare Chambers, Nicholas Cheeseman, Joshua Cherniss, Elizabeth Fraser, Michael Freeden, Andrew Hurrell, Jonathan Quong, Tiziana Torresi, and Mark Warren. I have presented my work at many conferences, too many to list here, but it is essential that I thank the participants of the Nuffield Political Theory Workshop conducted between 2001 and 2004, nearly all of whom engaged critically and seriously with my work.

Discussions with several scholars have been instrumental in shaping how I think about trust: Barbara Arneil, who generously shared parts of an unpublished manuscript with me, as well as Keith Banting, Chris Bertram, Avigail Eisenberg, Richard Johnston, Will Kymlicka, Finn Spicer, and Natalia Letki. I owe special thanks to Stuart Soroka, with whom I co-organized a workshop at Nuffield titled "Conceptualizing Trust: Interdisciplinary Perspectives." Stuart was instrumental in persuading me that a solely philosophical approach to the concept and phenomenon of trust would be inadequate, and his pressure to consider the concept more broadly is reflected in the first chapter in particular.

I prepared the initial manuscript over four wonderful years I spent as a lecturer in the Committee on Degrees in Social Studies at Harvard University, and I wish to thank several of my colleagues there for creating a collegial and supportive environment in which to work: Kate Anable, Anya Bernstein, Bo-Mi Choi, Noah Dauber, Michael Frazer, Glyn Morgan, Nicole Newendorp, Stefan-Bird Pollan, Thomas Ponniah, Verity Smith, and Scott Staring. I owe a special thanks to David Meskill, who guided me through the process of preparing and submitting a book proposal.

I completed the manuscript as a member of the Graduate School of Public and International Affairs at the University of Ottawa, and I wish to say publicly that it is a pleasure to be part of such a collegial and dynamic group of scholars and students. I owe a special thanks to my close friend and collaborator, Christine Straehle, whose good food, good cheer, and good ideas have propelled this manuscript (and several others) to completion.

The staff at Penn State Press are truly exceptional, and it is has been a pleasure to work with them. I would like especially to thank Sandy Thatcher, who first expressed interest in the manuscript, for his encouragement throughout the review process (and for many discussions of the lot of the master swimmer), and Kendra Boileau for supporting the manuscript through to its publication.

I'd like to thank several people personally as well. Margaret Moore, my first-ever professor of political theory, the supervisor of my undergraduate thesis, and now my friend and collaborator, has (among many other things) generously taken on the job of guiding me through the vagaries of professional academic life, for which I am ongoingly grateful. Angela Kaida, my closest friend since my first day of university, has confidence in me that I don't deserve, a confidence that is rivaled by the confidence I have in her, which in her case is richly deserved. My parents, John and Harriet Lenard, have offered unwavering encouragement to all of my intellectual decisions. Their pride in and love for me has been a source of support on which I have constantly relied and have always appreciated as one of my greatest resources.

And finally, my heart is racing as I try, and fail, to find a way to express the depth of my thanks to Jacob J. Krich. He is a perfect partner to me in every way. There is no idea in this book that hasn't been the source of extensive discussion with him. He once said to me that he wanted to be one of those spouses who can say he's read his partner's entire book. He can certainly say that—he's read many chapters more than once—and he can also say that he is the only person (myself included) who has *never* tired of discussing the ideas that I present here. It is in no way an exaggeration to note that this book would have never seen the light of day if it hadn't been for Jacob's support, enthusiasm, and love, for which I am grateful beyond words.

Parts of chapters 2 and 3 appeared originally in a somewhat different version as "Trust Your Compatriots, But Count Your Change: The Roles of Trust, Mistrust, and Distrust in Democracy," in *Political Studies* 56, no. 2 (2008): 312–32, reprinted here with the permission of John Wiley & Sons. Part of chapter 4 appeared originally in a somewhat different version as "Shared Public Culture: A Reliable Source of Trust," in *Contemporary Political Theory*, no. 6 (2007): 385–404, reprinted here with the permission of Palgrave Macmillan.

INTRODUCTION:
TRUST, DEMOCRACY, AND MULTICULTURAL CHALLENGES

No single incident prompted a British magazine cover to question whether Britain is "too diverse." No individual moment in Dutch politics created an environment in which a new book about immigration to the Netherlands could plausibly be titled *When Ways of Life Collide.* No particular event prompted some Americans to wonder if, after all, they should adopt English as an official language so as to encourage a greater degree, and rate, of immigrant assimilation. Yet it is clear that tensions among religious and cultural minorities, as they struggle with whether to integrate (or not) into Western multicultural democracies, have been rising for several years.[1] As this book will argue, these tensions and struggles can best be understood and evaluated through the lenses of *trust, distrust,* and *mistrust.*

Such tensions were evident in recent scuffles over whether, for example, to allow Muslim girls to participate in a variety of sports events while wearing the Muslim headscarf. In early 2007, five Muslim girls wearing headscarves were forced to withdraw from a Canadian taekwondo tournament in response to a ruling by tournament officials that, since the *hijab* is not permitted according to World Taekwondo Federation rules, the girls could not compete while wearing one. Similarly, in Quebec, Muslim girls were forced to withdraw from a soccer competition—the *hijab,* officials said, was not permitted, according to a FIFA rule that bans equipment and clothing that are dangerous to oneself and others. In both cases, officials contended the rulings were made in the spirit of safety: even though tucked under a helmet in taekwondo, and even though FIFA's own website at the time depicted images of women players wearing the *hijab,* the danger that the *hijab* could become loose and then be yanked in such a way as to seriously injure the girls' necks justified the ban. In both cases, advocates for the Muslim girls cried discrimination. A spokesperson for the Canadian Council of American-Islamic Relations argued that "this recent fixation on the *hijab* is only serving to marginalize Muslim women who wish to participate in athletic activity."[2]

This fixation on the *hijab* has also propelled Lisa Valentine to a certain kind of fame. Valentine, who accompanied her nephew as he appeared to defend himself against a traffic citation, was prevented from entering a Georgia courtroom because she refused to remove her headscarf. She was charged with contempt of court on the grounds that court regulations prohibited the wearing of head coverings of any kind, and was ordered to spend ten days in jail as a consequence (she did not ultimately do jail time). In response to the incident, Valentine reported that she felt "stripped of my civil, my human rights."[3] Faiza Silmi felt similarly when her application for French citizenship was denied on the grounds that her form of dress—in particular, the *niqab*, a face-covering veil that, in the words of the French minister for urban affairs (herself a practicing Muslim), is best described as a "prison" or a "straightjacket"— displayed her apparent commitment to a radical form of Islam that is incompatible with broader French republican ideals. She was therefore denied French citizenship on the grounds of "insufficient assimilation" into France. In an interview, Silmi asked the broader French public, the majority of whom claimed to support the court's decision, about her right to religious freedom: "Yes, I am a practicing Muslim, I am orthodox. But is that not my right?"[4] The appeals court concluded that she was not in fact entitled to this right, or at least that if she was, it didn't protect her from the requirement that her manner of public dress reflect a more obvious assimilation into French norms and values.

As these examples illustrate, whether the practices of religious and cultural minorities should be accommodated in liberal democracies is a source of ongoing public debate. These issues are only likely to increase as global migration, and the consequent diversity of liberal democracies, increases; they are issues that liberal democracies must face as they develop and modify the conditions under which increasingly diverse communities can live together peacefully, that is, under conditions of inclusive and generalized *trust*. Trust, I will argue, is of central importance in generating an inclusive, participatory, and efficient democratic politics, not least in situations where cultural practices are contested. Without trust, cultural and religious minorities will increasingly be the victims of discrimination, and so will fail to extend fellow citizens and political authorities the trust that is essential to securing stable multicultural democracies over time. Moreover, in the absence of trust between members of cultural minorities and cultural majorities, the majority may remain unwilling to consider the merits of permitting or banning contested practices, and legitimate compromise may never be reached. The discrimination faced by cultural minorities is often a consequence of a lack of trust in one direction, that is, from majority to minority; the consequence of this discrimination is equally a lack of trust in the other direction, that is, from minority to majority.

Across Western democracies, Muslims are increasingly singled out for challenging the models of accommodation and assimilation traditionally adopted in Western democratic communities.[5] To take one emblematic example, in an attempt to forestall demands to accommodate in the first place, a small town in Quebec declared a set of rules, or "standards," by which potential immigrants to their town must abide. Public stoning of women would not be permitted, nor would burning them alive or throwing acid on them. In explanation, a Hérouxville city councilor noted that the standards were not adopted in the face of an influx of immigrants—Hérouxville's thirteen thousand residents included, at the time, only one Caribbean family and a Haitian boy adopted by a local couple. Rather, he explained, the standards were essential because "we have to ensure that people who settle here are happy . . . we are not racists. We invite people from all nationalities, all languages, all sexual orientations, whatever, to come live with us, but we want them to know ahead of time how we live."[6] Muslim leaders across Canada were unsurprisingly incensed by the news of these standards. Salam Elmenyawi, president of the Muslim Council of Montreal, expressed anger: "I was shocked and insulted to see these kinds of false stereotypes and ignorance about Islam and our religion."[7] Measures like these, which deliberately portray false stereotypes and conjure up dangers that do not exist, are unfortunately increasingly widespread. As of March 2011, for example, thirteen American states had introduced or passed bills aimed at explicitly or implicitly protecting against the alleged incursion of Sharia law in American courts. According to a Texas state representative, women in the United States should fear "creeping sharia law" that threatens to strip them of their rights. The worry, apparently, is that courts will be asked in their rulings to respect Sharia rather than American law.[8]

In these cases Muslims are predictably and rightly outraged, *not* from the suggestion that newcomers should expect to integrate into a national culture, and *not* from the suggestion that newcomers should be subject to the legal authority of the state they join, but rather from a public portrayal of a deliberately insulting and inaccurate account of Islam, an account that the vast majority of

Muslims would not recognize as their own. Portraying Islam as a threat that we must guard against inevitably creates an environment in which trust between newcomers and the host society will prove difficult to build.

In response to the apparent integration challenges posed by Muslim newcomers, many European nations have moved toward adopting more robust citizenship integration regimes.[9] For example, the Netherlands has been at the center of controversy in its attempts to implement a civic integration regime that includes two citizenship tests, one of which must be passed prior to immigration, solely for immigrants hailing from non-Western countries. This first test demands the prior viewing of a video titled "Coming to the Netherlands," which controversially includes images of homosexual men kissing and female nudity, both of which are offensive to members of the Muslim faith. Those who defend it suggest that the capacity of individuals to pass the test is important to Dutch society: "it is in the interest of Dutch society" that newcomers successfully pass this test, said immigration minister Rita Verdonk.[10] Yet advocates on behalf of immigrants object that the test is discriminatory and, moreover, deliberately offensive. It is clearly targeted at Muslims who, some Dutch believe, are increasingly demonstrating that they are unable to adopt the secular norms that characterize Dutch society. Says a community activist who hails from Turkey: "They [Dutch officials] know that according to Islam, nudity and homosexuality are taboo. They know the feelings of Muslims on this subject. So, indirectly, they are saying that we are not welcome."[11] It is not that receiving countries are obligated to throw down a welcome mat in order to ensure that newcomers feel comfortable in their new environment, yet the apparently deliberate attempts to insult and offend newcomers do set a tone suggesting that newcomers can expect derision and rejection of customs associated with their religious and cultural communities, and that until these customs are discarded, newcomers will not be extended the trust that ought to flow between members of a democratic political community.[12]

The tensions reflected in the incidents reported above are not isolated to immigrant groups, nor are they restricted to Muslims. The support extended to the standards by some Québécois—one supporter of Hérouxville's standards announced "at last, someone is standing up [to religious and cultural groups] instead of prostrating themselves like certain ministers, judges, executives, and companies"[13]—is motivated by the same worries that are offered to justify a series of anti-Hispanic measures adopted across the United States. A recent law passed in Arizona bans the teaching of ethnic studies on the grounds that these classes discourage the integration of Hispanic students into the wider American society and encourages them instead to "resent or hate other races."[14] Several small towns in the United States have banned the flying of foreign flags; others have required that any public display of a foreign flag be accompanied by an even larger American flag. A member of the town board in one of these communities explained: "All of the illegal alien protestors are waving Mexican flags, and we just got tired of it. . . . This is the United States, and the Stars and Stripes should fly supreme."[15]

Attempts to formally deny the right of governments to provide services to citizens in languages other than English are ongoing. In 2009, for example, residents of Nashville, Tennessee, where 14 percent of the population does not speak English at home, just barely (by 53–47 percent) voted against a proposition that would have banned the provision of services to residents in languages other than English. At its best, the movement for the proposition highlights the importance of learning English as a path to full integration. At its worst, however, it translates into a virulent racism against immigrants who apparently display an unwillingness to learn English, a racism that is justified by their apparent threat to American public culture more broadly. Permitting, indeed encouraging, public officials to provide essential information in languages other than English, say these advocates, encourages fractionalization and ghettoization and therefore prevents the emergence of a cohesive American identity. Instead, English should be adopted as a national language as a first step toward ensuring that newcomers cannot resist integration by conducting their lives wholly in their native language. Similarly across Europe, political actors are focusing on the linguistic competence of newcomers, who must increasingly pass challenging language tests to acquire citizenship and, in some cases, the right to enter the territory as a legal migrant in the first place.[16]

The debates about reasonable accommodation of immigrant minorities, about whether to adopt English-only regulations, and about the value of citizenship tests in Europe stem from the *absence of trust*—a trust that should, in principle, emerge from shared values and norms, and that *must* underpin democratic, multicultural nations. The concern is that the trust necessary to sustain a commitment to shared democratic institutions, and to the cooperation and reciprocity that they secure, is under threat in the presence of ethnocultural diversity. In the face of increases in ethnocultural diversity (and, in some cases, of increases in the *salience* of ethnocultural diversity that has been present over a long period of time), diversity that brings new norms and values along with it, the worry is that the trust that is essential to well-functioning democratic communities is at risk.[17] When officials ban headscarves from sports environments, and so prevent the participation of Muslim girls, members of the Muslim community take them to be making spurious claims about safety that veil an unstated discrimination against and hostility toward—in other words, distrust of—Muslims. Newcomers interpret newly implemented citizenship tests, which target those from non-Western communities, as statements of distrust. They are forced to overcome additional obstacles to attain citizenship status, a status that, moreover, no longer easily translates into perceived trustworthiness.

The worries that motivate these actions are not necessarily stated in terms of trust, of course. Yet the central thesis of this book is that these conflicts and tensions are, at their heart, about trust. Once we reevaluate these conflicts in terms of trust (or a lack there of) among citizens who are largely strangers to each other, we can begin to see what is necessary to reduce tensions among them. Trust in a democratic society principally arises from shared norms and values, I shall argue, and when these shared norms and values appear to be under threat, trust is likewise under threat. My claim is *not* that shared norms and values are the only source of trust; rather, my claim is that it is the main source of widespread trust in democratic communities. Where it is perceived to be the case that these shared norms and values are at risk—as in conditions in which ethnocultural diversity is made salient as a marker of difference—so too is the trust that ought to derive from them. When nonimmigrant citizens suggest that the values held by newcomers are incompatible with integration, they are suggesting that newcomers are therefore unable or unwilling to adopt the set of values on which the trust "around here" is based.

One issue that ethnocultural diversity in contemporary multicultural democracies makes plain is that we have long been complacent in assuming that shared values and norms necessarily give rise to trust. The hyperbole that surrounds recent public proclamations of the "death of" or the "failure of" or the "backlash against" multiculturalism highlights that it is now essential to determine *which* among these values and norms must be shared in order for trust to emerge.[18] It is no longer sufficient that we proclaim the importance of shared norms and values as the source of trust—it is clear enough that not all norms and values must be shared among citizens in order for them to trust one another. As John Rawls has said, contemporary democratic communities are characterized by the "fact of pluralism"; the challenge, therefore, is to articulate a public culture that respects this fact of pluralism while at the same time offers the resources that are essential to underpin a democratic community.[19] This book takes up the challenge by identifying when, how, and why shared values, norms, and beliefs matter to sustain a public culture, which in turn is the major source of trust relations.

Why a Book About Trust?

Why, one might ask, is it important to recharacterize democratic relations—and the stresses upon them as a result of ethnocultural diversity—in terms of trust? Why is it important to offer an account of multicultural democracy in terms of trust in addition to or rather than simply in terms of justice or equality or liberty? The reason is this: trust is *the* fundamental, foundational quality of an effective, well-functioning democracy. For reasons that will be elaborated in later chapters, democracies rely *first and foremost* on trust relations that extend between citizens and between citizens and their representatives. As Daniel Weinstock suggests, "well-functioning liberal democracies provide people with reasons not to withdraw their support from common institutions . . . [and] what is required in order to increase the likelihood that citizens will not withdraw their allegiance and support from common institutions is not so much a shared identity as *trust*."[20] It is of course true that perpetual injustices or inequalities will tend to dampen or break trust relations. Yet without trust, there will be no collectively felt motivation to erase or rectify existing inequalities and injustices in the first place.[21] Trust, in other words, underpins the motivation needed to make attempts at removing injustices and easing inequalities. It is therefore *the* first, essential element of any properly functioning democratic community.

A review of contemporary political philosophy might appear to indicate that trust is of little interest to those among us who are concerned with the central aspects of democratic politics: trust is conspicuously absent as an issue in contemporary analytic philosophy. Only a few recent attempts to make sense of trust have appeared in the literature, and they have not been accompanied by an effort to account for its overwhelming absence as a key concept in political theory. In spite of its relative absence in contemporary political philosophy, however, it is a frequent topic of discussion in the history of political philosophy.[22] For example. Thomas Hobbes famously suggested that we can explain the state of nature as a state of war in part because of what he termed "diffidence," that is, the natural distrust that we feel toward others. Any promise or agreement made on trust is effectively invalid in the state of nature: "covenants of mutuall trust, where there is a feare of not performance on either part, are invalid."[23] We need a central authority of some kind, he argued, to create the conditions under which this distrust can be mitigated. In a recent analysis of Hobbes's conception of trust, Danielle Allen observes that Hobbes was well aware that securing the conditions under which trust is possible is an *ongoing* task, since "it is impossible ever to generate bonds of trust so firm that perpetual stability is assured."[24]

John Locke offered an alternative account of the role that trust plays in the political environment. He suggested that we ought to view the government itself as a kind of trust. The legislature, he wrote, acts "pursuant to their [the citizens'] trust"; the boundaries of its legitimate actions fall squarely within what it has been entrusted to do (Locke's well-known view is that government is trusted in particular with protecting the people's natural right to property).[25] This understanding of trust—that trust, when extended, gives others some discretion to act in our best interests—features again in Edmund Burke's distinction between the political representative as *trustee* and the political representative as *delegate*. It is the former, a *trusted* representative, who is offered the discretion necessary to act in the best interests of constituents in a flexible manner. A representative who is treated as a mere delegate has not yet attained the trust of his or her constituents.[26]

Skeptics might nevertheless point out that historically, trust has neatly coexisted with rampant inequalities and injustices. They might point to instances in which serfs trusted their feudal lords in spite of the injustices that sustained the feudal system. They might point to instances in which wives trusted their husbands in spite of a patriarchal, sexist environment in which gender inequalities prevailed. What these supposedly countervailing examples illustrate, however, is that inequalities and injustices prevail in a climate of trust only so long as they are not widely perceived as such. Once a spade is called a spade—once the inequalities and injustices come to be thought of as inequalities and injustices—the trust with which they have coexisted will either dissipate or, in the best of circumstances, support and motivate the willingness to change. Trust, as we shall see over the course of this book, is fostered only in environments in which it is extended and reciprocated on a regular basis.

Yet, skeptics might continue, historical and contemporary democratic countries illustrate that even democracy can be sustained in the face of great inequalities and injustices. While ideal democratic theory tells us that justice and equality are the sine qua non of democratic communities, reality shows us that democratic environments can be more or less just and more or less equal. Ongoing democratic audits, for example, measure democracy along certain scales, according to which some countries are more just and more equal, and therefore more democratic, than others. Even so, I will argue, democratic environments simply *cannot* sustain themselves without trust; *trust* is essential to solving dilemmas of injustice and inequality that are still a regular part of democratic political life. I will argue that without at least minimal trust relations, dilemmas of injustice and inequality will necessarily remain unresolved. Without minimal trust relations—and even in the case of merely minimal trust relations—a democracy at best will limp along, unable to provide the standard benefits we attribute to democratic political arrangements, and at worst will break apart.

The preceding paragraph is not meant to be apocalyptic, especially since one theme of this book is that the threat to multicultural democracies, created as a result of certain forms of ethnocultural diversity, can be managed with the right kinds of policies. The argument here is manifestly *not* that multicultural democracies are on the brink of breakup, although chapter 6 engages with severely divided democracies in which the threat of breakup is real. Rather, the argument is a less fateful—but equally provocative—one: the benefits we attribute to democratic institutions are at risk under conditions of ethnocultural diversity, and this is because of the ways in which ethnocultural diversity places stress on the trust relations on which democracies rely. The spirit in which this book is written is one of realism—many previous accounts of multiculturalism have been blithely optimistic with respect to the ease of integration over time. Yet the book is motivated equally by a deep commitment to the benefits of multiculturalism, as well as to the view that citizens of different races, ethnocultural groups, and religions can and will live together in a flourishing democratic environment.

This book intends to accomplish three broad tasks. The first defends the argument that democracies rely heavily on widespread, extended trust relations. In order to do this, some preliminary analytic work is essential, and this is accomplished in the first chapter of the book. The first chapter tackles the concept of trust itself—it is critical to begin with a clear sense of the way in which the term "trust" is defined and used through the book. The chapter will highlight the relational aspect of trust—namely, that it is a term that describes relations between people, rather than the interactions between people and institutions. The chapter will, equally, emphasize that there are both attitudinal—we might say psychological or dispositional—and behavioral elements to trust; in other words, in order to count as a trusting person, an actor must *do* something and must do it with a particular attitude. The behavior must reflect a willingness to place oneself in a position of *vulnerability* with respect to others. This willingness to place oneself in a position of vulnerability is connected to another central element of trust, namely, a willingness to do so only under the condition that we believe that others bear us good will, or at least do not bear us ill will. Finally, having evaluated—whether consciously or unconsciously—a situation as one in which trust is warranted, that is, that one is indeed willing to place oneself in a position of vulnerability, the belief or attitude that motivated trusting behavior will prove to be resistant to evidence.

In order to articulate the concept of trust that is at the heart of this book, chapter 1 also evaluates the techniques employed to evaluate trust. In part because trust is relatively underexplored in contemporary political theory, and in part because it is *heavily* explored in social science disciplines more generally, the book relies on some of the insights developed from within the social science scholarship. The social science literature relies on a range of strategies, all of which will generate important insights that help to bolster the arguments that make up the core of this book and that serve to motivate its central questions. It is no longer surprising—though it remains an issue of deep concern—to read of surveys detailing the decline of trust across Western multicultural democracies. Before relying on these reports, however, it is critical that we examine the information that they purport to communicate, as well as the conclusions that we can and should draw from it.

With these preliminary evaluative tasks completed, we can turn to the central argument of the book, namely, that trust is the foundational element of democratic communities. Citizens of democratic communities extend trust and display trustworthiness as a matter of course. I will argue in chapter 2 that the voluntary compliance on which democracies rely depends on the willingness of citizens to extend and reciprocate trust on a regular basis. It is sometimes argued that the benefits attributed to democracy stem from several commitments—to protect the equality of all citizens, to secure the stability of democratic institutions, to ensure that peace and security prevails, to provide for the basic needs of all, and so on—all of which depend on the existence of sanctions that reward certain behaviors and punish others. But it is a mistake to attribute these benefits exclusively to an effective system of rewards and punishments—rather, these benefits are provided in large part by the willing compliance of citizens in schemes that produce them. One essential feature of democratic communities is, in fact, that they choose against putting their limited resources toward enforcing compliance—to the extent that they put their limited resources toward the enforcement of compliance, they are constrained from providing a greater set of benefits that rely on voluntary rather than forced compliance.

The second task of the book is to illustrate the nature of *distrust* and *mistrust* and the dangers associated with the erosion of trust in a democratic environment. This task can be thought of as a corollary of the first. If trust is essential to the benefits of a democracy that can rely on widespread compliance with shared norms and laws, then the emergence of distrust erodes the ability of a democracy to rely on this compliance. The benefits that are provided from within a democracy characterized by widespread trust relations are therefore at risk. There are many sources of distrust, and sociological research has illustrated many of them in considerable detail. Eric Uslaner, for example, convincingly argues that widespread income inequality is negatively correlated with trust. He suggests not only that pronounced income inequality is correlated with the emergence of distrust, but also that pronounced income inequality—because it is correlated with a decline in trust—erodes the motivation to enact the social justice policies that might serve to alleviate income inequality (and so perhaps revitalize trust).[27] Mark Warren concentrates on the negative effect of widespread corruption on trust relations. It is not surprising to learn that the belief that widespread corruption exists negatively affects trust relations.[28] Whatever the cause of the distrust, however, chapter 3 intends to make clear the dimensions along which distrust is a problem for democracy. Here I argue against suggestions, which emerge in part from the game theory tradition that is canvassed in chapter 1, that distrust might well be reinterpreted as essential to democracy. Any interpretation that places distrust rather than trust at the center of democracy is profoundly mistaken.

In order to make sense of these apparently contradictory claims—my own, that trust is an essential component of democracy, and that of others, that distrust is an essential component of democracy—I shall distinguish between the two concepts mentioned above, distrust and mistrust, which are often confused in this debate. This distinction will prove central to the arguments that underpin the second half of the book. Whereas distrust is a solid and stable attitude that prevents opportunities for extending and rewarding trust to emerge in the first place, mistrust is a more precarious and unstable attitude; crucially, whereas distrust is largely insensitive to new information indicating the value of extending and rewarding trust, mistrust is malleable and can therefore shift considerably in response to new information. In order to develop a clearer understanding of the relationship of new information to attitudes that signal the absence of trust, then, we will need to assess the relationship between evidence and trust, mistrust and distrust. Trusters and distrusters maintain trusting or distrusting attitudes for an extended period of time in the face of evidence suggesting they should do otherwise; these attitudes are fundamentally evidence resistant. As we shall see in chapters 5 and 6, the failure of trust and distrust to respond to evidence poses challenges in communities divided by ethnocultural diversity.

As the opening examples were meant to illustrate, this book concentrates on the precise mechanisms by which *ethnocultural* diversity can lead to the erosion of trust relations. The argument is this: under certain conditions, ethnocultural diversity can generate the sense that the public culture—that is, the shared ethos that characterizes a political community and encompasses its values and norms—is no longer shared. Chapter 4 will illustrate that trust emerges from a sense of shared norms and values; if ethnocultural diversity threatens the sense that shared norms and values are widespread, it threatens trust relations as well. Whether it is the actual erosion of shared values and norms or the *perception* of erosion that matters is an issue that will be dealt with as well.

The concept of a public culture is controversial, however, and requires some defending.[29] Any multicultural democracy (indeed, any nonmulticultural democracy as well) requires an inclusive source of trust, and the main thesis of chapter 4 is that a public culture can be such a source. According to the public culture argument, democratic institutions function best when they find support among a population united by a public culture. This argument is of course the subject of a great many critiques, and chapter 4 will argue against them. More important, the chapter will rearticulate the concept of a public culture in such a way that it can, without illegitimate prejudice against newcomers, provide a cohesive, nonexclusive, and morally legitimate way to bind citizens in the relations of trust that are essential to well-functioning democracies.

This is an especially important task since most of us now live in political communities that are extraordinarily diverse." With only a few exceptions, states are heterogeneous, comprising a range of ethnicities, religions, cultural groups, and sub-state national groups. By accepting diversity as a fact, we are acknowledging the need to take seriously that cultural group members feel loyalty toward and solidarity with fellow group members, and that they may feel the bonds that join them as immutable and enduring; this is the case even though there is considerable evidence that cultures are constantly changing in response to many things, including internal tensions, external pressures, and interactions with other cultural groups. As a consequence, the bonds that group members feel, the nature of these bonds, and the obligations that attend these bonds are fluid and constantly in flux. Together, these two observations—that members of cultural groups often feel loyalty toward each other and that they often feel these bonds as enduring—give rise to two further observations that motivate the analysis in chapter 4. First, although it is true that "people identify and empathize more easily with those with whom they have more in common than with those with whom they have less in common,"[30] it is equally true that how we determine with whom we share values and beliefs is not fixed, but is instead malleable over time. Second, even as we may advocate multicultural policies, in doing so we must be careful to reject a reified concept of the culture that defines minority groups. Cultures (whether minority or majority) are amorphous and flexible; while individuals are influenced by their experiences within them, they are equally capable of reflection on the positive and negative aspects of their culture. In other words, we must be sensitive to the influence that culture has on people's formative experiences, without taking culture as entirely determinative of their values and behaviors.[31] These groups, the boundaries of which often overlap and are so difficult (if not impossible) to discern, have different views of what constitutes the good life and how this good life should be obtained. In the ideal, all of these groups nevertheless (I hope) share a set of common values and norms, at both the social and political levels, that enable long-term cooperation for the benefit of all. Yet as I shall suggest, there is a strong correlation between diversity and weakened trust relations within a population.

There is nothing inherent in the presence of ethnocultural diversity that makes it generate tension in the public culture's ability to act as a reliable source of trust. Yet there is considerable evidence that under certain conditions the presence of ethnocultural diversity makes trusting relations between citizens more difficult. Robert Putnam, for example, has recently suggested that ethnocultural diversity breeds mistrust among a population: "the bottom line is that there are special challenges posed to building social capital [one key component of which is trust, in Putnam's account] by ethnic diversity."[32] In chapter 5, the relationship between ethnocultural diversity and the decline of trust is accounted for as follows. An increase in ethnocultural diversity is accompanied by an increase in the diversity of norms and values within a community (and sometimes merely the *perception* that such an increase in the diversity of norms and values has taken place). As citizens of a shared community, we therefore are (or perceive ourselves to be) less able to count on others to behave in ways that we can predict and understand. At worst, we no longer feel that we are part of a genuinely shared community at all, since nothing recognizable appears shared among us.

Before turning to the final task of this book—an articulation of the strategies and mechanisms we ought to employ to strengthen, repair, and rebuild trust relations—I turn to an evaluation of trust relations in communities that are severely divided along ethnocultural lines. The chapter may appear to take us off course, but its objective is to show that severe divisions of the kind that characterize Northern Ireland, Sri Lanka, and so on, are at their base also divisions that pertain to trust relations. In these kinds of societies the challenges for building, or rebuilding, flourishing democratic relations appear to be more difficult than they do in the multicultural democracies that are the main focus of this book. Yet, I shall suggest, the divisions that persist in severely divided societies can best be understood in terms of trust relations or the lack thereof. The *weakened trust relations* that characterize ethnoculturally diverse societies will here be distinguished from the *distrust* that characterizes severely divided societies; the discussion will illustrate that trust and distrust exist on a kind of continuum, and that we can describe communities as more or less trusting and more or less distrusting.

After a thorough examination of the centrality of trust relations to democratic success, and the dangers posed by ethnocultural diversity to trust relations in a democratic environment, the book concludes with an account of how these damaged relations can be repaired. The final chapter concentrates on the principles and strategies that should guide us in our efforts to rebuild trust relations. The principles are drawn, in part, from the literature on deliberative democracy—a literature that remains ambivalent with respect to the relationship between trust and deliberation—and, in part, from the literature on cooperation building that underpins conflict resolution strategies in severely divided societies. Taken together, these literatures can guide us in producing a set of general trust-building principles that, if deployed in public policy, will serve to resolve the dilemmas of trust that characterize contemporary democratic communities. In a high trust environment, it is the public culture that serves as a source of trust; the public culture works to reduce the sense of vulnerability that we feel in extending and reciprocating trust. Thus, rebuilding trust relations requires that we identify mechanisms by which we can *mimic* the trust-building role played by the public culture. The objective is, similarly, to reduce the vulnerability that is inherent to trust, and thus to create the conditions under which trust can emerge. By way of conclusion, I shall suggest that among many other policies, well-designed multicultural policies can contribute to reducing this vulnerability.

TRUST DEFINED

Trust is central to human relations of all kinds. We trust our parents, our friends, our teachers, our doctors, and so on. We even trust people more generally, often people we have never met, as we go about our daily lives. We trust people on the street to provide us with accurate directions when we're lost (and we trust them to tell us when they don't know the directions to what we're looking for). We trust people not to steal our belongings when we leave them at the front of the store (even when the request to do so is because a store is trying to prevent shoplifting, which displays an explicit distrust of customers). We trust bus drivers to drive safely and to follow the right route. Without trust, to quote Russell Hardin, "one could not even get up in the morning."[1]

The reasons, moreover, that we extend trust to others are at least as wide-ranging as the situations in which we decide to trust. We trust people because our intuition tells us they're trustworthy; we think of our intuition as guiding us, for example, when we ask a stranger to watch our luggage when we use the washroom in the train station. We trust experts because they have credentials we recognize; health and legal professionals often post their diplomas where patients and clients can see them so as to give information on which they can base their trust. We trust people because our friends tell us they're trustworthy; people often meet for blind dates, for example, on friends' recommendations. We trust others because we have something important in common; conationals meeting in foreign countries often extend and reciprocate trust simply by virtue of finding themselves together as outsiders in a foreign country.

When we invoke trust, we are invoking questions connected to whether we are willing to rely on another person to do something, even if we do not have all the information to be certain that she will do this thing. We substitute our lack of information with an assessment of her trustworthiness, an assessment of our own relative confidence that she will do this thing that we are relying on her to do. Often when we think about the phenomenon of trust, we think about the people with whom we are closest, on whom we rely to carry out a whole range of tasks on a regular basis. We realize that we trust these people perhaps unthinkingly with the things—our children, our homes, our secrets—that we care most about.

Yet trust isn't only a feature of intimate, interpersonal relations; it is also a feature of our social and political lives. We extend trust on a regular basis to more than our intimates, and we do so with less information about who they are and what their motivations might be. We claim, sometimes, to trust doctors or priests or teachers, and in making these claims we are referring to categories of people rather than specific people about whom we have specific information. Trust is also invoked by political leaders, who attempt to assure us that they have our best interests in mind. On winning the race for governor in California, Arnold Schwarzenegger said, "I will do everything I can to live up to that trust. I will not fail you. I will not disappoint you and I will not let you down."[2] When, as of late, we hear claims that trust is generally declining, we are claiming that something has undermined our confidence in others in a general way.[3] We are claiming that something—whatever that something is—has affected the likelihood that we will assess someone or, more likely, a whole category of people, as willing or able to carry out some task. I hope these initial thoughts prompt readers to consider the complexity that underlies what, on its surface, may seem like a simple concept.

In this chapter, I consider the ways in which scholars from a range of disciplines have treated the concepts of trust and trustworthiness. Philosophers are concerned primarily with the role of reason and intuition in making trusting decisions, and the moral content (or lack thereof) of extending and reciprocating trust; experimental economists have worked in small-scale group settings to assess the conditions under which individuals can be encouraged to cooperate and those under which they will choose against doing so; sociologists and quantitative political scientists have worked to produce and evaluate responses to survey questions that ask people around the world to self-assess their trusting attitudes and trustworthy behaviors. A reading of these methods is instructive in illustrating the complexity of the concept of trust; gathered together, the multidisciplinary research provides a general sense of how and why trust matters, both in interpersonal relations and in political and social environments more generally. In this chapter I will suggest that trust is composed of six key features, and that the social scientific research in conjunction with philosophical investigations work together to elaborate their significance. Trust is relational; it involves vulnerability to the actions of others; it is part behavior, part attitude; it is evidence resistant; and (to some extent) it can be said to have a moral component.

Trust Is a Feature of Human Relations

Trust is a feature of human relationships rather than a feature of how people interact with the various institutions (for example, political and economic) that regulate their lives. To decide to trust necessarily implicates another person; the decision is made in relation to a specific group of others. It is sometimes suggested that we put our trust in institutions—for example, that we trust democratic institutions to yield the best decision or that we trust the judiciary to protect our rights. It is a mistake to think of institutions in this way, however. Institutions are themselves inert; they are not capable of acting in a trustworthy or an untrustworthy manner. Rather, what we mean when we claim that an institution can be trusted is that the *individuals* who operate the institution can be trusted to do so effectively. In claiming to trust institutions, therefore, we are offering a kind of shorthand for the idea that "I trust person X to operate this institution effectively."[4] We need only think of partisan debates in the United States around the composition of the Supreme Court to illustrate this point. At issue when Democrats or Republicans lobby in favor of or against a particular nominee to the Supreme Court is not whether judicial institutions can be trusted; at issue is whether the nominee in question can be trusted, for example, to judge in accordance with the U.S. Constitution, or to refrain from judicial activism.

To say that we trust others is not to suggest that we extend trust unconditionally. We might, for example, trust someone with a specific task with which we believe she has specific competence. We trust taxi drivers to drive us safely to the location of our choice, for example, and we trust a doctor to have the expertise necessary to offer good advice with respect to our health concerns. Or, while we might trust our friends or our parents in general, we can exclude some task from the general, unspecified tasks with which we trust them. I can trust my friend to carry out the duties typically connected to friendship without trusting her to drive my car. And we often extend our trust beyond individuals to groups of others that are generally identified (as will be observed more clearly below) by a set of shared, or presumably shared, characteristics and value sets. For example, if we claim to trust the group "Canadians" or "Muslims" or "teachers," we are trusting them on the basis of a set of shared norms and understandings about how we behave in relation to each other. Note here that it is consistent to say that I trust Canadians without it being the case that I trust all Canadians equivalently and without it being the case that I trust all Canadians all the time. The claim to trust a group of people—in which we do not have personal, intimate knowledge of each member—reflects a generalized attitude that may manifest itself in a variety of ways.[5] It is this final observation about trust that will serve to elucidate the roles that trust plays in large-scale democratic communities, as I shall observe in chapter 2.

Trust and Vulnerability

At its core, trust is about *vulnerability;* in trusting others, we are making ourselves vulnerable to the actions of others, and therefore to the possibility of disappointment or, even more starkly, betrayal as a result of their actions.[6] This vulnerability stems from two related sources. First, we trust others in response to evidence that we believe suggests they are trustworthy, though this evidence can never be perfectly predictive: "the condition of ignorance or uncertainty about other people's behaviour is central to the notion of trust."[7] Second, whether or not we are able accurately to judge that others are trustworthy, they will always retain their freedom to act as they please, and this is an additional source of vulnerability associated with extending trust. Those we trust necessarily maintain a "degree of freedom to disappoint our expectations."[8] As a result, extending trust to others, who may or may not prove to deserve that trust, necessarily leaves us vulnerable to disappointment and betrayal.

Consider the following example, which Jane Mansbridge describes in some detail in "Altruistic Trust." A young woman is walking along a dark street late at night. After some time a young African American man turns a corner, and as he approaches her the young woman considers "Jesse Jackson's point that he would worry more with a Black young man behind him than a young White, and the recent statistics on rape . . . which include many more rapes by Black men than White" (294). With this evidence, the woman ponders whether to cross the street. The young woman might conclude that given this evidence, she will cross the street; she reasons that "even though the probability of anything bad happening is low, the magnitude of the potential bad is great enough to warrant crossing the street" (294). She feels her vulnerability too starkly to extend trust, and in making a decision to refuse to extend trust to a class of people—young African American men—she is doing so on the grounds of their sex and race, at least in this situation. Alternatively, she might resolve to continue on her path, even as she would prefer to cross the street. She reminds herself of having heard her "Black men friends speak of their humiliation in situations like this, when women acted as if they were rapists simply on the grounds of their sex and race" (294). In choosing against crossing the street, the young woman is explicitly confronting her attitudes of trust or otherwise toward young African American men in general. Here the young woman extends trust—she reveals a "vulnerable area of herself" as a way to generate trust (294).

Now contrast two (terrible) scenarios. In one scenario, the young woman is assaulted in spite of having crossed the street; in another, the young woman does not cross the street (having made the decision not to do so) and is assaulted. In the former situation, the woman will certainly be angry with her assaulter (and perhaps also with herself for having put herself in a dangerous situation). Yet she will not describe her trust as having been violated; she is not betrayed by or disappointed in her attacker. Indeed, she made an explicit decision against trust—and backed up this distrustful attitude with untrusting behavior. On the other hand, if the young woman has deliberately extended trust and she is violated, she will rightly describe her attitude in part as one of betrayed or disappointed trust.

This example highlights two additional features of the trust relationship. First, trust relationships can survive a certain number of disappointments without breaking down entirely. We have all had the experience of being disappointed by a friend's behavior in a way that touches on the trust that is foundational to friendship—perhaps they have failed to keep a secret or failed to be there in our time of need. In most instances of a strong and ongoing relationship, an explanation or apology will serve to remedy the violated trust. Yet at some point the trust violations will be such that they do foretell the end of the friendship; we can all imagine saying, we used to be friends, but I just can't trust her anymore.

Second, it is often thought that trust and choice are incompatible. It is a mistake, on this view, to think of trust as something that one *decides* to do;

trust, rather, is something we extend intuitively and unconsciously. Karen Jones, for example, suggests that "trust cannot be willed."[9] In her view, once deliberate choice enters the equation, we are discussing something like probability or risk assessment rather than trust. There is an element of truth to this observation, at least insofar as it is plainly possible to make the decision to risk relying on another person to carry out some task by evaluating the costs and benefits of doing so. Here one is merely asking whether the benefits of successfully relying on someone outweigh—sufficiently to make the risk worth taking—the costs associated with their turning out to be unreliable.

However, trust is in fact characterized at least partly in terms of choice, as illustrated by how we often react to violated trust. Sometimes our response to violated or betrayed trust is to become angry with the person who has violated our trust. Other times, however, we blame ourselves—we say, I shouldn't have trusted this person in this way. Taking responsibility for misplaced trust suggests that we feel responsible for having made the choice to extend trust, and so can be blamed for a bad *choice*.[10]

Just as it is a mistake to argue that trust is devoid of choice, however, it is also a mistake to suggest that trust is characterized wholly by choice. Trust is best thought of as composed partly of conscious decision based on our estimation of the likelihood that our trust will be rewarded, and partly by an attitude that allows us to short circuit the decision-making procedure and therefore to willingly, but more or less unconsciously, place ourselves in a position of vulnerability to the acts of others.[11] The point to observe here is simply that choice per se is compatible with trust and that there are instances in which it is clear that choice plays an essential, even if only partial, role in extending trust to others. As we shall see, the element of choice is emphasized by many scholars whose research focuses on whether, and under what conditions, people extend trust to others; this emphasis is unsatisfactory, however, because it fails to capture fully what is essential to trusting relationships.

The Behavioral Element of Trust

To trust is to *behave* in a certain way, in particular in such a way as to make ourselves vulnerable to the actions of others. We can readily observe that some behaviors appear to display trust; for example, the willingness of plumbers or electricians to take payment *after* they have rendered service, or the willingness to leave contractors in one's home unattended. If a person claims to trust someone, it is meaningless if that person refuses to show it by trusting that someone with something. Correspondingly, if someone claimed to trust another person and refused to prove it by trusting her with something, the person would have, I should think, good reason to believe that she is not in fact trusted. Consider when parents refuse to lend their children a car, in spite of claiming to trust their driving abilities (and my guess is that most parents obscure this absence of trust by pointing to the unsafe practices of *other* drivers). In the following section, I shall suggest that trusting behaviors are accompanied by a trusting disposition; for now, let me concentrate on the ways in which behaviors do or do not display trust.

Trust is frequently not overt; the intimate, personal relationships that matter most to us are infused with trust, and this trust is generally not made explicit. As a consequence, there is not necessarily a specific, identifiable behavior that constitutes trust; we do not say of our loved ones, I trust you with this, and with this, and with this, and with this. We trust them, rather, in a more general and often unexamined way; if asked, we might say that we trust them to have our best interests in mind or perhaps to display goodwill toward us. Moreover, we tend not to think of the trust placed in these relations with much specificity; rather, it is characteristic of our intimate relations that the trust that characterizes them is especially unconscious, unthinking, and very deep. Yet if our trust is betrayed by our intimate relations, we would nevertheless be able in retrospect to point to the task with which we trusted our intimate, and therefore the specific behavior that violated this trust.

Observing and measuring trusting behavior are two of the objectives pursued by experimental economists. One conventional way of testing for supposed trusting behavior in small groups is via an experiment referred to as "the trust game," of which variations abound.[12] In its most basic form, two players are separated so that they can't see each other and are designated as either sender or recipient. The sender is given an amount of money and decides how much to send to the recipient. The sender makes the decision knowing that the amount will be trebled before the recipient receives it; if the sender chooses to send $10, the recipient receives $30. The recipient then returns an amount of money of her own choosing (including none) to the sender. A scale is designed to separate the senders into two general groups, the trusters and the distrusters; for example, those who choose to send more than half their money are designated trusters, while the rest are distrusters.[13] The players have no additional information about each other; there is no expectation of future interaction and there is no threat of punishment or public exposure for those who choose not to send money, either as sender or as recipient. In spite of these conditions, players repeatedly send some amount of money to an anonymous recipient, and they often choose to send the whole amount.[14]

The assumption going into this research is that individuals are self-interested rational agents, and therefore that in exchanges with strangers they will, all things equal, decide against engaging with others in any seemingly risky interaction; in these games, the prediction is therefore that we will see no trusting behavior. In this framework, trust is conceptualized as a purely rational conduct or attitude; any decision to trust others is merely an evaluation of the relative likelihood that people will reciprocate the trust placed in them by acting in a trustworthy way. In the presence of risk, rational self-interested individuals will *not* trust others when they engage with them, at least not without the presence of some form of constraint (formal or informal) that secures a stranger's cooperation in an exchange. Especially useful to the truster is information about whether it is in the self-interest of the trusted to reciprocate the trust placed in them.[15]

For those of us who are critical of these games, it seems misleading to describe them as trust games. Players are not trusting (or not) the other game players; rather, they are assessing the likelihood of certain outcomes based on the range of options they have available to them. I thus agree with how rational choice thinkers characterize the behaviors of trust game players. Although players are vulnerable to the decisions made by others, they do not display the right trusting *attitude*. Instead, their self-interest guides their decisions, and their decisions are based on an assessment of the risk associated with certain actions in relation to the possible gains and losses these actions can produce. They are simply engaging in a game in which the objective is to estimate the likely behavior of others: "my expectations about your behavior may be grounded in my belief in your morality or reciprocity or self-interest."[16] On this view trust is reduced to a rational assessment of the relative risk of certain decisions. For many, if not most, theorists of trust, however, this risk assessment procedure does not produce behaviors that are best described in the language of trust. Trust is not equivalent to the behavior that is prompted by rational self-interest, and genuinely trusting behavior is not produced simply in response to one's ascertaining that the risk of disappointment is low. Rather, it is at least accompanied by, if not also produced by, a trusting attitude.

The Attitudinal Element of Trust

In order to capture the essence of trust, we shall need to emphasize the *attitude* that prompts a trusting behavior. In particular, a trusting attitude is the disposition to think that others are trustworthy, so that we are therefore willing to place ourselves in a position of vulnerability with respect to their actions.[17]

It is sometimes suggested that we extend trust toward others because we believe that they bear us good will. On this view, in order to extend trust to others we must believe that they are "directly and favorably moved by the thought" that we are counting on them.[18] However, this is mistaken. Certainly, if we believe that others bear us *ill will*, we typically do not extend our trust toward them, and absent our belief that they have very strong self-interested reasons to do so, we do not expect them to behave in a trustworthy manner toward us. That said, it is not essential that others bear us good will in order for us to extend trust; rather, we simply must expect that others will "use their discretionary powers competently and nonmaliciously."[19] In an important sense, the attitude that matters to trust is about the truster rather than the trusted; whether I extend trust to others has to do with my own attitude toward them, an attitude that is in part dependent on my perception of their attitudes toward me. Generally, a good deal of the information that informs this attitude of trust comes from observing the behaviors, whether trustworthy or not, of others.

Recall, for a moment, the structure of the basic trust game. One person determines that she will send a certain amount of money, which she knows will be trebled, to the recipient. The recipient then decides whether to return money to the sender. During this experiment, as traditionally conceived, the players do not meet each other. One modification of the trust game, which tests for motivations beyond self-interest, examines the effect of perceived or real *social connectedness* between players. One example conducted in a university setting asked players to choose their own partners, thus increasing the likelihood that the partners are friends. Results indicate that even under conditions in which the amount sent is only doubled (thus supposedly increasing the incentive of the sender to keep the full amount), the fact of genuine social connectedness between the players increases the amount of money sent (and returned), in comparison to when these games are played between strangers. Experimenters conclude that trust (and trustworthiness) increases if social connectedness between players is real or can be established between them.[20]

An alternative modification relies on something called a "promise condition." A promise condition gives an opportunity for the receiver to indicate to the sender whether she intends to return the money entrusted to her, and if she will return some of it, the proportion of the money received she plans to return. This kind of study shows that there is a connection between the recipients' stated intention and the proportion of money sent. If the recipient promises to return a large amount of the money sent, she is more likely to be trusted with a large amount of money, even though there is no formal (or even informal) requirement that the recipient abide by her originally stated intentions (the supposedly rational decision here is to break a promise to return the money). Here, experimenters suggest, trust is extended on the basis of the perceived likelihood that it will be reciprocated.[21]

There are myriad more examples, far too many to report here, that offer modifications to the basic trust game based on the hypothesis that self-interest is not the sole motivating influence on people's trusting decisions. By altering the conditions of the trust game, researchers aim to show that motivations other than self-interested ones have an influence on trusting behavior; indeed, when the conditions under which people are asked to send and return money change, their decisions about whether to do so likewise change. In real life as well, external conditions are well known to affect trust; this result— that changing conditions influence whether people choose to trust others— will be significant in the final chapter. Note, however, that while the modifications suggest that self-interest is not always the lone explanation for trusting behavior, they nevertheless make it difficult to determine which attitude in particular is responsible for the observed changes in behavior. Although the modifications to the basic trust game *suggest* that more than self-interest is at stake in engaging with others, they do not decisively rule out the possibility that self-interest is the only factor at stake. None of these experiments successfully captures the various potential effects of the attitudinal component of trust on whether people do or do not trust others. None tests for attitudes about the world, the idea that people are generally trustworthy, or that, all things being equal, we should trust those around us; they merely capture information about how our inclination to trust others or not responds to certain, and often very specific, external stimuli.

Survey Research on Trusting Attitudes and Trusting Behaviors

A trusting attitude, when widespread among many people, is sometimes de-scribed as a "climate" of trust, an environment in which people determine that others are, more often than not, going to be trustworthy. In any given com-munity, even one that is pervaded by a climate of trust, there will be those who are genuinely trusting, and those who will be inclined to trust only some smaller category of people such as members of their family or ethnic group. In the sociological literature on trust, the former is typically termed "generalized trust," and the latter is termed "particularized trust." Whereas particular-ized trust refers to decisions to trust specific others with the aim of gaining some specific and immediate benefit, generalized trust refers to trust in "peo-ple whom we don't know and who are likely to be different from ourselves ... without expecting anything in return."[22] It is typically said that a democracy requires that citizens display a generalized rather than a particularized dis-position to trust; it is generalized trust that serves to "build large-scale, com-plex, interdependent social networks and institutions ... generalized trust is connected to a number of dispositions that underwrite democratic culture, including tolerance for pluralism and criticism."[23] So long as enough people have a generally trusting attitude, we can say that a climate of trust prevails (in chapter 6 I consider societies in which particularized but not generalized trust prevails).

The most conventional way of testing for trusting attitudes on a large scale is via survey research that often poses what is termed the "general trust ques-tion."[24] The general trust question is two-pronged: in general do you think that people can be trusted, or do you think that you can't be too careful in dealing with others? Yet there are reasons to be skeptical of the information gleaned from responses to this question.[25] In addition to allowing respon-dents only two possible answers (yes, people can be trusted, or no, people cannot be trusted), this question asks people to oppose two positions that are not obviously opposite or contrary opinions. It is possible to believe both that most people can be trusted—under some conditions to do some things—and that in specific dealings with others, it is better more often than not to be care-ful. Counting one's change when it is returned is not obviously a signal that people cannot be trusted, even if it is an example of being careful in dealing with others.[26]

A more general concern about survey research as it pertains to trust is the frequency with which different concepts are taken to report equivalent attitudes, even when the questions are clearly attempting to pinpoint distinctive ones. For example, Eric Uslaner claims that trust is mainly "based upon an optimistic view of the world and a sense that we can make it better,"[27] and he proceeds to rely on survey data detailing people's relative optimism about the world and their place within it to give him information about the presence of trust or lack thereof. Yet the link between trust and optimism is not straightforward; it is logically possible, and indeed plausible, for someone to be trusting and yet pessimistic about one's ability to improve the world, or distrustful yet persuaded that one can make the world a better place. Questions about other concepts that are sometimes taken to reflect levels of trust include honesty, fairness, and legitimacy. Each of these concepts may well have some relation to trust, but the nature of this relationship is by no means clear. Each of the terms that is used as a proxy arises from a different source, makes use of distinct judgments that we make about others, makes more or less use of moral appraisals of others, and so on. The consequence of using proxies, therefore, is an increased likelihood that the scholars who rely on them come to different conclusions about the relevance of trust in general and its role in democracies in particular. These conflicting conclusions suggest that the decision to measure trust by relying on proxies is at best inconclusive and at worst unreliable.

The general trust question is intended to tap into general trusting attitudes. Yet a (putatively) trusting attitude is not of use or benefit if it is not accompanied by trusting behavior, and if it is *never* accompanied by trusting behavior, it is not a trusting attitude at all. Consider two alternative large-scale approaches that take heed of the clear behavioral element to trust and offer methods to focus on trusting behavior on a large scale. The first approach to investigating trusting behavior takes its lead from the general trust question, but formulates questions that are intended to focus on behavior rather than attitude; for example, of the form: what did you do or would you do in this or that sort of situation? Affirmative responses to questions about putatively trusting behavior are taken as proxies for a trusting attitude. One set of researchers chose the following questions, positive responses to which were taken as signals of trusting people: "How often do you lend money to your friends? How often do you lend personal possessions to your friends? How often do you intentionally leave your rooming group's hallway door unlocked when nobody is home?"[28]

An alternative line of questioning likewise probes the extent to which people trust a range of others with whom they have interactions. It can therefore respond to the complaint that the radius of trust is unclear in the general trust question, that is, that it is not clear who individuals are thinking about when they respond to the general trust question.[29] Specifically, the research relies on responses to the following question: "Say you lost a wallet or purse with $100 in it. How likely is it that the wallet or purse will be returned with the money in it if it was found by a neighbor, a police officer, a clerk at a local grocery store, and a stranger?"[30] Unlike the general trust question, it asks respondents to focus on a *specific* set of individuals in a *specific* situation. By specifying individuals, respondents have the opportunity to consider context, and so their responses may reflect an evaluation of the relative trustworthiness of members of their local community versus members of a larger community. Second, by asking respondents to consider a specific situation rather than the general state of affairs, the question is attempting to get at the behavioral component of trust.[31] It asks respondents to assess whether trustworthy behaviors can be expected of others, and thus implicitly whether the respondents have a trusting attitude toward these specific people. Those who reply that all four people would return the wallet with the $100 in it are designated "trusting" and those who reply that none of the four people would return the wallet are designated "untrusting." Unsurprisingly, the researchers find that most people fall between these two extremes and, moreover, that there is disagreement among those surveyed with respect to which category of person is likely to be trustworthy. And, of course, it is logically possible to believe that others will return the wallet without believing that they are trustworthy.

Note however that these questions encourage respondents to think in terms of statistics—what is the likelihood that my wallet will be returned to me? In addition to excising the word "trust," the question does not capture the sense of vulnerability that comes along with trusting others; this is because the premise of the question does not require responders to consider whether they are willing to take on vulnerability. They have already lost the wallet; the only question is whether they expect to have it returned to them. In order for the question to capture the essence of trusting others, however, it must construct a situation in which the respondents are forced to think not only about who they are trusting but also about the vulnerable situation in which they are placing themselves in doing so. One option, for example, might be to ask: would you ask a police officer, a stranger, a neighbor, etc., to watch your jacket or laptop computer while you went to use the washroom? This question at least requires respondents to consider making themselves vulnerable to others based on a specific attitude toward them.

An Interjection: Social Capital as a Measure of Trust

An account of relatively large-scale methods by which we might measure trust would be incomplete without acknowledging the tremendous impact of social capital research on studies of trust. The argument there is well known: political communities characterized by widespread "social capital"—the "social networks and the associated norms of reciprocity and trustworthiness" that participation in these social networks engenders—are better able to support flourishing democratic communities.[32] Scholars of social capital generally see robust relationships between social capital and trust—in some accounts, trust is thought of as a component of social capital, and in others, social capital is thought to *produce* trust. Either way, they suggest, we should encourage participation in civil society organizations because the social capital that is thereby generated is accompanied by the trust on which democracy relies.[33] As a result the standard, or at least the original, method by which social capital theorists operate is simply by measuring the average level of participation exhibited by community members; citizens are surveyed for the number of organizations in which they participate, for the number of hours they spend participating, and so on. In communities characterized by high levels of participation in civil society organizations, social capital theorists suggest— whether they believe that social capital is defined by trust, or whether social capital produces trust—that we can predict that the community is a trusting one and therefore more likely to be a democratic one.[34] The central intuition of this approach is an important one: environments in which citizens have an opportunity to cooperate together to achieve common objectives are those in which trust can and often does emerge. The connection between cooperation and trust is left implicit, however, and in the final chapter I will offer an account of when cooperation serves to build trust.

For now, I will turn to a brief account of two important critiques commonly launched at the standard social capital approach. Dietlind Stolle highlights one such objection, namely, that it is perhaps the case that those who participate in these organizations already extend trust to others.[35] Since it is trusters who join organizations, participation in them is only apparently the source of social capital, and therefore of trust, and as a result the emphasis on voluntary associations as "producers of generalized trust" is unwarranted.[36] Although assessing levels of participation in civil society organizations may correlate with levels of trust in a community, it is on this view a mistake to encourage participation in these organizations as a way to produce trust.[37]

A second objection suggests that although trust might well emerge from participating in *some forms* of civil society organizations, it is a mistake to claim that trust emerges from participation in all civil society organizations. We should distinguish between two forms of civil society organizations: those that produce "bonding" social capital (social capital that forms "ties to people who are *like* you in some important way") and those that produce "bridging" social capital (social capital that forms "ties to people who are *unlike* you in some important way").[38] Organizations that produce only bonding social capital—ethnic organizations, religious organizations, and so on—may produce trust among members, but they do not produce the wider and more generalized trust on which democracy is said to rely. Moreover, we do not want to be in the position of having to argue that participation in morally objectionable or "bad" civil society organizations—the KKK, for example, or other organizations with explicitly racist objectives—is equivalent to participating in "good" civil society organizations, such as those that aim to deliver charity to people who are in need. Surely we want to be able to claim that however much these bad organizations are characterized by trust, or however much we believe they can produce trust, people ought to be *prevented* from participating in them as much as possible (even if this prevention is not legally enforced).[39] Although they may build trust, they are in other ways bad for democracy because they inhibit the development of other important democratic values, including tolerance, inclusion, and so on.

For the purposes of this book, we can rely on the data collected by those involved in social capital research to provide some direction as follows. First, where civil society participation is evidently high, we can infer that there is at least some trust—at the very least, among those who are participating (even if we remain agnostic with respect to whether it is the participation that is producing the trust or is the result of the trust). Second, we can see that the context of the participation matters—certain kinds of environments are at least correlated with generalized trust, and others are correlated only with particularized trust. In the final chapter of this book in particular, it will be important to recognize that—like social capital theorists concerned with flourishing democracies—we will need to pay attention to where trust is being built, and among whom. Third, it seems clear enough that the *institutional context*—whether democratic, for example, or severely divided in some way—matters to a considerable extent in determining whether the organizations in question exist and can serve as trust builders. Although it may be useful to rely on social capital theory to tell us when to expect trust to be widespread (under conditions of extensive participation), it is equally important to recognize that institutional structure can—and as we shall see in the final chapter, often does—have a significant impact on whether trust relations can and do emerge across a community. The emergence of trust will depend on an institutional structure that prompts the right kind of participation.

Trusting Attitudes and Their Resistance to Evidence

How do we come to have a trusting attitude? I suggested that when we extend trust, we typically do not think of ourselves as counting up evidence in favor of and against trusting before we do so. Rather, trust has the appearance of being more intuitive or unconscious; we become aware that we have trusted, typically, when we realize we have misplaced this trust and find ourselves disappointed by someone's failure to reward our trust. Although we frequently describe our "decisions" to extend trust or otherwise, for most of us, and in most cases, doing so is not a matter of overt decision making. I suggested earlier that thinking of trust in terms of a risk assessment, in which we weigh evidence to extend trust or otherwise, is a mistake frequently made by economic experimentalists persuaded by rational choice theory.

Yet it would also be a mistake to deny a relationship between evidence and trust. Trust is not blind to evidence; indeed, we are frequently critical of those who extend blind trust to others. Trust emerges in the first place in response to considerable evidence, even if this evidence itself is not collected consciously or deliberately. We interact with others in ways that give us the opportunity to get a sense of what they are like and how they will behave in certain kinds of situations. Over time, we learn "when and how much we can rely on them and trust them."[40] Once we have a belief about the trustworthiness of others, however, this belief is often sustained in the face of evidence indicating that change is warranted.[41]

Moreover, most of us will have had experiences in which the evidence suggests that we ought to extend trust, but where we nevertheless have not been able to do so. New parents, for example, contemplating leaving their children at home with highly recommended babysitters, or even their own family members, have ample evidence to support a decision to trust others with the care of their children and still may not extend this trust. In this type of case, there is no *evidence* that warrants a lack of trust, yet new parents frequently display a lack of trust in would-be caretakers. The example suggests that the relationship between trust and evidence is not straightforward: evidence of trustworthiness is insufficient in many cases to generate a trusting attitude. As Diego Gambetta has written, "rational individuals cannot simply decide to believe that they trust someone if they do not."[42] As we shall see in later chapters, if it were simply the case that evidence could solve the problems of trust, then there would not be a real dilemma posed by trust in the first place.[43]

Our trusting attitude shapes the way in which we experience our environment: these attitudes "shape our understanding of various events, leading us to experience the world in ways that tend to reinforce the attitudes [of trust] we already hold."[44] These attitudes act as a kind of bias that shapes how we interpret and respond to events we experience; our bias in favor of friends, colleagues, neighbors, family members, and so on leads us to interpret evidence in such a way that it confirms our beliefs about their trustworthiness.[45]

Additionally, this bias can lead us to describe our friends as trustworthy even if they fail to carry out some of their responsibilities toward us; we excuse an otherwise trusted co-worker if she fails to do her work well, we forgive elected politicians for compromising when we believe they generally have our interests in mind as they do so. In other words, it is not simply that trust is a stable attitude that can survive disappointments over time; rather, it is additionally resistant to evidence in some sense. Its virtue—that it underpins the support we offer our friends, colleagues, co-workers, conationals— can also be its vice. If our trust is consistently betrayed, and yet we continue to place this trust in others, we can rightly be accused of gullibility; we are guilty of a kind of blind trust that we should, but aren't willing to, revisit in light of evidence. Our trust acts as a kind of interpretative lens through which to evaluate the actions of others, but it can be so insensitive to evidence that it opens us to accusations of gullibility, and worse, to considerable (and in principle avoidable) disappointment and harm.

Consider, as Judith Baker suggests, a situation in which a friend is accused of some wrongdoing. Our trust in our friend presses us toward rejecting what might be considerable evidence of this wrongdoing; in this case, and others like it, we can say that "trust is robustly resistant to evidence which is counter to trusting belief" that we have already formed over time.[46] If sufficient evidence of a wrongdoing emerges that suggests that even friends should abandon their trust in the wrongdoer, the truster is opened up to accusations of gullibility, as above. But part of what it *means* to have friends (characterized by trusting relations) is to sustain trust in the face of evidence that suggests it is to a considerable extent unwarranted. In the case of trust, and as we shall see later, in cases of distrust, a willingness to shift our attitude in response to evidence that it is unwarranted means more than simply shifting an attitude. It also means shifting the character of our relationships with certain others; since trust is foundational to so many relationships, the effect of shifting our attitude toward distrust can have the effect of undermining it entirely. The same is true of distrust; when we agree to work with those with whom we have a past history of distrust, we are moving from refusing to extend them trust toward the possibility of forging a trusting relationship with them over time.

The Moral Components of Trust (and Trustworthiness)

There is a final and perhaps more controversial aspect of trust to observe, and this is its apparent connection with morality. Our intuition might suggest that trust is morally good in some way; we might be tempted to say that more trust is better and less trust is worse. I do believe that, all things equal, more trust is better than less trust. However, upon examination it is clear that more trust is not always better: while strong trust relations can lead to good outcomes, they can also lead to bad ones. On the one hand, trust serves to solve collective action problems of the kind that plague democratic political action, among other things. On the other hand, the expression "honor among thieves" highlights that strong trust relations can facilitate negative or objectionable outcomes just as they can facilitate positive and valuable outcomes. As a result, there will be occasions in which the right thing to do, from a moral perspective, is to build trust, and others where the right thing to do is to break it down. In light of this reality, let me simply highlight two ways in which trust is thought to be good from a moral perspective.

First, in some situations, it is *better* to trust others than to refuse to extend them trust. We can imagine a situation in which members of a community recognize the value in some good or some set of interests that can be achieved only cooperatively, and so make a concerted effort to trust others as a way to achieve that good or to realize these common interests. Here we might be tempted to say that trust maintains a morally neutral status, since it is playing a mere instrumental role in achieving a morally valuable good of some kind. In my view, however, this valuation would be mistaken in cases where the good in question would be *impossible* to achieve without trust relations; in this case, trust has moral content by virtue of its role as a facilitator in achieving a morally good end. In later chapters, I will argue that there is at least one genuinely valuable end, namely, democracy, which can only be achieved under conditions of widespread trust. Because democracy is a valuable good, the trust that underpins it contains important moral dimensions.

A second so-called moral aspect of trust emerges from the fact that trustworthiness is typically thought of as a virtue to which we aspire and that we admire and seek in others. In principle, when we assess the trustworthiness of others we could simply be asking about the probability that they will fulfill the trust placed in them; we could be evaluating the conditions in place that will ensure their willingness to fulfill the trust; we could be replaying past experiences with them to assess whether they have proved reliable in the past. This evaluative process, which sometimes transpires consciously and at other times unconsciously, goes into making decisions about whether to trust others; it can in principle take place without engaging moral considerations at all. We need not ask, does this person seem trustworthy to me? This is by and large what Russell Hardin means to highlight when he describes trust as "encapsulated self-interest"; for Hardin, we decide to trust others when we believe that our interests can be encapsulated in theirs.[47] We believe that others have an *interest* in fulfilling our trust. In the case of doctors, for example, we may often believe that their motivation to behave in a trustworthy manner stems from a desire to act in the best interests of patients generally, even when doing so is transparently self-interested, as it might be in the case of doctors who want to secure the willingness of patients to continue to visit their practice. Or in the case of parents, their motivation to behave in a trustworthy manner may stem directly from their perceived desire to secure the best interests of their children.[48] Yet these examples suggest that our evaluation of trustworthiness stems in part from an assessment of the motives others possess and in part from a general evaluation of the sense of trustworthiness that others exude. This latter evaluation will often have at least a moral inflection, and it is thus a mistake to ignore the moral elements that are often implicated in the decisions we make with respect to trusting others.

Consider another example from experimental economics. In order to understand the conditions under which trustworthy behavior can be induced, we can look to studies that focus on what persuades people to participate in public-good dilemmas. Goods are described as "public" when they are provided to a community as a result of the participation of all or most members (i.e., they are jointly provided), where the benefit cannot be denied to those who choose against participating (i.e., they are nonexcludable), and where the use of the goods by some members does not diminish their availability for others' use. Both national defense and environmental cleanliness are standard examples: in partaking of security or clean parks, I do not diminish the security of others, nor their access to clean parks, and should I choose to free ride on the cooperation of others, the goods will be provided so long as I am among a minority who choose against participating. Free riding here can take at least two forms: I can actively make the provision of the public good more difficult (e.g., by littering in a park, by failing to ensure that my car meets emission standards), or I can refuse to contribute to the upkeep of a public good (e.g., by refusing to remove litter for which I am not responsible).

In public-good experiments, the objective is to assess the conditions under which people will willingly contribute to a public good. In a typical public-good dilemma, participants are provided with some money (or something that stands in for money), and if they donate some portion of it to the public, it will be doubled (or tripled) and then redistributed to all participants without regard for who donated the money in the first instance. So if each of five participants is given $100, a decision by all participants to contribute all their money to the public—money that is then doubled and redistributed—will result in each contributor having $200. Or if one person contributes her money, she will find herself with $40 and everyone else will have $140. In most standard formulations of the game, participants all do well when everyone contributes to the good in question.[49]

One common variation of the game evaluates whether people respond to the expectations, which are announced publicly, that others have in them. In one study, experimenters asked participants to play under three different conditions: some were told that their partners would never know of their decision, others were told that their partners would learn of their decision, and still others were informed that not only would their partners learn of their decision but they would also have the opportunity to meet their partner once the experiment was complete.[50] Predictably, results from studies like this indicate that there are those who cooperate regardless of the external conditions and there are those who refuse to cooperate regardless of the external conditions. What is interesting, and what matters ultimately for this project, is that many people who are initially designated "low trusters," who choose not to cooperate under conditions of anonymity, will often behave in a co-operative fashion upon learning that either their choices will be known or their choices will become known and they will meet those with whom they have played the game. Researchers conclude from these results that the absence of a trusting attitude (as reflected by those who choose not to cooperate given the condition of complete anonymity) is not necessarily the only factor influencing trusting behavior. In other words, people can under certain conditions be induced to adopt what appears to be trustworthy behavior (i.e., contribute to the public good) even though they are not initially unambiguously trustworthy people (i.e., they won't contribute to the public good unless they know that some form of monitoring exists, as I shall elaborate in chapter 7).

This kind of research highlights the difficulty in extrapolating in general from behavior to feelings of trust—in particular, apparently untrusting or untrustworthy behavior is not necessarily evidence of an entirely distrustful attitude toward others, and apparently trusting behavior is not necessarily evidence of a trusting attitude. Those who extrapolate too quickly from apparently untrustworthy behavior to the presence of distrustful attitudes will fail to see the importance, and perhaps even the ease, of generating the conditions under which low trusters too will cooperate with others. Research on trustworthiness suggests that the possibilities for cooperation, given conditions of apparently low trust, can be solved by a focus on what induces—or what sort of attitude underpins and motivates—trusting and trustworthy behavior.

In sum, as with many other values—freedom, equality, or friendship, for example—all things considered, we have good reason to prefer trust over distrust, even if in some cases the absence of trust (and trustworthiness) will produce preferable outcomes. Not only does trust often underpin goods that we value, but trustworthiness is also typically thought of as a virtue. As we have also seen, trust often emerges from expectations that others have of us. We behave in trustworthy ways when we believe that others expect us to do so. In later chapters, I will suggest that these expectations can be produced in relatively large democratic communities via what I, and others, term a "public culture." I will say more about how public culture works in chapter 4.

Conclusions

Trust has been widely explored in a range of disciplines, even as it has been relatively ignored in contemporary political theory. A theory of trust such as the one this book is offering cannot be developed in isolation of the important work that has thus far been done to explore the real-life implications of widespread trust and its absence. The review conducted in this chapter is certainly not exhaustive, but it is, I hope, instructive. Its aim has been to highlight some central insights generated from within a range of disciplines with respect to the concept of trust.

The concept of trust that I've identified has six features:

1. Trust is relational; it describes relations between individuals (rather than between people and institutions).
2. Trust is intimately linked with deliberately chosen vulnerability to disappointment and betrayal.
3. Trust requires a specific behavior.
4. Trust requires a specific attitude.
5. Trusting attitudes are resistant to evidence that they are unwarranted.
6. There is an important moral component to trust in two ways: our assessment of others as trustworthy or otherwise is generally at least partially a moral assessment, and there are morally desirable ends that can be attained only in the presence of widespread trust.

In later chapters, we shall revisit each of these essential elements of trust. The next chapter elaborates why we should think of the trust that characterizes democratic political communities to be between people, rather than between people and the institutions that structure political activity. We shall also see that the *good* of democracy depends on extensive trust relations, and therefore that building trust can be a valuable activity from a normative perspective (chapter 4 relies on the plausibility of this claim as well). In chapter 3, we shall consider the complicated relationship between trust (and distrust) and the evidence that underpins decisions to extend trust (or not). This complicated relationship will be obvious in the multicultural communities I consider in chapter 5 and the severely divided societies I describe in chapter 6; over the course of these chapters we shall be able to trace a decline in trusting attitudes along with a decline in overt trusting behaviors. The source of trusting attitudes, in democratic political communities, occupies us in chapter 4.

We shall return to the relationship between trust and evidence, which frames the argument in chapter 7, when I consider how we can build trust in environments in which the evidence suggests that distrust is warranted instead. Chapter 7 will equally highlight the distinction between the behavioral and the attitudinal component of trust (and distrust); as I shall suggest, one way in which to build trusting attitudes is to prompt trusting and trustworthy behaviors, and we shall do so *in particular* by attempting to reduce the vulnerability connected to extending trust to others.

TRUST AS A FOUNDATIONAL DEMOCRATIC VALUE

The thesis of my book is that trust is important to social and political communities, in particular to the cooperation and reciprocity that typically underpin communities when they function for the good of their members. The previous chapter examined the methodologies employed by social scientists who are concerned with the concept and phenomenon of trust. These methodologies make connections between the existence of trust and the smooth functioning of communities both large and small: they typically find that the more trust is present, the more likely it is that members will cooperate with one another, and therefore the more smoothly these communities will run.

But these studies tackle the role of trust in political relations only indirectly, and in particular, only in *democratic* political relations. As such, no argument is made that clearly places trust (or the lack of trust) at the center of democratic politics, even if the research is concerned to provide insights for social and political relations in democratic communities more generally. The objective in this chapter is therefore to provide a systematic argument for placing trust at the heart of democratic politics. I suggest that the voluntary compliance required in order for democratic institutions to function, and for citizens to implement and abide by democratically determined legislation, depends on trust. Democratic theorists generally agree that voluntary compliance with democratically established rules is central to democratic efficacy. The purpose of the chapter is to illustrate that trust is at the heart of collective voluntary compliance, by suggesting that it is central to the three basic features of a democratic system of governance: power transition, representative government, and minority protection. Any attempt to build a more robust, egalitarian democracy will depend at least on the effective functioning of these three features.

Trust and Voluntary Compliance

There is more than one explanation for citizens' apparent willingness to abide by shared rules. On one view, states generate a set of regulations, and there are punishments of various severities associated with breaking these regulations that serve as incentives to abide by the sometimes inconvenient or disagreeable regulations. States with powerful police forces and militaries can afford to institute unpopular legislation with the knowledge that they have the resources to enforce compliance aggressively; these states can, therefore, operate without widespread trust. A stronger version of this view emphasizes that widespread trust is not only unnecessary, but is also in some ways problematic for the efficient running of a state system. On this Hobbesian view, trust is a liability rather than an asset, since widespread trust allows for rampant free riding in such a way that some citizens are suckered into extending trust to untrustworthy cocitizens and, in particular, to untrustworthy political actors. Coercive institutions, therefore, uniquely serve to combat free riding, and without coercive institutions to protect citizens from one another's untrustworthiness, widespread (but naïve and misplaced) trust will quickly be undermined.

Coercive power in a *democracy* is limited in its capacity to secure compliance, however, and so democratic authorities must rely on the willingness of (most) citizens to defer to their decisions under most circumstances. As is well known, decisions made by democratic institutions (and legislators) are difficult to enforce. In order for democratic decisions to regulate the behavior of citizens and to govern their interactions, citizens must voluntarily comply with them.[1] If citizens withdraw their compliance, democratic authorities in general would be hard pressed to coerce them (aggressively) into doing so. While it is true that democratically-made laws cannot be thought of entirely as obligations that are voluntarily incurred, and while it is likewise true that violation of these laws is subject to punishment, it remains the case that in order for a democracy to work effectively, citizens must consistently choose against free riding on the willing compliance of others, especially "in situations where they are fairly certain of escaping detection."[2]

There are two questions that arise here. First, why would citizens agree to abide by democratically made decisions? Second, what is needed in order for citizens to abide by them? The first is not the main concern here, though we can see that in general democratic decisions are imbued with a certain kind of legitimacy. Theorists attribute this legitimacy to various aspects of democracy: its fair procedures, its beneficial outcomes, its fundamental acceptance of the equality of all people. Thus, one very important reason why democracies are successful over time is that the decisions made within democratic institutions are perceived to be legitimate, and this perception is central to any account of the voluntary compliance on which democracies rely. Yet the legitimacy of democratically made decisions does not alone secure compliance with them. Compliance is made more likely when trust exists among citizens and between citizens and their democratically chosen representatives. As Miller writes: "For this activity [voluntary compliance] to be successful, the citizens must trust the state, and they must trust one another to comply with what the state demands of them."[3] Let me explain in general how this can be the case, and then in the next section I will offer a more precise analysis of the specific democratic features that rely on trust.

In order to comply with regulations and laws when there is no way to secure against free riders, we need trust, and we need trust even if every person individually thinks that the law is independently a good idea. This is what I mean when I suggest that the legitimacy of a given regulation or law is insufficient to secure compliance in a democracy. It is possible for me to agree that a law is legitimate—morally perhaps, or because it has been decided in some forum that I regard as legitimate—without being willing to abide by it. More than simple legitimacy is required to secure my compliance. When I consider whether to abide by some law—when abiding carries some cost for me, and when I know that I cannot know without a doubt that others will abide by the law—I choose to abide (at least partly) because I trust that others will do so as well. I know that the benefits to be secured from collective compliance will arise *only if* most of us comply. Yet since I can never know for sure whether others will themselves comply at any given moment, I must trust them to comply. We reason to ourselves that others are likely to abide by democratically established rules and thus that the risk that we alone comply with a particular rule (and so are taken advantage of by others) is low. We even acknowledge the existence of some free riders, since the system can support a small number of them, so long as their number is small enough that their existence is too small to undermine the system. We may see, for example, people jumping over the turnstiles to get on the London Tube, but go on paying for the service nevertheless in the expectation that others generally do so as well. We offer our tickets to the train conductor when he asks whether there are tickets he hasn't yet seen, knowing that he has no way (other than his memory) of determining whether you've displayed your ticket. Free riding is easy to accomplish in these situations, but most people choose against it, at least as long as they believe that most others are likewise choosing against it.

In general, it seems plausible to think that even if I'm willing to comply with some rule—where one important condition of my compliance is my belief that others are likewise in general complying with the same rule—my willingness will survive only so long as I believe that others are doing the same.[4] Consider the yellow box by way of example. In some British cities, a yellow box covers the area in the middle of busy intersections to indicate the area that must be kept clear of traffic when lights change. So, when I approach an intersection, I must know that I can get through from my side of the yellow box to the other side of the yellow box before the light changes. If I cannot be sure I will be able to exit the yellow box, I ought to stop before entering it so that, if the light changes, I am not blocking the intersection. This sort of norm is in everyone's best interest *so long as* most people are willing to abide by it. As people decide to violate the norm—to cross the yellow box before they can see that they will not block the intersection when the light changes—the incentive for others to abide by it decreases. My decision to abide by this traffic norm, therefore, is contingent on others' willingness to do the same. Here the (mainly visual) perception that others are, in fact, not willing to abide by a shared rule contributes to the decision others make to violate it as well.

Recall the six features of trust that I identified in chapter 1, and note how these are central to securing widespread voluntary compliance. Trust requires the acceptance of a certain amount of vulnerability. It transpires under conditions of imperfect information and uncertainty. It is expressed in relation to other people. There is a behavioral component to trust, and we must therefore actively express our trust in others. There is an attitudinal element to trust, which often involves some kind of moral evaluation. And, finally, trust (and distrust) is resistant to evidence that it is unwarranted. This, I think, is an accurate description of what occurs when people voluntarily comply with regulations: they are behaving in such a way as to make themselves vulnerable to others, who may choose not to comply themselves. They are reflecting on others, and determining that in all likelihood others will turn out to be trustworthy—they are adopting an attitude of trust toward them. They can never know for sure whether others will comply, and since the system can and does support a certain number of free riders, they can never be certain that any specific person has complied with a given regulation. They are regularly complying with democratically established legislation with incomplete information concerning the behaviors of others. In other words, trust is the central feature of widespread, collective, voluntary compliance with democratically established regulations, principles, and norms. On the other hand, when trust is absent, democratic institutions will prove unable to secure the compliance they need to function efficiently (and they may be forced, as a consequence, to resort to more coercive techniques to secure compliance): "if trust is low . . . institutions will be mere formalities, lacking compliance and effectiveness, as most people defect from obedience in the expectation that almost everyone else will" as well.[5] A democracy thus requires that citizens display a generalized disposition to trust; although regulations are generated at a political and general level, it is the voluntary compliance of trusting citizens, on an individual basis, that tends to ensure their effective implementation over time.

Basic Democratic Features and Trust

Now that I've made the general case for democracy and trust—since democracy relies on voluntary compliance, and voluntary compliance relies on trust, trust is central to democracy—we can turn to a closer look at the basic features of democracy to assess how trust is required for them to function effectively.

Democracy refers to a complex set of institutional mechanisms, principles, and norms, and there is plenty of theoretical and practical work that assesses the merits and weakness of various forms of democratic arrangements. Some models of democracy emphasize deliberation, others emphasize identifying and implementing the common good, and still others emphasize measures to secure fair but competitive bargaining among self-interested parties. In all cases, however, there are basic features we can identify without which no model of democracy can survive; indeed, without these features, the system is not fully democratic. They are as follows: the willingness of the governing party to give up power when it loses an election, the requirement that citizens accept the basic legitimacy of the representative system, and the existence of formal protections for the group of people who end up in the minority in any given election (and in any given legislative decision). My contention is that these basic features rely on trust.

Trust and the Electoral System

The willingness to give up and take up power in accordance with the preferences of the electorate is fundamental to democracy.[6] In order to be willing to participate in electoral politics to begin with, a party must believe that the other(s) will give up power if the electorate votes that way. In a basic way, trust is involved here, since political leaders must trust one another in particular to give up power upon losing an election; the vulnerability stems from accepting minority rather than governing status. Note, moreover, that the willingness to give up power in the face of electoral loss implies that a given representative will not then refuse to participate in government or withdraw her (and her group's) willingness to accept the winner and its subsequent decisions as authoritative: in order democracy to be effective, we require the loser's consent.[7] It is not only political leaders who must trust that others will give up power. In order for citizens to believe the electoral system is functional, and therefore to vote, they must likewise trust that the losing party will give up power; citizens who end up on the losing side must accept the legitimacy of the elected governors. The trust that underpins the willingness to comply voluntarily with the preferences of the electorate equally underpins the willingness to comply with the subsequent decisions made by the winner.

In consolidated democracies, where power transitions are a matter of course, the possibility that losing parties would refuse to step down in the face of electoral loss is not considered seriously. We thus might be tempted to say that losing parties have no choice but to step down, and therefore they are not well described as extending trust even if they are evidently vulnerable to the now governing party. Yet this is a case of trust at its best in democratic politics, where the basic trust that extends among citizens and political actors is so strong that the likelihood of violating it appears impossible and therefore as choiceless. The ongoing practice of effective democratic politics relies on this "choiceless" trust as a matter of course.

To say that we have trust in those who participate in and organize our electoral system describes more than simply the relationships that underpin the willingness to give up power after electoral loss and the willingness of losers to accept the winners' decision making. For one thing, trust is integral to the effective functioning of the electoral system—by which I mean the people who run the electoral system—which facilitates the selection of certain legislators over others. Consider, at a very basic level, what goes into a legitimate election: Voters' lists must be compiled—we trust that the compilers do their best to ensure that everyone is entitled to one vote, and no one can secure more than one vote. Electoral officers must monitor the voting process—for example, we trust the electoral officers to ensure that ballot stuffing does not occur and that no votes are deliberately discounted. And electoral boundaries must be drawn fairly—we trust that boundaries are not drawn to deliberately prevent one or another person from being elected. The purpose of this list is not to offer a comprehensive list of the ways in which the system for choosing governors is based on trust. It is merely to illustrate that the electoral system—the basic, democratic operation—is based at a very deep level on trust. Not only must each person who participates in securing the legitimacy of an election trust that others are doing the same, electors must also trust election organizers to take their job seriously. That the people who operate the elections can be trusted gives rise to a sense that the legislators were chosen fairly and so underpins the trust we extend in the political environment.

Trust and Political Representatives

Representative institutions permit the political participation of large numbers of people.[8] They permit groups of citizens who are presumed to share a set of interests in some way—generally, representatives are territorially based, on the assumption that citizens of a given territory have interests in common—to select a few individuals to do their bidding (in what sense, I shall soon discuss). Representatives are central to effective governance in modern democracies in large part because they serve to give voice to citizens' assorted preferences and values, and also because they work to produce legislation that will meet citizens' various needs and wants as best as is possible. Democratic representatives have "the potential to unify and connect the plural forms of association within civil society, in part by provoking citizens to reflect on future perspectives and conflicts in the process of devising national politics."[9] Representatives thus aim to convert the citizenry's divergent preferences and values into a coherent political program that can gain their widespread support.

The conventional way of thinking about the representative's role is typically attributed to a distinction drawn by Edmund Burke in his "Speech to the Electors of Bristol." Having won the controversial and narrowly contested election, Burke explained to his constituents how one might think of the representative's role, and how he himself thought of his own role. One way to think about the representative is to think of him as having been granted, through election, a set of "authoritative instructions . . . which the Member is bound blindly and implicitly to obey, to vote, and to argue for, though contrary to the clearest conviction of his judgment and conscience."[10] On this view, which is now conventionally referred to as the *delegate* model of representation, representatives are charged simply with carrying out a very specific mandate. As a result, this model "binds representatives to their constituents through elections and communication between elections."[11]

In a complex modern democracy, this is in general an impractical standard, even if aspects of some political processes do function according to this model. Consider the American Electoral College, for example, according to which voters choose electors to the Electoral College who then vote for the president of the United States (the precise way in which this happens differs by state). These electors are bound—more or less formally—to vote for the presidential candidate chosen by the voters (electors who vote against the wishes of the voters are termed "faithless electors," but this is infrequent and, to my knowledge, has never affected the outcome of a presidential election); in this case, we might say that the electors are representing voters as delegates. In most cases, however, it is near impossible to imagine that our representatives are charged only with registering our preferences as we express them via an election. Not only are election platforms so expansive that it is difficult to imagine that any one elector agrees with *all* of any one candidate's positions, but representatives are also too frequently called upon to make quick decisions concerning policies and questions about which no mandate has been provided. Instead, we have come to think of representatives as having discretion to act in our best interests, in a model of representation typically referred as "trusteeship." For Burke—who worried that the masses would prove unable to understand the depth and importance of decisions that representatives would be called upon to make—representatives must be granted extensive discretion to act as they see fit. Burke says a representative must

> live in the strictest union, the closest correspondence, and the most unreserved communication with his constituents. Their wishes ought to have great weight with him; their opinion high respect; their business unremitted attention. It is his duty to sacrifice his repose, his pleasures, his satisfactions, to theirs; and, above all, ever, and in all cases, to prefer their interest to his own. But, his unbiassed opinion, his mature judgement, his enlightened conscience, he ought not to sacrifice to

you. . . . Your representative owes you, not his industry only, but his judgement; and he betrays, instead of serving you, if he sacrifices it to your opinion.[12]

Thus, although representatives are morally obligated to be in constant discussion with their constituents, to gather their views, and to inform them of the relevant considerations, they are not simply charged with doing the bidding of those they represent. Instead, representatives are chosen because of their judgment skills, and in being elected they are authorized to exercise this judgment as a member of the legislative body to which they are elected. "Government and Legislation," Burke says, "are matters of reason and judgement, and not of inclination."[13]

Representation thus serves to mitigate the dangers of direct democratic rule in which the mere preferences of citizens—rather than the considered judgments of representatives—would be permitted to direct national legislation, and therefore diminish the likelihood (or even possibility) of policy making in the long term and the best interests of a national community in favor of short-term self-interested policy making.[14] The trustee model is so named because in selecting a representative, electors are interpreted to be extending their trust to a person who will then be charged with making decisions in their best interest. As Burke suggests, the trustee is not extended absolute free agency—he or she must be in constant touch with constituents in order to stay current with respect to their views and preferences.

Rather than free agency, the legislator is trusted to use her or his discretion wisely. In political environments where a particular legislator, or legislators in general, are granted the trust of their citizens, they are given discretion to make decisions, with which citizens agree to comply, about how the community in question should be governed. Given the constraints set by a series of accountability mechanisms that serve to prescribe limits to this discretion in advance (which I'll elaborate in the next chapter), legislators who are trusted to act within them are assumed to be able to make good political judgments. The benefits to the legislator should be clear: not only are they given a good amount of flexibility in making political decisions but they also do so with the knowledge that, because they are trusted, their decisions will likely elicit voluntary compliance. Further, under conditions of high levels of political trust, legislators know that even when political decisions are contentious (as they are often bound to be), citizens will be inclined to give them the benefit of the doubt.

Critics might suggest that it is a mistake to equate the trust that we extend to intimates with the trust we extend to political representatives. When we extend trust to our friends, family members, neighbors, and so on, we do this on the basis of personal experience—we witness these people in close proximity, responding to a range of situations, on a near daily basis. The encapsulated interested model of trust rightly points us to the fact that we trust those who are close to us in part on the basis of our belief that they share interests with us, or have our interests in mind when they act.[15] The same may not seem equivalent in the case of political representatives: if the trust we extend to them is based in personal experience, it is manifestly not the same kind of experience that is at work in our intuitive relationships; and insofar as we believe we have interests in common, or that they are motivated to act *by our* interests, it is not in the same way. Rather, our experience comes in the form of what is frequently one-way communication (since so few citizens choose to interact directly with political representatives) that we receive via a range of media, including newspapers, the Internet, radio, and television.[16] The messages that political legislators offer us, as a way to evaluate their capacity to act on our behalf, are evaluated for their plausibility and credibility. Our inability to trust this information cripples our capacity to act effectively in the political environment.[17] As Warren writes, "the representative's role is, in part, to provide citizens with the information they need to judge when they should trust."[18]

Typically, we extend trust to our political representatives because we believe that we share a set of interests in common, namely, an interest in preserving the democratic political community that defines us, as well as in promoting the national interest broadly understood. Of course, we do not typically trust all representatives to agree with our views on the content of policies that are in our national interest (although there are exceptions, and these will occupy us in chapters 5 and 6). There are legitimate disagreements that we can have on the direction our state should take that will not erode our trust in our representatives. The reason for this apparent disconnect is simply that the trust we extend to representatives is not necessarily based in policy agreement as much as it is based on a shared sense that we are all motivated by a commitment to protecting and promoting our collective interests.

At a very basic level, in order to extend political trust to their legislators, citizens must believe that they are committed to standard democratic principles and norms—as noted above, as one main democratic norm, is the willingness to share or give up power in the face of electoral loss. This form of political trust, however, does not derive simply from the belief that legislators have internalized, and demonstrated, a commitment to democratic norms and principles. In the main, citizens must believe that whatever their party affiliation, legislators intend to operate with the national interest in mind. So, even if representative democracy requires that individuals compete for election on the basis of specific platforms, and that one consequence of this is that some leaders appeal to some constituents but not to others, any winner must (seem to) be committed to the interest of the whole community, rather than merely the interests of the segment that elected her or him. Winners are trusted not to take a narrowly partisan position once in power; they are expected to legislate in the national common interest.[19] That trust in Tony Blair, for example, declined over the course of his tenure in office was due to the perception that he no longer had the national interest in mind, or that his perception of the British national interest was at odds with a more widely held view of British national interests, rather than because Britons were worried that he would subvert the basic norms of democracy (by refusing to give up power if faced with electoral defeat or by encouraging supporters of the Labour Party to stuff ballot boxes, for example).

Recall that as with trust in general, it is possible to use the term "trust" to refer to an individual person or to categories of people. We can also select one person to trust, even when this person falls into a category of people we more generally deem untrustworthy, and we can trust a category of people in general, for example, doctors, even if we don't extend trust to one particular member of this group. Thus, it is coherent to say both that we trust politicians as a group or that we trust this particular politician, and we can claim simultaneously that we do not trust politicians in general, but that we do trust this or that politician (and vice versa). It is possible, for example, to say that we trust members of the Democratic Party but not Barack Obama; equally, we could say that we trust Barack Obama, but not members of the Democratic Party in general. If, on the one hand, we claim that we trust politicians in general, the basis for this claim is, first, a belief that they have internalized the norms and values that underpin our community and, second, a belief that they have the national interest in mind when they make policy decisions; we trust politicians *because* they have internalized these norms and values and because they act in the national interest. We expect that the decisions made by politicians, in general, are guided by a recognition, if not an acceptance, of the "way we do things around here" and what's best for all of us. If, on the other hand, we claim generally to distrust politicians, but to trust this one in particular nevertheless, then the basis for our claim is that politicians in general do not successfully act in the best interests of the community and that this politician does do so nevertheless, and so can be granted our trust.

Often, the claim that we trust only one particular legislator is based on more than the simple claim that she seems to have internalized the norms we think are valuable or has the national interest in mind when acting. Rather than being a simple attitudinal claim, as it might be (but need not be) when we refer to politicians in general, we are making a moral evaluation of a particular politician that is akin to the evaluation we make in the interpersonal trusting relations I described in chapter 1. We gather information about the specific individual we trust, and we use this information to make what looks like a moral evaluation about whether to trust a particular legislator. In this case, our general attitude toward politicians—that they are untrustworthy—is trumped by the results of a moral evaluation in which we might conclude that, nevertheless, *this* politician is trustworthy. In the political environment, as is the case more generally, the moral evaluations we make in determining whether specific rather than general others are trustworthy are given greater weight in our decision-making process than is the general trusting attitude with which we approach people or a category of people.

Trust and Minority Protection

Trust in the political environment doesn't refer solely to the relations between political leaders or between legislator and citizen, however, though it may do when we're referring to a competitive, associational sort of democratic arrangement. In outlining the trust we extend in the political environment, we are also denoting the trust relations that extend among citizens who believe that fellow citizens have internalized democratic norms and values. By trusting their legislators, citizens offer legislators the opportunity to use their discretion in generating legislation appropriate for our political community. By trusting fellow citizens, citizens indicate their belief that others will be willing to implement decisions made by legislators. If trust among citizens exists, then legislators will have the freedom not only to exercise their discretion but also to generate decisions that will garner voluntary rather than coercive compliance. This is the general story about trust that I told in the opening section of this chapter, and it is this widespread trust among citizens that secures the long-term stability of a democratic community. Because very few formal constraints exist to mediate citizens' political relations, it is sometimes difficult to recognize fellow citizens' commitment to democratic norms and values and to signal one's own commitment to these same norms and values.

What is the basis of trust among citizens? In any democracy in which decisions are made by some variation of majority rule, there will always be losers, people whose first preferences in leaders or legislation are not reflected in the outcome. Any defense of the majority rule principle recognizes that a certain proportion of people will turn out to be in the minority on any given decision; ideally, the makeup of people in the minority—given the large number of decisions that need to be made on a regular basis—on any given decision is in constant flux. These people accept and abide by decisions made by majority rule because the procedure is perceived as legitimate and fair, and they have a reasonable expectation that they will turn out to be in the majority when future decisions are made. In spite of this expectation (which is often not realized), those in the minority need some kind of guarantee that they will not suffer abuse or discrimination for being in the minority. Moreover, the conditions of stable democratic participation, as well as peaceful living, are generally connected to there being a set of rights and freedoms that cannot be altered without overcoming significant obstacles. These are guaranteed for members of the majority and members of the minority. The third basic feature of democracies is the existence of minority protection—that is, some mechanism to protect those who either lose an election or whose preferences are not ultimately reflected in legislative decisions. The long-term objective of this sort of protection is to ensure that citizens can live together peacefully even if only some of their preferences are reflected in legislation at any given time: the minority is to be free of discrimination and their basic rights will remain protected.

Thus, trust among citizens derives in part from the existence of a formal mechanism to protect minorities from abuse and discrimination by majorities. The existence of this formal mechanism, however, is insufficient in and of itself to generate trust among citizens. The formal commitment to protecting equal rights must be accompanied by citizens' demonstrated willingness to object to policies that instantiate abuse and discrimination of others. One main way in which citizens demonstrate their commitment to a constitution that enshrines the equal rights of all citizens is by refusing to offer support to political parties that have in mind to reject this principle. The emergence of political parties that campaign on a platform of reducing the rights of certain groups (implicitly or explicitly) is often a signal that the trust that underpins a commitment to the protection of minorities (whose rights will be reduced) has been (or is being) eroded.[20] We trust our fellow citizens to reject the suggestion that oppression of some citizens by others is acceptable.

To take an example—consider Jean-Marie Le Pen's success in qualifying for the second round of the 2002 French presidential elections. Le Pen is widely known in France for his anti-immigrant views, and has frequently been accused of harboring both anti-Semitic and anti-Muslim views. Yet he won just over 15 percent of the vote in 2002, and thus qualified to participate in the second-round vote.[21] Much of the French public was horrified that someone with such objectionable views had been this successful in electoral politics and in response took to the street to protest. Le Pen was soundly defeated in the final round of the presidential election. We can rightly interpret the response by the French public to the possibility of a Le Pen-led France in terms of a commitment to mobilize against electoral candidates who aim to restrict the rights of minorities; here the trust that extends among citizens was secured by the French public's response to the possibility that the rights and privileges of minorities would be jeopardized.

While the two previous conditions of democracy rely on trust (and allow the development of deeper trust), this final basic condition may seem to have a different relation to trust. At first glance, it may seem that the main role for minority protection is to act as a precondition for the development of trust relations among a democratic populace. On this view, there would be a clear paradox: isn't the need to institutionalize a set of effectively unalterable rights and freedoms, most likely in the form of a constitution, an expression of distrust? How can so clear an expression of distrust serve as a precondition for trust? The next chapter considers the relation between distrust and democracy in greater detail. For now, let me say only that when citizens can know *beyond a doubt* that certain behaviors are prohibited and certain rights are unambiguously guaranteed, they might feel themselves as more free to take the risks associated with trusting others: some of the vulnerability associated with extending trust will be mitigated by the existence of constitutional rights protections. (I shall suggest that this is the case with a series of multicultural policies, for example, in the book's conclusion.) But the constitutional protection of minority rights itself likewise *relies* on trust. In Mill's words, "political checks will no more act of themselves, than a bridle will direct a horse without a rider... if the public, the mainspring of the whole checking machinery, are too ignorant, too passive, or too careless and inattentive," the constitution (among other institutions intended to protect against abuse) cannot function properly.[22] If citizens are unwilling to comply with what the constitution demands of them—by, for example, refusing to insist on the equal rights of all citizens—the constitution itself will fail to protect minorities. We must trust others to abide by, and to work toward the full implementation of, constitutional provisions. It is one thing to have a constitutional provision protecting against discrimination on the basis of race, it is another thing to ensure that no discrimination on the basis of race occurs. The latter condition in a democracy requires voluntary compliance in order to obtain, and this voluntary compliance, as with the other two minimal conditions for democratic support, relies on trust.

Whereas the two prior conditions apply mainly to the political realm, the compliance with minority protections, which clearly often has political implications, is often also carried out in less obviously political domains. Many rights and freedoms that are constitutionally entrenched do not pertain exclusively to the political environment and require a broader commitment on behalf of the populace in order to be effective (I will return to this in the next chapter). We need citizens to refrain from discrimination in hiring and education, to allow the free practice of religion, and so on. Although these rights may be protected, it is in practice impossible to secure them without the voluntary compliance of citizens in what is sometimes described as the social domain. This form of trust is frequently referred to as *social trust,* that is, the trust that we extend to and expect of others in a wide range of situations that aren't obviously political.

At times, it may prove helpful to distinguish between social and political trust—but there is little genuine difference between the content of political trust that defines the relations among citizens and the social trust that is said to define relations among citizens living together more generally, even as many other scholars prefer to effect a neat separation between them.[23] We might think of social trust as the trust that underpins the set of norms and understandings that guide how citizens interact with one another when they meet in the street, when they engage in exchange relations, when they participate in volunteer associations, and so on—in other words, in situations that are to some degree apolitical. If you enter a library and leave your coat on a hook by the door as you search through the stacks, the trust in operation here is well captured by the term "social trust." Similarly, if you fall on the sidewalk, and someone offers to help you, you might be described as relying on social trust in accepting her helpfulness. In general—and this is an idea that will be examined in more detail in later chapters—when you determine that others can be trusted by virtue of an expectation that they operate by the same broad community standards that guide your own behavior, you are engaging in, or relying upon, social trust. As a result, insofar as there is a distinction between political trust and social trust, it pertains to *what* is being trusted to others, that is, actions consistent with our shared *political* norms and values, rather than norms and values more generally, and not to whom it is being extended. The distinction between political norms and values and norms and values more generally will, moreover, be imprecise, as we shall see in later chapters; many of these shared norms and values will guide actions in both political and more obviously social domains.

Conclusions

As I have argued, trust is at the foundation of democratic communities, and the effectiveness of democratic political institutions depends on the existence of widespread trust among members of the community. In particular, democracies rely on citizens' voluntary compliance with democratically established rules and regulations, and central to voluntary compliance is trust: I comply with what is asked of me, at some cost to myself, because I trust others to do the same, and at some cost to themselves. The three basic conditions for democracy—the belief that a losing party will give up power and abide by the rules set by the winner, the belief that the electoral system fairly chooses legislators who, in turn, have the national interest in mind, and that protections for the minority exist, generally (but not exclusively) in the form of a constitution, and are largely unalterable over time—rely on trust. They also provide the basis for the broader and more extensive trust that underpins successful democratic communities.

The reason to think carefully about the role of trust in democratic communities is in part so that we can understand how we should think about the evidence that trust is declining across democratic communities, as well as the evidence that this decline is in part a result of increasing rates of ethno-cultural diversity. We must first, however, settle on an account of the apparent opposite of trust—distrust—and assess its role, if any, in democratic political communities.

3

DISTRUST, MISTRUST, AND DEMOCRACY

In the preceding chapter, I argued that trust is central to assuring the smooth functioning of the most basic of democratic institutions, and that trust is among the central public attitudes that must prevail in order for these institutions to maintain support over time. When there exists widespread trust among a population, legislators can act knowing that their decisions will elicit voluntary compliance, compliance offered because citizens trust legislators to make good decisions and because they trust their cocitizens to abide by these decisions. This is, clearly, an optimistic picture—some might even think it naïve—and often does not pertain within democratic communities. We have reason, after all, to believe that any democratic community will need to survive the ebb and flow of trust relations as citizens and their legislators react to changing political and social circumstances that can have positive and negative effects on trust relations.

One reason to suspect that some amount of distrust or mistrust can be handled by democratic regimes is provided by recent empirical evidence announcing declining trust relations across democratic communities. Polls reveal a decreased sense of trust and confidence in legislators and the institutions they operate, an increased sense of alienation from the political system, and an increased cynicism about the motivation of those who choose to enter politics.[1] Although some claim that distrust may be healthy—perhaps it is the case that "too much trust may be a bad thing for our liberties"—the belief that others can be trusted in general, or that the government can be trusted to do the right thing, is increasingly rare.[2] The general worry is that without trust the voluntary compliance that secures an efficient and effective democracy will plummet.[3] Absent trust, "citizens may begin to withdraw voluntary compliance with the system, including voluntary compliance with other laws, and thus set in motion the downward spiral of worsening performance and more withdrawal from collective action of all kinds."[4]

In the first section of the chapter, I analyze the concept and phenomenon of distrust, and the closely related concept and phenomenon of mistrust. In the past, many political theorists have suggested that distrust is central to democratic politics; I unpack this argument and then suggest that distrust is instead inimical to democracy. Democracy certainly does rely on vigilance: citizens must be watchful of their representatives. I suggest, however, that this vigilant attitude is itself motivated by mistrust rather than distrust, and I then argue that this vigilant, mistrustful attitude in fact depends on extensive trust relations among citizens and between citizens and their representatives. Whereas certain forms of distrust clearly damage trust relations, the mistrust that underpins vigilance supports rather than undermines strong democracy.

Distrust and Mistrust: A Conceptual Analysis

Chapter 1 began by exploring the concept and phenomenon of trust. I suggested that in order to understand the implication of social science research indicating a widespread decline in trust and confidence in others, we first needed a clear understanding of the meaning of trusting others. I offered a way to understand trust, as well as a guide to understanding the way in which social science and philosophical research has treated it. This chapter turns to concepts that are deployed to signal the absence of trust, namely, distrust and mistrust; as I shall suggest, they signal the absence of trust in quite distinctive ways, and their respective absences therefore have distinctive implications for political practice in democratic communities.

The first observation to make is that an absence of trust does not automatically translate into distrustful or mistrustful attitudes; in this sense, neither of these concepts is, strictly speaking, the opposite of trust. There are plenty of people in whom we do not place our trust on a regular basis simply because we do not find ourselves in situations in which it is appropriate to extend trust, or otherwise, to them. In these kinds of cases, it would be odd to say that we distrust them, even though trust may be not be actively present; having neither met nor interacted with the citizens of Iceland, for example, I may not have a trusting attitude toward them (except, perhaps, insofar as I trust people in general), but this absence of trust is not equivalent to distrusting them. Whatever it is that distrust and mistrust mean, it is not simply the absence of trust in others.

Defining Distrust

Distrust is best interpreted as an attitude that reflects suspicion or cynicism about the actions of others; people are deemed untrustworthy in part because they have over time provided (what is taken as) evidence that they cannot be trusted.[5] When we say that others are not trustworthy, we are expressing suspicion or perhaps doubt about their motives and intentions. If my community is characterized by a generalized distrust, I will actively believe that people are untrustworthy, and so view them with suspicion or skepticism. If I believe it is unsafe to walk outdoors at night because I may be mugged, I have a distrustful attitude toward others. If I believe that, given the opportunity, others would break promises or otherwise try to cheat in their dealings with me, I distrust others. Approaching interactions not just with caution, but in particular caution infused with skepticism and cynicism, is to approach them with a distrustful attitude. It is a mindset that propels people to believe that most interactions carry risk, perhaps substantial risk, and that the risk of harm and disappointment is far greater than the likelihood of success in any interaction. Distrustful people will often believe that others are inclined to exploit or harm them should the opportunity arise: "when we distrust someone, we regard even those acts and gestures which should be benign as sinister underneath . . . what is said is not taken 'straight' because we assume that the other is trying to deceive, mislead, or manipulate us."[6] Distrust can derive from multiple sources. For example, distrust can emerge when we question another's competence (he will not be able to carry out the task), when we question another's willingness (he will not be willing to carry out the task), or when we question someone's stated intentions (we suspect someone of lying or obfuscating the truth of his intended actions, or believe that he is simply unaware of his own relative competence to carry out some task).

Also, trust and distrust are not necessarily incompatible. As with trust, distrust can describe both a general attitude and an attitude directed toward specific people or categories of people. It is thus possible to have a distrustful attitude toward people in general, while maintaining strong trusting attitudes toward certain others. This is the story, for example, reported by Edward Banfield of Montegrano, a small rural village in southern Italy where, as of the late 1950s, the 3,400 inhabitants had failed to develop any sense of community or camaraderie. Montegrano is an example of a community pervaded by a climate of distrust. To cope with their belief that virtually all other members of the community were untrustworthy, and so unwilling or unable to help them in their times of need, village members relied exclusively on their immediate families for help.[7] Banfield characterized village members as distrustful in general, which was not incompatible with the selective trust that village members tended to display toward their own family members.

We can also observe that a generally trusting person (someone, for example, who trusts her fellow Hungarians) can simultaneously have an attitude of distrust toward a certain category of people (someone, for example, who doesn't trust Hungarian politicians). And one can be distrustful of a category of people, say politicians or journalists, but determine nevertheless that Tony Blair and Wolf Blitzer deserve trust. It is also possible to have, at the same time, an attitude of distrust and trust toward the same person in at least two different ways. I may trust your willingness to carry out some task but not your competence to do so, and so determine that in spite of a general attitude of trust toward you I will, nevertheless, not trust you in this case. I could, for example, trust my best friend in general, but believe that she ought not to be trusted to drive me home safely. Or I could trust someone in relation to some set of tasks while *explicitly* distrusting him in relation to certain others. For example, I could trust someone to drive me home safely, while not trusting him to return items I have lent him.

Like trust, distrust is evidence resistant, that is, resistant to evidence that it is unwarranted. Once distrust has emerged—once we believe we have reason to distrust others—we will, as with trust, interpret their behavior through this lens, and will therefore read their behavior as confirming our bias against others. But there is an important difference, at least in principle, between trust and distrust and their relation to evidence. Although trust is *resistant* to evidence, in most cases it does not remain absolutely closed to evidence that it is unwarranted. Over time, and with sufficient evidence, unwarranted trusting attitudes can and often do shift. The same is not straightforwardly true of distrust, however, since the effect of distrust is to close off opportunities to gather evidence that it is unwarranted. As I shall describe in more detail in later chapters, distrust is "difficult to invalidate through experience" since it "prevents people from engaging in the appropriate kind of social experiment," that is, experiments in which people can prove themselves trustworthy and therefore deserving of trust rather than distrust.[8] Or as Trudy Govier explains, "distrust has a strong tendency to be self-perpetuating ... distrust impedes the communication which could overcome it."[9]

Consider a benign case, for example, in which we agree to lend our class notes to a friend who wasn't able to attend class on a given day; if that friend fails to return the notes (ever, or even in a timely fashion), the chance that we shall lend our class notes a second time is low. We will simply not provide an opportunity for this person to indicate that she has changed and can now be trusted to return notes. In a more extreme form, this attitude of caution underpins more deeply distrustful attitudes as well, such as those that are reflected in actions intended to insulate actors from the dangers (apparently) inherent in interacting with others. These are actions that are characterized not only by an unwillingness or reluctance to trust others, but also by the intention to prevent the opportunity to witness that others are trustworthy or otherwise. This is what Thomas Hobbes had in mind when he described an unstable and insecure environment in which people lock their doors at night and keep their valuables locked in their homes, even when they are there: "When going to sleep, he locks his doors; when even in his house he locks his chests; and this when he knows there be laws and public officers, armed, to revenge all injuries shall be done him; what opinion he has of his fellow subjects, when he rides armed, of his fellow citizens, when he locks his doors; and of his children, and servants, when he locks his chest."[10] In this sort of environment, we believe that people are untrustworthy and that we must guard against giving them opportunities to prove it, rather than giving them an opportunity to prove us wrong.[11]

As we shall see in chapter 6, the conditions in which we live have an influence on whether we are generally trusting or generally distrusting. Where we have good reasons to distrust others, as in the case of severely divided societies, considerable evidence will have to be furnished to justify one's willingness to shift one's attitudes. And since distrust closes us to opportunities to receive disconfirming evidence, we shall have to pay attention to the conditions under which trust can begin to seem plausible. Doing so will entail creating the conditions under which distrusters can, at a minimum, open themselves to disconfirming evidence; distrusters may be forced to act "as if one trusted, at least until more stable beliefs can be established on the basis of further information."[12] How such trust building operates is the subject of the concluding chapter of this book.

Defining Mistrust

We can distinguish distrust from a closely related concept, mistrust. Mistrust describes a precarious and indecisive attitude, characterized by approaching others with suspicion and caution. Mistrusters experience an unwillingness or an inability to commit to trust or distrust, and, as I shall describe, are therefore highly susceptible to new information. Mistrust and distrust are both characterized by a lack of trust, but there are at least three main differences between them. First, while distrust is a fairly stable attitude, mistrust is more variable, and so more sensitive to contextual changes. Second, in approaching a situation with an attitude of mistrust, one is doing so with caution and doubt or perhaps a generally questioning mindset rather than with the suspicion and cynicism that characterizes distrust. Third, while distrust is by and large inimical to democracy, mistrust can be good for democracy. I will explain the second and third of these distinctions in the next two sections of this chapter. First, however, let me say more about distrust as a stable attitude and mistrust as a variable one.

While distrust often refers to a general long-term attitude that tends to color a person's overall outlook, mistrust is a more precarious attitude. Mistrust is more likely to translate into ambivalence about others' trustworthiness rather than into a perception that they cannot be trusted at all. Mistrustful people then may sometimes decide to trust others or not to do so; often the context in which the decision is made will matter substantially. A mistrustful person is unsure about a given situation—she may not be sure whether delaying her decision will result in the emergence of information that might aid her in making a determinate decision—and instead of being committed to an attitude of distrust, she wavers between trusting others and distrusting them. A person with a mistrustful attitude is therefore characterized by indecision. Often this indecision is due to a seeming paucity of available information, and so is highly sensitive to the possibility of acquiring further information. In sum, mistrusting people are characterized by a frequently shifting attitude toward extending trust and/or no clear attitude toward extending trust.

Consequently, one clear distinction between distrust and mistrust is the effect of new information on the attitude. While both mistrust and distrust can emerge from lack of information, they differ with respect to their relative sensitivity to new information. While distrust is often described as evidence resistant, the same is not true of mistrust.[13] When people are mistrustful, they occupy a kind of limbo state in which the alternatives are: to take what seems to be a leap of faith and decide to trust with what they view as insufficient evidence indicating the wisdom of this decision, or to be reluctant to make decisions that could result in harm or injury of some kind. They consider a range of questions before making a decision, among them: What sort of immediate risks seem to be involved with the decision that must be made now? How great is the benefit associated with trusting, and how bad are the consequences of misplaced trust? What sort of safety net exists if I place trust, and my trust is betrayed or violated? What kind of information do I have with which to make this decision, and am I likely to be able to gather more in the near future?[14]

One consequence of this wavering attitude is that mistrust can turn into either trust or distrust if, over a series of individual and often difficult decisions, the trust turns out to have been well placed or misplaced. If a mistrustful person decides not to trust, the opportunity to identify whether others deserve to be trusted does not arise, and if this decision is made repeatedly the attitude can eventually be described as distrustful. For example, a person who, after much deliberation, repeatedly determines against hailing taxis on the street will eventually best be described as someone who is distrustful of taxi drivers.

In general, we may find that behaviors motivated by a mistrustful attitude are difficult to distinguish from those that are motivated by a distrustful attitude. Since a mistrustful attitude is typified by a wavering or vacillating stance in a given situation, it has to be possible that a mistrustful attitude could nevertheless result in what for all intents and purposes seems a trusting behavior, and that given very minor changes in condition a mistrustful attitude would not exist in the first place. Since mistrust arises from lack of (or minimal) information, a small change in the amount of information provided should alter not only the attitude but also the consequent behavior. Whereas I may decide not to trust anyone in a given situation, I may change my mind upon learning, for example, that the person I am being asked to trust is a member of my own ethnic group. Since a mistrustful attitude is so sensitive to small changes in the decision-making environment, mistrustful people are constantly seeking further information that might give them insight into whether trusting or distrusting is the best option for them.

The terms distrust and mistrust likewise apply not only to individual interactions but also in the context of group relations. On the one hand, group distrust—an environment in which individual members of a group adopt an attitude of distrust toward members of another group—arises as a result of a political or social context in which group relations are characterized by antagonism, often (although not always) the result of a power imbalance in which one group forcibly marginalizes and excludes the other from political and social life. African Americans provide one stark example of group distrust: as a group, African Americans display the highest levels of distrust of any group in the United States.[15] Melissa Williams describes the black American reaction to the failure of white American legislators to act in the best interests of blacks, even after slavery was abolished and African Americans were admitted to the ranks of equal citizenship: "they could not, after all, depend on Whites to represent them fairly. . . . Whites simply were unable to understand Black concerns and interests." Blacks, as a result, came to "doubt and distrust" the whites who claimed to speak and act on their behalf.[16]

Group mistrust, on the other hand, characterizes relations between groups of people when they are each unsure about whether in general it is best to trust members of the other group(s). It is an attitude that emerges under conditions of uncertainty—citizens do not feel themselves to have enough information to assess accurately the risk involved in trusting others—when members of discrete groups prefer to remain watchful of others and on the look out for information that might make it clear whether they ought to trust them. This sort of environment characterizes the relation between citizens and the legislators they elect to govern them. The former adopt an attitude of mistrust toward their legislators because it is perpetually unclear whether it is best to extend them their trust. They therefore prefer to remain watchful of their legislators rather than commit to trusting or distrusting them in advance.

Democracy and Distrust

In chapter 2, we saw that trust is central to democratic political communities. However, critics will undoubtedly observe that many democracies can survive in the face of some distrust—an attitude that is often reasonable, as in the case of Northern Ireland and Canadian Aboriginals. However, distrust is in fact inimical to the ongoing functioning of a democratic political community. We can explain how it is that democracies can function in the presence of *some* distrust by observing that distrust exists on a kind of continuum: as we shall see, the more widespread the distrust and the deeper it runs, the more we need to worry about our democratic communities.

Remember the three specific benefits of the voluntary compliance that prevails in democracies characterized by trust. First, we can expect an inclusive attitude to prevail; attitudes of trust will be extended generally rather than to specific individuals or categories of individuals. Second, we can expect that citizens in a trusting environment will choose against free riding even when there are no specific monitors or sanctions preventing defection. Third, we can expect that a general attitude of reciprocity prevails whereby members of group Y are willing to participate in group X's project here and now in the expectation that in the future, members of group X will likewise be willing to participate in group Y's project. A sense that the community is ongoing, and that trust and cooperation will prevail within this community over time, is central to supporting the loose reciprocity that characterizes trusting democracies.

The same is not the case in a distrusting environment, however. Citizens will either be generally distrustful of others or trust only specific, identifiable others. Free riding will be rampant; citizens will take advantage of opportunities to defect from legislation when they believe others will not comply with it (beyond the general limits of enforced compliance). Citizens will not be willing to invest in the projects of others since they will not trust that others will do the same for them. The voluntary compliance that typifies democracies will not characterize those in which distrust rather than trust prevails.

Of course, in most political communities, distrust is unlikely to be wholly absent. While the voluntary compliance that democracies *need* to function well depends on stores of trust, democracies can persist in the face of some, and perhaps even a great deal of, distrust. Once reports of distrust begin to emerge in a democracy, the institutional structure will not immediately crumble. Instead, it is more likely that some of the benefits of widespread trusting relations will dissolve over time; free riding may become more rampant, reciprocity may be extended less frequently. Over time, we may witness the weakening of a democracy in the face of widespread distrust, but the weakening will be neither immediate nor irreversible. One way to make this clear is to note recent research highlighting the apparently rising levels of distrust in Western liberal democracies. Among those (including me) who worry about these rising levels, the concern is not that our democracies will break up immediately, but instead that we will witness a steady decline in a democracy's capacity to provide benefits to its citizens, the provision of which relies on widespread trusting relations.[17]

Rather than being all or nothing, trust and distrust exist on a kind of continuum, as a result of which communities can be characterized by more or less distrust or by deeper or shallower distrust. Trust violations can range from (mere) reneging on agreements that are founded on trust relations through treating others in such a way that the emergence of trust becomes impossible, making it so that any decision to extend trust to others is transparently irrational. The more distrust that prevails, and the deeper it runs, the more we need to worry about our democracies. Chapters 5 and 6 will focus specifically on the stresses on trust relations in multicultural and severely divided communities respectively. Here I offer a general account of the strategies by which we can evaluate the depth of distrust in political communities. There are three dimensions along which we can evaluate the depth of distrust: the severity of trust breaches, the number of trust violations (or, instead, the length of time our community has been characterized by distrust), and the presence or not of power imbalances. Analysis along each of these dimensions enables an assessment of the depth of distrust within a community, as well as the extent to which we ought to worry about the democratic politics within it.

First, trust breaches may be severe. In a divided society, perhaps in one that has recently been characterized by sectarian conflict in which a set of competing ethnic groups are engaged in violent and hostile actions against others, the breaches will be severe. The distrust that pervades such environments has emerged as a result of acute breaches of trust in which members of one community carried out acts of tremendous violence and hostility against the others. At the end of such a conflict, citizens are asked to lay down their arms and work together as a community, and the challenge is in overcoming the deep distrust that now prevails. Each community thinks of the other: Recently, you behaved violently toward me and toward those about whom I care deeply. How can I trust that your attitude toward us has changed, just because the war has been declared over by some third party? Why should I feel justified in placing myself in positions of vulnerability—remember that willing vulnerability is a key feature of trust—in relation to you, you who have so recently behaved violently against me? This community is characterized by a deep distrust that has emerged as a result of serious life-threatening breaches of trust. The distrust that has emerged in this instance can reasonably be called *proportionate,* in the sense that the distrust seems more or less proportional to the harms caused by the breaches.

Alternatively, breaches of trust may produce disproportionate distrust. These are cases in which a breach of trust has occurred, but the level of distrust that has emerged is disproportional to the harm caused by the breach.[18] For example, disproportionate distrust may emerge as a result of a mistaken equation between certain behaviors and their relation to untrustworthiness. Take competence in a language other than the national language(s), as evidenced by an accent in the national language. Assuming a basic level of competence,

however, accented speech should not affect the development of trust relations among citizens in a democratic polity, since no one is impaired (because of difficulty in communication) from carrying out the tasks associated
with democratic politics. It is a behavioral difference that does not generate
any good reason for imputing a lack of trustworthiness to others. Members of
ethnic minorities nevertheless report feeling uncomfortable, distrusted, or
excluded based on ethnocultural characteristics including their accent in a
national language.[19] The distinction between proportionate and disproportionate distrust helps us to determine whether the response that citizens have
to breaches of trust is reasonable.

A second distinction, between rational and irrational distrust, helps to
assess the severity of the distrust, and on occasion overlaps with the propor-
tionate/disproportionate distinction. In severely divided societies in which
we determine that the distrust is proportional to the harms caused by the
breach, we are also likely to describe the distrust as rational. In other words,
a risk assessment along the lines recommended by rational choice thinkers
will, in these instances, lead to the determination that the distrust is rational.
Yet in other cases distrust may be irrational. In these situations, a formal risk
assessment might reveal that the level of distrust is unwarranted, yet the parties to the relationship continue to extend distrust.[20] The irrational distrust
in this situation has been "decoupled from assessment of the other's interests or past behavior," and instead "represents a form of presumptive distrust
that is conferred ex ante on others."[21] The irrationality that characterizes the
distrust in severely divided communities accounts for the ease with which
they turn (and return) to violence. Divided societies therefore are often in
part characterized by environments in which small breaches of trust generate
irrational or disproportionate responses.

A second way to consider the depth of distrust is to measure the frequency
of trust violations. This method of assessment considers the history of interaction between citizens; if the history is replete with violations of trust over
time, a climate of deep distrust may prevail, whereas if trust violations are a
recent phenomenon, the distrust may be shallow. For example, Northern Ireland is a severely divided society characterized by deep distrust. Both Protestants and Catholics can point to repeated examples of trust violations that
have transpired over an extended period of time. Both, moreover, are reluctant to make further attempts at extending their trust to the other only to see
it violated again and again.[22] Because the groups do not trust each other and
have not done so for an extended period of time, there may be few recent ex-

amples of trust violations; thus we cannot rely exclusively on the frequency of trust violations to measure the depth of distrust. We must therefore be careful to recognize situations in which distrust is so deep that trust is no longer extended between members of competing groups. In this context, the refusal to extend trust is a clear indication that the distrust runs deep and that we ought genuinely to worry about the eventual disintegration of the community. Moreover, the commission of wrongs—in addition to the unwillingness to condemn past wrongs—serves to increase and confirm the existence of severe distrust.

A third consideration in assessing where communities lie on the continuum between trust and distrust concerns the nature of the power relations between the parties. Significant power imbalances frequently exacerbate distrust or prevent the emergence of trust, since they are frequently accompanied by the oppression and marginalization of one community by another, as in the case of Aboriginals in Canada. Approximately half of Canada's Aboriginal population lives in concentrated areas, called reserves, where they are by and large isolated from the wider Canadian community. The reserves are widely acknowledged to have poor living conditions: on-reserve Aboriginals are unambiguously economically marginalized and their long-term political marginalization is evident as well.[23] Relations between Aboriginals and non-Aboriginals are characterized by extensive distrust. On the one hand, many non-Aboriginals are (wrongly, in my view) persuaded that Aboriginals are unwilling to help themselves and choose instead to survive from tax dollars the federal government redistributes from the pockets of non-Aboriginal Canadians. On the other hand, Aboriginals continue to display deep suspicion (not without reason) that the Canadian government and people are interested only in destroying their culture and assimilating them into the greater Canadian community. They point to the government's repeated failures to provide for Aboriginal groups; the history of Aboriginals in Canada is one of systemic exclusion from all domains of social and political life for over a hundred years. The relations between Aboriginals and (representatives of) the Canadian state are thus characterized by extensive distrust, a distrust that is exacerbated by the power that the Canadian state can exercise, and has exercised, to the disadvantage of Aboriginal Canadians.[24] In more general terms, a power dynamic in which one party chooses to abuse or misuse its greater numerical and political influence is likely to create an environment within which distrust runs deep.

In sum, we can measure the depth of distrust in a political community by considering the severity of trust violations, the frequency of trust violations, and the existence (or not) of power imbalances in relations between parties. I shall keep these measures of distrust in mind as I assess the trust relations in multicultural societies and in severely divided societies (in chapters 5 and 6, respectively).

Democracy, Mistrust, and Vigilance

Attempts to connect distrust and democracy abound. Vivien Hart offers a paradigmatic account of the apparent link between the two: "The dilemma of democracy which is the central concern of this political distrust is the ancient question of who guards the guardians. The answer of the distrustful is that the people must and can."[25]

In this section, I argue that it is a mistake to associate democracy so intimately with distrust. I am guided here by some insights articulated within contemporary republican political theory, according to which it is vigilance rather than distrust that is central to liberal democratic institutions. Republicans such as Quentin Skinner and Philip Pettit take seriously the observation that citizens cannot extend a blanket trust to one another and to their legislators: it would be naïve and dangerous to do so. At the same time, they recognize that the attitude democratic citizens take toward one another cannot accurately (at least not in well-functioning democracies) be characterized as distrust. Distrust, remember, is associated with betrayal and deep disappointment. Republicans argue that it is more accurate to refer to vigilance than distrust in an assessment of liberal democratic institutions. I shall suggest that vigilance is motivated by an attitude of mistrust rather than distrust. Because vigilance relies on the existence of robust trust relations among citizens, trust is therefore central to democratic theory.

In general, republicans are concerned to refute the claim that the best method by which we can secure the freedom of individuals is via a set of constitutionally entrenched rights. Even if helpful, this sort of mechanism fails to secure us against the possibility, and indeed likelihood, that our institutions of governance will come to be populated by people who are concerned to further their own interests rather than the good of the community. The worry that a constitution will fail to protect us from self-interested governors motivates Skinner to argue that we must "cease to put our trust in princes, and instead take charge of the public arena ourselves."[26] The danger of failing to take "charge of the public arena" is that we will lose our status as self-governing, since we will not be directly responsible for making political decisions. He writes: "A body-politic, no less than a natural body, which entrusts itself to be defended by someone else [i.e., unaccountable governors] is exposing itself gratuitously to the loss of its liberty and even its life. For no one else can be expected to care as much for our own life and liberty as we care ourselves."[27] Vigilance—"the virtue of remaining alert, especially in dealing with powerful authorities, to the possibility that others may be behaving in a corrupt, sectional fashion"[28]—thus occupies a central place in republican political theory. The immediate question that emerges for those who equate democracy with distrust is: doesn't the vigilance described here imply a distrust of others?

There are two ways in which vigilance is thought to be predicated on distrust, one institutional and one interpersonal. First, republicans advocate the creation of institutions that constrain the behavior of authorities, and these institutions are sometimes referred to as institutions of distrust. Second, republicans argue for the importance of an active citizenry that takes responsibility for monitoring authorities in spite of the existence of protective institutions of various kinds. It is not sufficient that citizens discharge their responsibility for vigilance by requiring legislators to abide by institutional constraints on their powers; their attitude must always be critical as well.[29] This attitude is sometimes described as distrustful. Let me consider and reject each of these claims in turn.

If it is correct to think of our representatives as invested with our trust and to interpret government in general as a trust—as Locke wrote, "the community put the legislative power into such hands as they think fit, with this trust, that they shall be governed by declared laws"[30]—we will need to worry about the violation of this trust. There is, after all, considerable danger in extending trust toward those holding legislative power. Thus an interpretation of government as a trust whereby representatives have discretion over the lives of many people must be accompanied by a formal and rigorous system of checks and balances. The various systems of checks and balances that have been proposed over the years all share the idea that it is, all things considered, best to constrain the behaviors of legislators so that they are dissuaded from abusing the power granted them. Democrats concerned with establishing fair procedures for adjudicating among competing interests recognize that checks and balances are especially necessary to secure a domain in which trust is possible. This is not coincidentally sometimes referred to as the paradox of trust and democracy: in Geraint Parry's words, it appears odd that "one entrusts government to those one distrusts."[31] It seems that we need to implement institutions that suggest a deep distrust of what our legislators will do when offered an opportunity to control the levers of power. In Vivien Hart's words, "the philosophy of democracy . . . may depend for its fulfilment on a sustained suspicion of the vulnerability of men and institutions to the temptations of power."[32]

When scholars argue that distrust is an essential element of democratic practice, they often point to the presence of accountability mechanisms, which serve to limit the actions of political actors. In chapter 2, I suggested that political trust underpins the discretion that political representatives depend on to operate in the political environment. This discretion is not absolute, and in the political environment it is constrained in part by institutions that render political representatives accountable for their actions. As J. S. Maloy explains in his account of the emergence of modern treatments of trust: "discretion and accountability are mutually necessary" in any modern liberal democracy.[33] The motivation to focus on accountability mechanisms stems from an awareness of the power we entrust to political representatives, and therefore from a fear that they will betray our trust, for example, by subverting the political system in which they operate: "our attention moves to the safeguards that are supposed to protect us when we trust others."[34] The desire to protect ourselves from the discretion we ultimately offer our representatives stems from a fear of betrayed trust, and this is a fear that we have learned in good part through our experience, both in our political lives and in our private lives. Peter Johnson writes that "our experience of the vulnerability involved in trusting another permits an insight into the dangers of political trust, which are exposed on a larger scale. Human attachments and allegiances in both public and private life involve a possible surrender to as yet unnoticed harm."[35] It is fear of the extraordinary harm that political actors can inflict that suggests the importance of accountability mechanisms that institutionalize vigilance.

Thus, we authorize our political representatives to act on our behalf, but we do so subject to a set of conditions that aim to constrain their actions in three broad ways; one in advance of their actions, one during their actions, and one after their actions, and it is the latter two that are typically referred to as accountability mechanisms. In the first place, legislators are constrained simply by our having placed limits on what they are able to do—in practice, these constraints are outlined in constitutions and associated legal documents that delimit the legitimate range of actions for political representatives.

Political actors are further constrained by accountability mechanisms that aim to increase transparency and monitoring or surveillance in the form of various auditing procedures. Transparency mechanisms demand that political actors make their internal communications public, for example, and that they make public the source of their financial support. Surveillance or auditing mechanisms demand that political actors be subjected to auditing procedures that provide a third party with "full disclosure of information and circumstances needed to judge" whether the proper procedures have been followed.[36] The objective of these institutions is to protect the perceived *trustworthiness* of public actors, and therefore permit us to extend them warranted trust.[37]

Of late we have seen calls to deepen the scrutiny to which political actors are subject, in response to apparently increased political cynicism. This increased cynicism can press in two directions: it can "encourage a salutary civic vigilance and thus oblige government to pay greater heed to social demands, yet it can also encourage destructive forms of denigration and negativity."[38] The *danger* is that these institutions serve to "economize on trust," since they serve to "guarantee" trustworthiness, and therefore make it such that "placing trust will be simultaneously risk-free and unnecessary."[39] In the absence of trust, and additionally in the presence of distrust, accountability institutions serve to reduce the trust that is needed to enable a political system to function effectively.

It is a mistake, however, to suggest that these institutions permit political systems to function in the absence of trust. As I shall soon describe, we will also need to maintain an engaged, vigilant attitude in order to sustain an effective democratic system. A dependence on expansive accountability mechanisms is thus dangerous for suggesting that citizens can disengage from the political system without penalty, that is, that they can abandon their own responsibility for sustaining an effective democratic system.[40] However effective its accountability mechanisms, an effective political system will require a vigilant attitude, and this attitude depends on stores of available trust. The demand for accountability mechanisms may well emerge from an absence of trust, and often from the presence of active distrust, and they can serve as a last resort to protect the stability of a system in which citizens have little trust. As we shall see, moreover, under the right conditions, they can also serve to provide opportunities for trust to emerge. In the ideal they are seen as a partner to the vigilant attitude that characterizes active and engaged citizens, which I will soon describe.

More generally, however, the decision to structure institutions to constrain the behavior of legislators is not motivated by distrust as much as it is motivated by a realism about the nature of political life. For one thing, it would be politically naïve to extend blanket trust to all legislators, and the institutions of constraint serve to protect us from those who are unable to resist the temptation to abuse their powers. This observation is consistent with my earlier claims, that is, that it is possible to trust categories of people, for example political actors, without trusting each and every one of them. Second, although people are in general trustworthy—those who agree to legislate, therefore, are not inherently untrustworthy—they are corruptible under certain conditions, including conditions under which they are given a substantial degree of power. This response suggests that while I trust others in general, I do not trust them in certain conditions, and therefore protect myself when they arise. This insight drives republicanism's central tenet that citizens must, *themselves*, be willing to engage in politics: citizens must actively protect their own freedom since no one else can be expected to be willing (or able) to do so on their behalf. Third, we can intend to trust our legislators to carry out some activities and not others, and so we constrain them as a way to signal the boundaries of the discretion we extend them. In this case, the claim is that we judge this category of people—legislators—to be trustworthy in carrying out a particular set of tasks (presumably what they have been mandated to do, broadly understood), and we wish to take precautions to ensure that they act to carry out only those tasks. Moreover, even if we take precautions to prevent legislators from overstepping boundaries, we are well aware that the conditions of representative democracy in general are such that there will *always* be room for trust. The discretion we offer, articulated in chapter 2, is such that even within the boundaries created by the institutions of constraint just described, there is plenty of room for trust.[41] Fourth, it may simply be that in political life the stakes are so high that while we trust political actors in general, we may prefer to establish a set of backup institutions in cases where this trust proves unfounded.

Together, these observations suggest that while we trust legislators in general, we insist on constraining them via a set of institutions because not all legislators are trustworthy; because even generally trustworthy legislators might be inclined to overstep the boundaries of the tasks with which they have been entrusted; and because even if we do constrain some of their actions, we leave plenty of room for trust. We can conclude, therefore, that these sorts of constraining institutions do not fundamentally express our distrust in our legislators. But what do they express, if not distrust?

Primarily, these constraining institutions express our *mistrust,* a mistrust that reflects a "healthy suspicion of power upon which the vitality of democracy depends."[42] Recall that mistrust is reflected in a constant unwillingness or felt inability to commit to trusting or distrusting; it is an unstable mindset in which a person finds it difficult to determine whether she should take the risks associated with trusting. When this kind of attitude is translated from the individual level, as described in the first section of this chapter, to the political or group level as described here, it serves to motivate the kind of vigilance now being elaborated. The inherent uncertainty in politics generates an attitude of mistrust in citizens, an attitude that in turn generates the requirement that citizens adopt a vigilant attitude. Because citizens are perpetually unsure that their governors can be trusted and because they are unsure that they will agree that their decisions are the right ones, they must adopt an attitude of mistrust toward them, and this attitude of mistrust translates into vigilance. At the political level, a mistrustful attitude translates into vigilant behavior, and one way in which this vigilance is formally instantiated is via the institutions described above. And so we can say that as democrats our intention is, in general, to institutionalize vigilance—which we are motivated to do because of our mistrustful attitudes—when we insist on implementing institutions that serve to constrain the behaviors of legislators. Having made these observations, we can notice two things about vigilance. First, vigilance *does not require* an attitude of distrust toward our legislators, and second, the vigilance we display in constraining our legislators *is not inconsistent* with having an attitude of trust toward them.[43]

Institutional vigilance is a passive way in which citizens express their mistrust, but as republicans observe, the protection of a flourishing democratic community depends equally on an active citizenry.[44] It is not sufficient that citizens discharge their responsibility for vigilance by requiring legislators to abide by institutional constraints on their powers; additionally, their attitude must be critical on an ongoing and continuous basis. A generally mistrustful attitude acts as a kind of backup mechanism of constraint for legislators; if legislators know that citizens are paying attention—via media, by demanding public input and consultation, for example—they will feel themselves constrained in a way that is somewhat analogous to formal institutions of constraint. Insofar as these mechanisms are motivated by a desire to routinize vigilance rather than to express distrust, so is this vigilant mindset motivated by an attitude of mistrust rather than distrust.

A public commitment to vigilance depends on trust in two ways. First, citizens must believe that the unfair restriction of the rights of some individuals is an affront to the community as a whole. Citizens, especially those whose rights and privileges are being constrained, must trust that others will commit themselves to campaigning against rights-restricting policies that unknowingly burden or deliberately target them. Note how it is reciprocity—the reciprocity that is central to democratic communities, especially those in which a public culture exist—at work. This observation is an extension of John Stuart Mill's explanation of the proper behaviors of citizens living under representative institutions. He writes, "the rights and interests of every or any person are only secure from being disregarded when the person interested is himself able, and habitually disposed, to stand up for them."[45] If citizens cannot stand up for themselves and their rights because they are prevented from doing so by an unreasonably burdensome policy, others must stand up on their behalf. Second, citizens must be willing to commit their time and energy on behalf of others without the clear knowledge that their efforts will be reciprocated. They must trust that the citizens they are aiding would be willing, if the need arose, to act on their behalf in return.

Consider, by way of example, the mechanisms by which democracies protect minorities within their communities. Minorities are *formally* protected when there exists formal legislation outlawing discrimination against them. Since, however, it is virtually impossible for the state to enforce full-scale compliance with antidiscriminatory regulations, we must rely on citizens to comply voluntarily with them. Thus minorities are *actually* protected when this legislation is willingly implemented by citizens in the domains of their lives over which they have control. For example, although legislation exists that prevents discrimination in employment hiring practices, citizens must in general be trusted to refrain from engaging in discriminatory hiring practices on their own. Not only are citizens trusted to implement voluntarily nondiscriminatory legislation when that legislation governs their actions (say, as an employer who faces little formal evaluation, but nevertheless is obligated by law to hire on a nondiscriminatory basis), but citizens must likewise be vigilant in observing that this legislation is being followed in general and that any legislation that generates an undue burden for—that is, discriminates against—citizens who are unable to object on their own behalf is jointly rejected, on their behalf, by the entire community. Persistent vigilance thus depends on our trusting others to protect our rights from being violated.

There is also second way in which vigilance depends on trust. I have in mind the trust that comes into play when interest groups identify policies that they believe will have a detrimental effect on the community as a whole.

This interest group is willing to campaign against a policy it believes to be generally harmful, and is willing to raise awareness in the community at large concerning the specific ills likely to be caused by this or that policy. Here, trust goes in at least three directions. First, we must trust fellow citizens *in general* to be willing to assess policies for possible detrimental effects when these effects are brought to their attention. Second, members of the interest group who have taken on the burden of fighting the policy must trust that citizens,[46] once made aware of the possible detrimental effects, will be willing at the very least to consider the merits of the information (they need not, necessarily, be trusted to agree with the interest groups' conclusions). Additionally, if the information is judged accurate, members of the interest group should be able to trust that they will be given support in their efforts: fighting to overturn a policy that is judged detrimental to the community as a whole cannot be left only to those who are willing to bother with it or those who are adversely affected by it. Third, citizens themselves must trust that members of interest groups raising concerns about policies that (allegedly) have detrimental effects on the public at large are acting sincerely and honestly in their campaigns.[47] There is no requirement that citizens agree with the assessments presented by the interest groups; that is, citizens are not trusted to act on behalf of whatever policy is deemed detrimental (by others) in some way. Trust is what ensures that citizens are willing to consider the views of an interest group, and to participate with them in fighting detrimental policies if, after careful consideration, they agree that these policies are indeed detrimental.

Conclusions

The most likely objection to a view that places trust at the center of democratic political activity is that it is distrust, rather than trust, that is central. We need distrust, say these critics, because trust only breeds a kind of apathy that allows political actors to act as they wish rather than in the interests of citizens. My goal in this chapter was to debunk this claim. Trust is central to the voluntary compliance that underpins all effective democratic politics. Voluntary compliance, I suggested in chapter 2, relies on trust along two dimensions: citizens must trust their legislators to have their best interests in mind and citizens must trust one another to abide by democratically established rules and regulations. Yet it is not that citizens should look the other way as political actors make decisions that have profound and lasting impact; rather, citizens must be vigilant with respect to their legislators and fellow citizens, that is, they must be willing to ensure that the institutions are working fairly and that people continue to abide by shared regulations. This vigilance, which is reflected both in a set of institutions and in an active citizenry, is motivated by an attitude termed "mistrust." Mistrust is a cautious attitude that propels citizens to maintain a watchful eye on the political and social happenings within their communities. Mistrust *depends* on trust: we trust fellow citizens to monitor for abuses of our own rights and privileges just as we monitor for abuses of their rights and privileges. We are, therefore, right to worry about widespread reports of the decline of trust, and wrong to conclude that distrust is somehow good for, or central to, democracy. Just as distrust is harmful to human relations of all kinds, and just as trust is central to positive human relations of all kinds, so is distrust inimical to democracy and trust central to its flourishing.

Chapters 5 and 6 consider the sorts of difficulties polities face in the absence of trust relations. Chapter 5 considers the difficulties faced by multicultural polities, and chapter 6 considers the difficulties faced by severely divided societies. Over the course of these chapters, it will be essential to recall that I am describing a continuum with trust on one side and distrust on the other; democracies, as I have described them in this chapter, must sustain a healthy level of mistrust, since this mistrust fosters the vigilant attitude that protects the democratic process. As we shall see, severely divided societies are defined by distrust, and our objective will be to press them toward trust, whereas multicultural societies are defined simply by weakened trust relations; the worst-case scenario is that multicultural societies will pursue policies that will press them toward severe division. In order to understand the difference between the dilemmas faced by multicultural societies and severely divided societies, however, we must turn to a prior question: if trust relations often break down along group lines, is there a way in which we can surmount this problem? In the next chapter, I turn to one possible solution, namely, the creation and maintenance of a public culture that can serve as a reliable and inclusive source of trust relations within a citizenry.

4

PUBLIC CULTURE AND TRUST

Earlier chapters suggested that trust is central to democratic political activity, and that even if a political community can sustain a certain degree of distrust for some time, distrust is by and large inimical to democracy. We now turn to an assessment of the source of trust in democratic political communities. Although there is disagreement among political theorists on this point, many do agree that shared norms and values play an essential role in sustaining democratic communities—the sum total of these shared norms and values is frequently termed the "public culture" of a democracy. This chapter offers a *qualified* defense of the public culture argument, namely, the argument that liberal democracies function well primarily when its institutions are supported by a public culture of the right type.

In chapter 3, we saw that trust is not merely an important feature of democratic success, but that it is also a necessary feature of democratic survival. Here I shall argue the following: *a public culture, properly articulated, can be a genuine and meaningful source of the trust that plays a critical role in sustaining liberal democratic social and political institutions over time.* Typically, it is merely assumed without question that a public culture is a source of trust, and this assumption opens the argument to a range of objections to which it appears not to have the resources to respond. A careful evaluation of the reasons *why* a public culture can give rise to trust makes it less vulnerable to critics who prefer to equate the public culture with homogenizing and marginalizing tendencies. That said, a preliminary caveat is in order: a public culture, while being an important source of trust, is not the sole source of trust; moreover, not all public cultures are able to serve as a source for trust. The chapter aims, therefore, not simply to account for *why* a public culture can underpin trust relations, but also to offer an account of the features it must possess in order to do so; in offering this account, I shall also shed light on why and when public cultures *fail* to act as a source of trust.

The chapter begins with an outline of the public culture argument, and why we might think that public culture can serve as a source of trust. Two general critiques are then refuted. The first critique suggests that democracies do not require a public culture in order to function effectively; all that is required is a shared commitment to liberal institutions. The second critique suggests that a public culture is too *thin* to underpin democratic politics; for those who launch this critique, public culture is merely a community of *sentiment,* and sentiment alone is insufficient to explain why citizens are obligated to one another. I then evaluate a more sustained attack on the public culture argument, according to which public cultures are not, and cannot be, a reliable source of trust. It shall become clear that this latter critique fails, even if it does suggest that the public culture argument needs a restatement, and this restatement will occupy the second half of the chapter.

The Public Culture Argument

For many liberal democratic theorists, one important feature of the state is that its members share a range of characteristics, among them a set of beliefs and values that are reflected in what is generally called a shared public, or political, culture. Specifically, a public culture refers to "a set of understandings about how a group of people is to conduct its life together."[1] Often the set of understandings includes an ethical component, as Francis Fukuyama has emphasized: we can think of a public culture as composed of, or as producing, "inherited ethical habits" among members.[2] When people have a public culture—when people share a set of understandings about how their collective life will progress—they will likely feel bound together not because physical or material necessity demands it, but rather because they share a "dense web of customs, practices, and understandings."[3] This view of public culture has been accused of being unreasonably thick, demanding, and homogenizing, but there are three distinctive features of the public culture that should assuage these criticisms: it does not require uniformity of all beliefs, it is publicly determined and expressed, as a result of which it is fluid rather than static over time. In the next section I will offer an account of why the public culture can give rise to trust; here my first goal is simply to define its central features.

Perhaps the most difficult aspect of a public culture to understand is what, precisely, must be shared, since a public culture does not require uniformity in all beliefs or lifestyle choices. In the first place, members of a public culture must believe (in sufficient numbers) that they belong together: political communities, writes David Miller, "are constituted by belief," and therefore "exist when their members recognize one another as compatriots."[4]

A public culture is typically defined not only by a shared sense of belonging, but also by a set of characteristics and customs that should be identifiable by members if they were asked to enumerate them. That said, we need not overemphasize or exaggerate the extent to which they are all encompassing: a public culture does not mean, writes Miller, "that everyone follows exactly the same conventions or adheres to the same cultural values."[5] Instead, it is defined by a "set of overlapping cultural characteristics—beliefs, practices, and sensibilities—which different members exhibit in different combinations and to different degrees."[6] Put differently, some but not all beliefs and characteristics must be shared; as I shall suggest, which ones in particular are shared is a matter for communities to define on their own.

These characteristics emerge over time, and often differ according to the various, contingent circumstances that communities have historically faced, including, among others, climate, access to material resources, friendly or hostile neighbors, and so on. Yet a public culture is more than a mere product of history; it often garners respect in the eyes of members because it contains an important, present, active, and public dimension. There are three senses in which this public culture is, indeed, public. First, the content of a public culture may develop from contributions from all the segments of society who are subject to it. The understandings and values that characterize a public culture often emerge from deliberation in the public sphere;[7] they are to a significant extent "a product of political debate" and can "be reshaped over time."[8] Ideally, the process by which a public culture is determined "involves inputs from all sections of the community, with groups openly competing to imprint the common identity with their own particular image."[9] In practice public cultures often emerge from imperfectly inclusive processes; this is because the historical elements of a public culture developed in an era in which democratic inclusion was not a widespread commitment, and in part because democratic communities are not yet as inclusive as they ought to be, as a result of which minority members continue to struggle to interact on equal terms in the domains in which the public culture is shaped and reshaped. There is

therefore a predictable consequence of imperfectly inclusive political environments: the production of policies that continue to exclude and marginalize certain minority populations. To the extent that minorities struggle to
gain access to these environments, the public culture is not adequately shared.[10]
Second, the content of a public culture "concern features of a society whose
existence is dependent upon political action."[11] The decisions we make, for
example, about whether we value large public spaces or wide boulevards will
have an influence on the political decisions legislators make about how to use
shared space. The decisions we make about whether education is a public or
private good has an impact on how politicians determine it ought to be funded.
Third, a public culture is public by virtue of how we communicate its content to
one another and how this content is communicated to us. Much of the learning
we do as part of growing up as a member of a public culture is in some sense
private (we learn from our families, our neighborhoods, and so on). Yet it is the
transmission of these beliefs—via "cultural artifacts which are available to
everyone who belongs," including "books, newspapers, pamphlets, and more recently the electronic media," as well as publicly provided education[12]—that
enables a culture to be publicly shared, and the public transmission of these
beliefs will prove important to integrating newcomers, as we shall see in subsequent chapters.

Emphasizing the manner in which a public culture develops over time
highlights its fluidity. There is no reason to think that advocates of public culture are suggesting, as critics sometimes claim, that the content of the public
culture remain stagnant or unchanging over time—critics sometimes accuse
public culture advocates of arguing for "strong preservation," a view according to which cultures should be insulated from change of any kind.[13] It is
rather the case that an important feature of a public culture is frequently connected to pride in having changed something among its key features and sur-
vived. American public culture might, for example, pride itself on having rid
itself of slavery and having become instead a relatively integrated society.
South African public culture might pride itself on having moved from a ra-
cially segregated to an integrated political community.[14] The evident fluidity
over time of the content of public cultures should be sufficient to make it clear
that communities bound by a public culture can sustain themselves over time
even if core values sometimes change. There is, surely, considerable debate
about the manner in which core values change, and the extent to which how
they change matters to their shared sense of themselves, but this is not of relevance here except insofar as it is important to point out that the public cul-

ture argument does not require or even imply stagnation. It instead relies on the widespread participation of its members in order to remain both legitimate and important to those it affects.

Avoiding Three Common Mistakes

Yet the notion of a public culture as a key aspect of democracy is frequently criticized, and I shall enumerate these criticisms and respond to them here.

Can't Institutions Do the Work of the Public Culture?

One objection to the public culture argument questions its emphasis on fellow feeling and mutual concern, insofar as they arise from a public culture, as the critical components in securing the stability and enduringness of liberal democratic communities. There is no reason, according to this critique, to think that a public culture is uniquely able to secure support for liberal democratic values. Instead, an emphasis on a public culture can be, and frequently is, morally objectionable: it encourages and sustains cultural homogeneity, which is often forced on minority communities against their will, via illiberal and coercive attempts to stamp out diversity of values and norms.[15] One *consequence* of this homogenization demand is that the cultural element of the public culture "will be promoted in a coercive and oppressive manner."[16] As a result, protecting a public culture demands accepting the inevitability of unjustly coercing minorities, who would otherwise reject the norms and values of the dominant group, into compliance. And, according to critics such as Andrew Mason, the unjust coercion is ultimately in the pursuit of something that is irrelevant, since citizens do not need to subscribe to the "belief that there is some special reason why they should associate together which appeals to something other than, say, that they happen to live in the same polity," in order that a liberal democratic community functions perfectly well over time.[17]

Instead, it is sufficient that citizens accept the legitimacy of the institutions that bind them into cooperative activity. Daniel Weinstock, for example, argues that "we ought to accept that citizens living under common institutions may very well share nothing *but* a stake in those institutions. When these institutions function well and justly for the good of all, this may very well be enough to sure institutional viability and social stability."[18] This commitment *to the institutions* is sufficient to ground something that A Mason terms "belonging to a polity," according to which the perception that members themselves belong together is "parasitic on a sense of belonging to a polity" (128). In describing the meaning of "belonging to a polity," Mason writes: "a person has a sense of belonging to a polity if and only if she identifies with most of its major institutions and some of its central practices, and feels at home in them" (127). When a person feels at home with a set of institutions and practices, "she is able to find her way around it, and experiences participation in it is as natural" (127). For example, in Belgium and Switzerland, to the extent that citizens believe they belong together, the belief is derivative of a sense of belonging to a polity. Each country is characterized by complex institutional machinery that encourages cooperation and consensus and that over time has generated the sense in its citizens of belonging together.

Yet it is not clear that this account of commitment to shared institutions represents a genuine alternative to the public culture view described earlier. Note that to "belong to a polity," citizens must feel at home in its central institutions and some of its central practices, and must experience participation in them as natural. A shared practice is described as a habitual, customary, regular action or set of actions or behaviors of some kind. These actions persist in the absence of formal institutional backing or sanction, but express our (perhaps unique) way of committing to a set of values or shared understandings that themselves may be institutionalized. For example, if we have shared religious practices, we mean to express our commitment to a codified faith in specific, communal, and mutually acceptable and recognizable ways. We feel at home in a set of practices if they adequately reflect our shared values and understandings; *these* practices are comfortable for us because they reflect what *we* value, and we experience participation in them as natural. Inherent in this way of conceptualizing a practice is that many people adhere to it; *we* share a commitment to these practices. Although it is possible to claim that each person individually commits to a given practice or set of practices on his or her own, it is unlikely that a practice gains the support of a populace because of its independent worth. It is inherent in the value associated with at least some practices that they have worth because they are *shared*.

At issue, at least in part, is causal direction: do institutions require the support of a public culture or do they create the public culture? It is not clear, however, that much hinges on this dispute. What matters, instead, is that the stability of a regime depends on a public culture of some kind, whether it is prepolitical or whether it is generated by shared institutions (indeed, that the latter proposition is possible is a critical component of the argument in chapter 7). After all, what is at issue is what is needed *in the present* in order to secure support for a shared democratic polity, rather than competing stories about how liberal democracies got where they are. That Belgians may have come to see each other as compatriots because of a shared commitment to a given set of institutions and practices does not ultimately say much about the long-term viability of the Belgian democratic system. It may be true that Belgians have, over time, developed a sense that they belong together, and that this sense can be attributed primarily to the presence of well-designed institutions; it is still plausible that the ongoingness of the Belgian democracy can be attributed to the public culture that has developed over time.[19] Perhaps, after all, "parasitic" is not the correct metaphor; perhaps what is going on is a symbiotic relation between Belgian institutions and Belgian public culture wherein Belgian public culture has emerged from well-designed institutions, and wherein these institutions are effective over the longer term because a public culture has emerged.

The Belgian example reveals what is unpersuasive about the suggestion that shared institutions alone are adequate to secure the stability of a democratic polity over time. It is simply implausible to think that a community that doesn't conceive itself as belonging together will, indefinitely, support common institutions that force consensus and moderation on its citizenry.[20] It is certainly true that elements of a public culture that are exclusionary, or otherwise morally objectionable, are not essential to underpinning democratic communities—I suggested earlier that public cultures ought to be defined by their commitment to norms and values that are *inclusive*. But it is a mistake to equate this sort of thinning of the public culture (i.e., the excising of elements of the public culture that are exclusive or otherwise morally objectionable), with the claim that a public culture itself is unnecessary; rather, the examples considered above suggest that the stability of a community over time ultimately depends on a public culture.

Doesn't the Public Culture Argument Imply that Mere Feeling Determines Membership?

Another objection describes the public culture as *merely* subjective, as a result of which membership in the public culture is determined entirely by how the majority feels. If members share a public culture because they feel they do, then whether they feel positively toward someone determines whether that person is a member. Members can therefore reject or deny the membership status of others based on how they feel. The main worry here arises from the supposed emphasis on sentiment in determining who counts as a member of a community. This critique relies for its plausibility on the idea that a public culture defines solely a community of sentiment (and therefore that members only *feel* bound together and believe they belong together). New members are admitted (or not) based entirely on the preexisting feelings of present members. Yet this is a mistaken interpretation of the public culture argument; as we saw earlier, a truly *public* culture is subject to a commitment to inclusivity that precludes the reliance on sentiment alone in bestowing membership on newcomers.

In particular, we should reject the equivalence between sentiment and membership in a public culture, and this has an essential bearing on the argument that I shall make in the next chapter. Depending on *sentiment* as the sole criterion in determining membership suggests, after all, that mere feeling is sufficient to identify who counts (and who can count) as a member. This would appear to suggest that anti-immigrant, or antidiversity, sentiments that a public culture can express are prima facie legitimate. On this view, if a majority simply *feels* that a minority group does not belong, that would be sufficient to exclude them legitimately from membership on a *moral* basis. To recognize the initially skeptical attitudes toward newcomers as the relevant attitudes on which to base obligations seems to privilege preliminary and unreflective sentiments over publicly debated reflective positions that a community arrives at over time. Not only is this straightforwardly objectionable from a moral point of view, but it also fails to account for empirical reality, namely, that public cultures frequently take time to adapt in response to new members and the practices and norms that accompany them. Earlier we saw that the public culture develops over time in response to inputs from all (or at least most) relevant parties, and it is a mistake to privilege the public culture *prior* rather than after this input has been collected and publicly debated. There is no doubt that public cultures will often make decisions about minorities (and their associated cultural practices and norms) that are objectionable from a strictly liberal point of view, and this is a real danger associated with privileging democratic norms over liberal ones.[21] The point here is simply that the legitimacy of the views that a public culture adopts is subject to certain publicity and inclusivity conditions that work to counter the majority's desire to demand exclusion of minority practices and norms on the basis of mere sentiment.

What If a Public Culture Doesn't Build Trust in the First Place?

The argument that places trust at the center of a well-functioning democracy is this: democracies function only when citizens voluntarily comply with a range of laws and regulations, and each citizen must trust that others will abide by these laws. I shall argue that the trust that exists between citizens arises in large part from ties of community, that is, a sense that they belong together even if they do not have personal knowledge of one another. Characterized in this way, trust is a condition not of straightforwardly self-interested action; rather, it facilitates the cooperation, founded on a sense of loose rather than strict reciprocity, that is central to democracy's functioning. As I will argue, this sort of trust is likely to emerge in modern states only if they have a public culture (of the right kind, as I shall describe later in the chapter). It is *because* of the shared culture—and its content—that the requisite sort of trust is able to emerge. In the past it has been assumed by so many that it is, writes David Miller, "virtually self-evident that ties of community are an important source of such trust between individuals who are not personally known to one another and who are in no position directly to monitor one another's behaviour."[22] Without an account of *why,* however, not only will we not be able to develop the tools we need to rebuild efficiently trust relations in distrusting communities, but we will also not even know, more basically, whether a public culture can do this work in the first place.

There are, say its critics, at least two reasons to reject the claim that public cultures can act as a source of trust. One reason is that trust can emerge even if a shared culture does not exist. Witness, for example, an Iranian journalist charged with violating censorship laws; this journalist would surely trust a German judge over an Iranian judge, and this trust has emerged in spite of the absence of a public culture. Further, aside from not being necessary to generate the trust needed to trust institutions, a public culture may not even be sufficient to generate the interpersonal trust cocitizens ought to feel toward one another. Witness consumers within one cultural group who believe that merchants from within their culture are corrupt, and so choose to engage in exchange relations with members of another, more trustworthy (at least in terms of participating fairly in exchange relations), cultural group. Again, a shared culture fails to prove a sufficient condition to generate trust.[23] These examples illustrate that not all public cultures serve as a source of trust and that sharing a public culture does not automatically entail that we offer blanket trust to all members of our culture on *all* issues.[24] That a public culture in general might serve as a source of trust is not incompatible with our making some selection about the circumstances under which we do trust other members of our cultures.

These examples do not illustrate that a public culture fails to act as a reliable source of trust; at most, they illustrate that the content of the shared culture matters in whether it is or is not a source of trust. Not only will it be the case that some public cultures will have a more positive effect on trust than others; it is equally true that some public cultures will be characterized by distrust rather than trust. The public cultures that characterize many post-Communist societies seem poor at generating the trust needed to support democratic institutions. Consider the features of the public culture of a typical post-Communist country such as Hungary, by way of example. At least in a general way, it is possible to identify features of a Hungarian public culture. These features include an appreciation for and commitment to music (consider the list of well-known Hungarian musicians), pride in the difficulty of learning the Hungarian language, pride, likewise, in the disproportionately high number of Hungarian Nobel Prize winners, the belief that things can always, and in general tend to, get worse (there is a well-known saying in Hungarian that "Hungarians cry even when they have a good time"), and a continued suspicion of the motives of others. But even though it is possible to identify a list of features, values, and interests that characterize the Hungarian public culture, only 23 percent of Hungarians report that they trust others (for comparative purposes: Western liberal democracies report trust levels that hover between 65 and 75 percent). In this example, a public culture has not (yet) given rise to trust relations among its citizens.[25]

One bad way to diffuse this objection to the public culture argument—the objection that it simply is not true that a public culture always gives rise to trust—would be to suggest that, in fact, public cultures *by definition* generate trust. It would then be possible to conclude that any supposed public culture that does not generate trust is in fact not a real public culture. It might even be possible to point to the characteristics of a public culture in general, and then identify a specific feature missing from a potential public culture. But this would be ducking the objection, since one main feature of a public culture is that it is recognizable by its members as such. The Hungarian example suggests that even where there exists a vibrant public culture—shared norms and values, and perhaps even a shared affective identity—generalized trust may not emerge.

In sum, attempts to refute the claim that a public culture is a reliable source of trust in democratic political communities fail; they fail in large part because they interpret the claim made by public culture advocates to be comprehensive along multiple dimensions, that is, that *all* public cultures build trust, and that trust *only* emerges from within environments characterized by public cultures. And, as I have suggested, defenders of the public culture argument do frequently argue in ways that suggest they are committed to these views. I believe, however, that they mean to offer a less comprehensive claim on its behalf, or at least that they ought to do so, and I shall now articulate the conditions under which a public culture *of the right type* can underpin trust in democratic political communities.

The Public Culture Argument: Concessions

As we saw, critics question whether a public culture is the sole way in which liberal democratic institutions can maintain support over time, and they question the claim that a public culture is the best source of the trust that is central to the ongoing support of liberal democratic institutions. Another challenge to relying on trust as a source of democratic support has to do with its contingent nature. Although it is possible to create conditions under which people are more likely to extend trust to others (and to reciprocate either by being trustworthy or by extending trust in return), it is in the nature of trust—and especially in its relation to conditions of uncertainty—that we can never guarantee that it will emerge. In order to make it plausible, therefore, we need to make two refinements to the public culture argument: first, we must be clear with respect to why a public culture can indeed serve as a reliable source of trust, and second, we need an account of the specific characteristics required of a public culture in order for it to serve as a genuine source of trust.

One reason that a public culture can serve as a source of trust has to do with its capacity to provide information to members concerning the *motivations* for actions undertaken by fellow members. People can be motivated by a variety of psychological and social factors to pursue a range of goals for a range of reasons. If we think we have insight into someone's motivations, the claim we are making is that we have some understanding of the likely factors that motivate her to act in a certain way, mainly because we have some sense of the range of objectives she might be pursuing. We trust a doctor, for example, because we have some sense that her interest is our health, that she is competent (because we understand the methods by which she has developed her credentials), and that she is constrained by various features of her profession (she is bound by a professional code of ethics, she is interested in securing further patients, and so on). We trust coreligionists because we have an understanding of the creed that guides our collective lives. In general, our knowledge of the shared social environment, and the way in which it shapes what others think is valuable and desirable, gives some insight into how people are motivated to shape their lives.

Insofar as trust relies on having some kind of insight into people's behaviors and attitudes, the ability to predict with reasonable certainty how others will behave can enable or facilitate the emergence of trust. It is useful as information, whether conscious or unconscious, in our determinations of whether others ought to be trusted. As of yet, there is nothing in what I've suggested that implies that some (however minimal) understanding of the root of someone's motivations will *necessarily* lead to trust. It could, equally, lead to distrust. The initial claim here is only that there is good reason to think that an understanding of how others are motivated in general, an understanding that emerges from a public culture, might facilitate the emergence of trust relations.

It is not only that information about motivations serves to narrow the range of options that others may face that matters for trust. It is also secondarily important that when motives are imputed to others, they must be assumed to be benign. As we saw in chapter 1, the belief that we must impute positive motives to others is at the heart of some analyses of trust. Annette Baier, for example, builds good will into her explanation of trust: "When I trust another, I depend on her goodwill toward me."[26] As I suggested earlier, however, we need not presume that others feel positively toward us and our interests; we need only believe that others do not bear us active ill will, and therefore that they are not likely to violate our trust out of a desire to frustrate our capacity to meet our objectives, whatever they may be.

Empirically, this sort of relation has been amply demonstrated; repeatedly, experimental and survey research indicates that in situations where others are expected to make decisions, we trust them to make the right ones especially when we expect them to have positive motives toward us or in general. For example, in studies asking workers to evaluate the quality and fairness of their supervisors, workers will consistently identify their supervisors as trustworthy when they are thought to have positive motives toward workers and their shared work environment. Likewise, surveys of citizens who evaluate the actions of politicians demonstrate that when citizens believe politicians are motivated by positive qualities—a desire to help citizens,

honesty, impartiality—they are likewise inclined to identify them as generally trustworthy.[27] If this phenomenon is translated to public culture, it
seems clear that people must believe that on a general level others bear them
good will, or perhaps that they have their best interest in mind, or even that
they are inclined to act out of fairness, in order to trust them. Some reason is
necessary in order to impute nonnegative motives to them, but the motives
need not correspond to the motives that are ascribed to all trusted people.
What is critical is only that these motives are generally nonnegative.

A second reason why a public culture facilitates trust relations has to
do with the role that communities of all kinds play in sanctioning—in both
senses of the term "sanction"—the behavior of their members.[28] Community
norms and values encourage certain behaviors and values, and they discourage others. Sanctions are generally informal, in the sense that the penalty for
violating them is generally social disapproval or exclusion rather than legal.
Often, moreover, these sanctions are unexpressed; although they are sometimes expressed in the form of social norms to be observed, at other times they
are implied. Consider the joke, when do Jewish children become adults? When
they are granted their advanced education degree. (Or as my now college-age
cousin was told when he was younger: he could have a profession as a baseball
player when he grew up, so long as he studied for a university degree—
preferably in math or computer science—before he tried out for the team.) The
implication (and punch line) is that education is a central value of the Jewish
community, and there is strong pressure on children to be successful in higher
education. There are informal sanctions against abandoning education, and
considerable encouragement of various kinds to pursue it (my Hebrew school
instructor gave prizes to the children with the best attendance record at the
end of every year).[29] In each case, the existence of these norms provides
information about how members of a community are likely to react and
behave in a range of situations.

Negative sanctions—sanctions against particular behaviors and values—
play similar role.[30] Not only do they serve to provide information about a
set of choices fellow members are likely to steer away from, but they likewise
act as a kind of constraint on behavior. They affect not only me as an interpreter
of your likely actions; they likewise affect you in the range of actions you are
likely to undertake, since you are aware that some actions will attract the
disapproval of fellow community members. (I'm making no claim here about
whether this is a good or bad thing—I presume that in some cases these sanctions are good and in others bad.) For example, evidence suggests that many

Americans choose to vote in part because they are concerned that they will be frowned upon by their neighbors if they do not the same worry encourages participation in recycling regimes.[31] Both positive and negative sanctions, the source of which is the public culture's content, enable us to develop behavioral expectations that encourage the emergence of trust relations.

A final reason why public cultures engender trust is connected to their capacity to generate the sense that members share something important in common. This is not a surprising claim: to say that we share a public culture is to say that we have certain things in common, and therefore that we view others in the group as in some way like us. The reason that sameness matters is that for better or worse, people are more inclined to cooperate with, and extend their trust toward, people they perceive to be in some way like themselves. Many political theorists and social scientists worry about the ways in which perceptions of sameness affect political communities: as they observe, when people are perceived to possess the wrong characteristics, whether religious, ethnic, or cultural, they are seen to be legitimate targets for *exclusion*. There is a dark side to acknowledging the importance that resemblance can play in building trust relations, in other words, to acknowledging the ways in which those who do not possess the relevant characteristics can be, and historically have often been, excluded. In my view, it is too easy to abandon as objectionable the relevance of sameness or resemblance in building trust relations, given the evident malleability of the content of sameness. Those who are critical of relying on sameness as a foundation for trust relations suggest that we aim for something less than trust that can nevertheless underpin democratic political communities; as we saw earlier, they frequently suggest that political stability can be attained through shared participation in institutions.[32] I suggested in response that over time political institutions will generate the public culture (if a public culture doesn't yet exist—I denied the importance of determining the causal order between shared political institutions and a public culture). In other words, participation in political institutions can generate, if need be, the relevant sameness, which can in turn be deployed to further political benefit, for example, in underpinning the willingness of members to participate in social justice policies that demand the sacrifice of some interests on behalf of others.

Extensive research into the resolution of social dilemmas, for example, indicates the "beneficial effects of social identification on cooperation."[33] In one experimental situation that typically confirms this observation, participants are divided into groups and each participant is provided with small amounts of money or something that stands in for money. Participants are then told that they can decide whether to keep the money or give some portion of it to the group. If some predesignated amount of money is contributed to the group—this will require, for example, that each participant contributes approximately half of their initial holdings—the group will receive a bonus that will be distributed equally among the group members without regard for who chose to contribute. In one variation of this game, groups were told one of two things: that the study's objective was to *compare* contributions of student groups at Southampton University (where the study was being conducted) to contributions of student groups at other universities across the country, or that the purpose of the study was to assess the relative contributions of individual students in general. Two results emerge from this study. First, group members who were given some reason to think of themselves as members of a defined group (students at Southampton University) with which they identified rated the interests of the group higher in a postexperiment survey than did those who were given no such reason to prioritize the interests of the group. Second, group members who had been given some reason to identify with the group contributed considerably more to the group than did those who did not have such a reason. Groups in which an attempt was made to create a sense of belonging were considerably more likely to find that members had contributed enough to earn the group bonus.[34]

Two things can be concluded from these kinds of studies. First, a sense of belonging matters—people who perceive themselves as belonging to an identifiable group are interested in promoting its best interests. Second, people appear to be more willing to cooperate with people who they believe are similarly motivated to promote the interests of the group.[35] How does this relate to the role played by a public culture? A public culture is often able to create the sameness that is necessary to ensure that people are willing to participate for the greater good of the community and to secure their belief that others likewise are concerned to prioritize the greater good of the community. In this kind of situation, the shared sense of belonging (and by extension, shared interest) serves in reducing the risk associated with trust; in particular, it makes it likely that trust among members of the group will generally be reciprocated since no benefit is thought to emerge from violating it.[36]

I have suggested that the three features described above serve to explain *why* a public culture serves to build trust among its members: it provides information about the motivations for the actions of comembers,[37] it generates both positive and negative sanctions that provide information about the range of behaviors likely to be undertaken by members, and it generates a sense that something important is shared among members. Recall that a central component of trust is the willing acceptance of vulnerability; the mechanisms I have described account for how the public culture serves to mitigate the vulnerability associated with extending and rewarding trust. When a public culture is present, it serves as information that others can in general be trusted; it enables us to think of the behaviors of others as more or less predictable, and therefore that in trusting them we are not very much at risk of being betrayed or disappointed. That we have institutional protection against loss or betrayal in only some of our interactions with comembers means that the risk in extending trust is not reduced to zero, and therefore that there is ongoing room and indeed necessity for trust. As longtime members, we may experience participation in the public culture as natural in some sense, and therefore we may think of the trust we extend to comembers as in some sense intuitive or unconscious. Yet that it is in fact *information* that can in principle and in practice be imparted to newcomers tells us that the norms and values that define a public culture have an important cognitive element, and therefore can be learned and adopted over time by those who join us. Long-term members may focus on what "we" have in common, and therefore attempt to harness the emotional or sentimental foundations of trust, but in integrating newcomers it will be essential to focus on the cognitive underpinnings of trust.

Two Additional Features of the Trust-Generating Public Culture

We have now seen three reasons to think that a public culture will facilitate, but not guarantee, the emergence of trust relations. There are, in addition, two main features of a public culture that it must possess in order that it genuinely serves as a source of trust: a willingness to cooperate and a commitment to a set of institutions intended to instantiate this cooperation. Without these two features, a public culture cannot be a source of trust; any public culture that is a source of generalized trust will necessarily have these two characteristics.

In chapter 2, I pointed to a distinction that scholars frequently draw between social trust and political trust. The distinction between political trust among citizens and social trust among citizens was, I thought, minimal: whereas we might reserve political trust to describe relations among citizens in political domains alone, social trust describes relations among citizens more generally. The direction in which the trust is being extended—to fellow citizens—is the same, however. In order to be a source of trust in general, then, a public culture must give rise to trust relations that can be relied on in both political and social environments. I indicated that there are two *essential* features a public culture must possess in order that it provides a source of trust: a willingness to cooperate among citizens as well as a willingness to commit to a set of institutions that will instantiate this cooperation. We can now see that there is a relation between trust in a general social environment and the willingness to cooperate, and between trust in the political environment and the willingness to submit to institutions that will instantiate this cooperation. Together, these distinct features of a public culture accounts for its capacity to serve as a source of generalized trust in a democratic community. These distinctions are largely analytic; in practice, they will overlap and interact in messy ways. But it will be useful to keep them in mind as we consider building trust in communities that are suffering from a decline in trust relations, as we shall do in chapter 7.

A caveat is in order, here: my claim is not that if these two features are present, trust is guaranteed to emerge, since the contingent nature of trust relations makes it impossible to make this strong a claim. My claim is simply that these are the two features a public culture must have if it is to be a source of trust, and that we therefore ought to foster these features first and foremost if we are concerned to generate a public culture capable of underpinning liberal democratic institutions. To state the claim clearly: these features are necessary, but not sufficient, to secure the emergence of trust relations. Defenders of the public culture argument might think that their articulation of public culture already includes these two elements; certainly Miller could not be faulted for thinking that he has accounted for them. However, although these features are accounted for in the description Miller gives of public culture, they are not described as central to producing trust. Insofar as part of the effort in this chapter is to assess more deeply the claim that ties of community are a source of trust, therefore, we need to examine how it is that these ties can be credited with being a genuine source of trust.

The first feature a public culture must have is a commitment to cooperation of some kind, however minimal. Cooperation obviously has a complex relation with trust[38]—and in the first instance, it may not be obvious that a willingness to cooperate can precede trust. Oughtn't we to say, for example, that trusting people cooperate? Or perhaps that trust is the lubricant needed to secure cooperation? The answer is indeed yes to both these questions; it is obvious that certain kinds of cooperation require trust to proceed. But what matters here is that an initial willingness to cooperate need not emerge from or require trust; even if trust is a lubricant for some kinds of cooperation, which it undoubtedly is, it is not *necessary* to secure cooperation. Consider an example borrowed from David Hume: if both of us need to row this boat to get across the river, and both of us want or need to get across the river, we may decide to cooperate without trusting each other. What we have in this kind of example are two people who have the exact same objective that cannot be achieved without the cooperation of the other. Both people know this. All that is required in this example is that both people are willing to cooperate for a mutual objective; given their mutual desire to achieve this objective, there is very little required in the way of trust. The more general observation is that cooperation describes a willingness to work together to achieve some common end, even if trust is not present and available. Even if trust need not be present, however, successful cooperative interactions tend to provide the right kind of environment for the growth of trust.[39]

This cooperation, however, cannot be restricted to interpersonal relations if it is to serve as a more general source of trust. The motivation to cooperate must exist at the macro level, one consequence of which is that in order to produce cooperation there must be common institutions able to do so. Thus, a second key feature of any public culture that can serve as a source of trust is the willingness, by the group of people in question, to submit to common institutions that will facilitate cooperation. This is, for example, the noticeable absence in the public culture that characterizes many of the post-Communist countries. While they often display the willingness to cooperate with one another (and, correspondingly, some display relatively high levels of inter-personal trust), they are reluctant to accept and participate in the common institutions charged with effecting cooperation.[40]

The willingness to accept common institutions to effect cooperation is one of John Stuart Mill's central insights in his account of the stability of representative institutions.[41] For Mill, there are three necessary social conditions for the creation and ongoingness of representative governance. First, any people who will be governed by representative institutions must be "willing to receive" them. Second, these people must be "willing and able to do what is necessary for its preservation." Third, these people must not only be willing to act to preserve a representative arrangement, but they must also be "willing and able to fulfill the duties and discharge the functions which it imposes on them." He writes, in summary, that "when people have no sufficient value for, and attachment to, a representative constitution, they have next to no chance of retaining it." Moreover, unless decision makers are "backed by effective opinion and feeling in the country," we cannot expect that common institutions will have the desired effect; "the executive has always the means of setting them aside" if public opinion does not support them.[42] In other words, the willingness to cooperate to secure the ongoingness of representative institutions is critical to the public culture's capacity to produce widespread trust relations.

At this point, readers may not be satisfied with the account I've provided of the mechanisms necessary to secure cooperation. I shall elaborate in chapter 7 by offering an account of how we can measure whether these features are present, and therefore by illustrating the *failure* of public cultures to produce trust in their *absence*.

Conclusions

This chapter has attempted to show that a tidied version of the public culture argument is defensible. Properly understood, a public culture is characterized by its fluidity over time, in particular in response to public contributions to its content. It does not require uniformity of commitment or belief among citizens. In fleshing out the implications of these characteristics, I refuted suggestions that the public culture argument is implausible or indefensible. For example, the argument is not vulnerable to the claim that it justifies an interpretation of obligations to fellow citizens as voluntary, because it is based on more sentiment nor is it vulnerable to the claim that alternatives are necessarily better suited to unite members of a political community. Moreover, the suggestion that a public culture can and does serve as a source of trust does not commit us to the view that *all* public cultures are able to do so.

The ways in which a public culture can serve as a reliable and inclusive source of trust motivates the analysis in the final chapter of this book, and so it is worth repeating them here: a public culture gives us insight into the motivations for peoples' actions, a public culture provides behavioral and attitudinal sanctions for its members, and a public culture increases the likelihood that the benefit of the community and the benefit of the individual are compatible and overlapping, since identity is shared among members. Moreover, if we look more deeply into the content of a public culture, we can identify two characteristics in particular that serve to make a given public culture more likely to be a source of trust. These are a willingness among a populace to cooperate and a willingness to allow for common institutions to secure this cooperation. The willingness to cooperate is in large part responsible for generating social trust; the willingness to allow for common institutions is in large part responsible for generating political trust.

The elaboration of a plausible source of trust marks the end of the first portion of the book. We have seen that trust rather than distrust is at the center of democratic political activity, and we have seen that a public culture is a reliable source of the trust on which this activity relies. Next we turn to an elaboration of some of the sources of distrust within a democratic community and how we might remedy them.

5

TRUST AND ETHNOCULTURAL DIVERSITY
IN MULTICULTURAL DEMOCRACIES

Since democracy relies on vibrant, robust trust relations, we have cause to worry if the presence of ethnocultural diversity erodes them, and impractical as it is fosters distrust instead. The debate, which is prominent in contemporary academic and political discussions, is most often framed in terms of immigration, in particular in terms of the *rate* of immigration. Perhaps, suggest some thinkers, if rates of immigration are high, especially if rates of immigration from nondemocratic countries are high, our social cohesion may suffer. In particular we may witness increased hostility toward, and discrimination against, new immigrants—a discrimination and hostility that discourages their social and political integration—as well as a less effective democratic system and, especially worrisome for egalitarians, a decreased commitment to material redistribution among citizens. This chapter explores these claims; it focuses on the struggles presented by ethnocultural diversity (and therefore may appear to have an unduly pessimistic tone), an understanding of which we need if we are to develop effective strategies by which to secure trust in ethnoculturally diverse political communities. I will explore these strategies in chapter 7.

As we saw in chapter 4, the public culture is composed of norms and principles, some of which describe ways of behaving in shared social space, and others of which describe the principles we hold and the ways of behaving in specifically political environments. This complex of norms combines to describe a unique public culture that newcomers meet on arrival and learn, and often adapt and modify, over time. This chapter's first objective is to evaluate whether ethnocultural diversity poses challenges to the trust that is central to the ongoing support of democratic institutions. As I have stressed, widespread trust is an essential ingredient of a successful, robust democracy. Absent this trust, a political community will suffer in a range of ways, in particular from a decreased willingness to contribute to the public goods that often define successful, robust democracies. As I will describe, we may sometimes observe a continuum from the weakened trust relations generated simply from the presence of ethnocultural diversity, to a further weakening of these relations as a result of the politicization of ethnicity, and ultimately to something that looks more like the distrust that motivates and accompanies the adoption of policies that encourage isolation and separation rather than integration across difference.

In the second section of this chapter, I consider one possible casualty of increased diversity, namely, support for redistributive policies to which egalitarian democrats are committed; since redistributive policies demand robust trust relations in both social and political environments, there is cause to worry for their stability in the presence of strained trust relations. Some scholars have responded to this accusation by suggesting that the stress on support for redistributive policies derives from multicultural policies rather than ethnocultural diversity per se; on this view, multicultural policies suggest and emphasize the differences between citizens, and thereby weaken the basis for trust relations among citizens. For these critics, the solution is to abandon multicultural policies. I reject this solution, in part by citing research suggesting that there is no *necessary* connection between the adoption of multicultural policies and the retreat from redistributive policies (although, as I do suggest, there are cases in which apparently multicultural policies do exacerbate the challenges citizens face in developing and sustaining trust relations). I suggest, however, that we have reasons to expect that ethnocultural diversity, rather than multicultural policies per se, will correlate with decreased support for redistributive policies, and that we must be, as trust builders, attentive to these reasons. The conclusions to be drawn from these discussions require that we recognize that although there is no inherent connection between ethnocultural diversity and weakened trust relations, ethnic diversity can in some instances weaken trust relations between citizens in multicultural democracies. The reason for this connection, I suggest, is that too often an individual's ethnic or cultural category is mistakenly taken to signal a commitment to values that are incompatible with those that define the public culture.[1] In general, an understanding of *why* ethnocultural diversity can have a negative effect on trust relations is essential to laying the groundwork for the final chapter of the book, in which I identify the principles that should underpin trust-building strategies in diverse communities.

Ethnocultural Diversity and Trust

This section offers an account of the struggles faced by trust in the political and social domains in response to increasing rates, and salience, of ethnocultural diversity. An understanding of these tensions, I believe, is essential to developing the best tools with which to sustain, or build, healthy diverse communities. I trace a dangerous progression that begins from the challenges posed simply by the arrival of newcomers who behave in alien ways in social and political spheres, and whose behaviors are frequently taken to be proxies for values and principles that are incompatible (or at least in tension) with those that define the public culture they have joined. Even at this point, the capacity of the public culture to produce trust is weakened slightly. If these perceptions (or misperceptions) remain unchanged over time, and thus if weakened trust relations are permitted to persist, we may witness attempts to capitalize on these differences in the political sphere. Over time representatives may emerge who are perceived to represent certain ethnically or culturally defined groups rather than the broader interest, and they may mobilize around issues of relevance to those groups alone (whether majority or minority). Although descriptive representation of this kind relies on trust to some extent (for example, between representatives and those who are represented), its emergence can also represent the erosion of the broad and inclusive trust on which democratic political communities depend.[2] In time, ethnically motivated politics can produce policies that serve to exacerbate rather than mitigate the challenges to trust in diverse societies, as I will explain. Readers may recall that chapter 2 described a continuum between mistrust and distrust along which communities can be located; as diverse societies move in the direction of politicizing ethnic divisions, they move from the weakened trust that frequently accompanies higher rates of immigration to the distrust that characterizes the divided societies I describe in the next chapter.

Preliminary evidence suggests that heterogeneous communities are indeed characterized by low levels of trust. Recent work conducted in the United Kingdom, for example, observes that in ethnically heterogeneous communities, the levels of reported trust in neighbors are lower than in ethnically homogeneous communities.[3] These studies suggest first that diversity is correlated with low trust, and second, that as ethnocultural diversity increases within a community, levels of trust decline. In the United States, we see a correlation between high levels of diversity and low levels of trust, as well as the behaviors with which trust is frequently equated, including participation in civil society associations and political participation.[4] How can we explain these decreased rates of trust?

Erosion of Shared Norms and the Weakening of Trust Relations

When the immigrant population becomes large enough to be noticed, the first danger is simply the perception that "we" no longer share the norms and values that underpin a public culture.[5] In many instances, this perception is simply borne from the growing pains associated with integration, a process that inevitably takes time. Take a relatively benign case, for example. Norma Hernandez, who directs an organization that facilitates the integration of Hispanic migrants in the United States, explains that even the norm of showing up on time for a scheduled appointment must be learned. In Mexico, people arrive for doctors' appointments many hours after the scheduled time because they know they will not see the doctor until then, whereas the same is not (generally) true in the United States: "it's just not knowing these little cultural things," she says, that prevent smooth and effective integration.[6] It is not surprising that newcomers arrive with their own conceptions of how interactions take place and find altering these conceptions difficult or impossible without some form of instruction. These norms are, obviously, more difficult to communicate than formal rules; they are, moreover, less likely to be openly articulated than are formal rules.

This example is innocuous of course, and an inevitable consequence of migration. A more challenging situation emerges when minorities are *unwilling*, often for good reason, to adopt new social norms when doing so appears unnecessary to demonstrate their loyalty and commitment to the receiving state. There is no reason, for example, to believe that a sari-wearing woman from the Indian subcontinent should wear jeans as a way to show her commitment to the United Kingdom. We are equally familiar with the challenges posed by culturally specific dress, for example, in cases where Sikh men have requested— and have been granted—permission to wear turbans rather than the head coverings associated with the traditional uniforms of the Royal Canadian Mounted Police or the American military.[7] The difference between the former example and the latter is that the sari-wearing woman is taken to be making a personal decision to which all citizens are entitled, and that the Sikh man in uniform is taken to be a representative of the state; for some, extending the accommodation to Sikh men who wish to be a Mountie or a soldier amounted to decreasing the value of these vaunted national symbols.[8] In general, though, this accommodation has been taken to be reasonable in a multicultural society that takes seriously the integration of newcomers.[9] Although the choices not to don normal dress patterns and to continue many cultural practices that are (thus far) alien in the social sphere are certainly *not* evidence of the untrustworthiness of newcomers, they are sometimes perceived in this way. In these cases, the wider community refuses to extend trust based on a perception that newcomers are rejecting shared norms, a misperception that often grows from a misinterpretation of minority cultural practices.

Generally, of course, multicultural countries recognize the difficulties newcomers have in adopting new cultural standards and so facilitate this learning to some extent. Citizenship classes are one way that communities attempt to fill this gap, although they have difficulty in imparting some of the most basic of social norms, for example, norms associated with who steps aside on the sidewalk when there's room for only one person to pass or norms associated with procedures (if there are any!) for queuing for the bus. Multicultural countries may also embark on campaigns intended to highlight the benefits provided by immigration and diversity as a way to provide a welcoming environment for newcomers. These are policies that aim at preventing the weakened trust relations that frequently occur as a result of migration.

When rates of immigration are high, and when the challenges posed by integrating newcomers are made salient, we may also find that newcomers' *willingness* to adopt the norms and values that characterize a host country remains unacknowledged or misinterpreted, and that demands are publicly made for immigrants to do *more* to indicate their commitment to the host community. After the murder of filmmaker Theo van Gogh by a Muslim extremist in Holland, Bert van den Brink describes a "crisis of civic integrity," between Dutch Muslims and the non-Muslim Dutch, partly fuelled by three misperceptions: "Dutch Muslims' presumed approval of the murder of van Gogh, their presumed unwillingness to integrate into [the] larger society, and the presumed incompatibility of Islamic religious beliefs and democratic constitutional citizenship."[10] The misperceptions described by van den Brink can be fostered in a variety of ways. By way of example, take an op-ed written by Ayaan Hirsi Ali (a Somali-born former member of the Dutch parliament whose life was threatened in a note left by the murderer on van Gogh's body).

She argues that the perception that Muslim minorities are unwilling to adopt the liberal, pluralist norms that characterize the Western democracies to which they have immigrated is heightened by their unwillingness to publicly condemn violent acts committed in the name of Islamic justice. She asks, "Where *are* the moderates? Where are the Muslim voices raised over the terrible injustice of incidents like these?"[11] Or, in response to a recent murder of a Muslim teenager for her failure to behave in accordance with Islamic rules of dress, an editorial writer in a Canadian newspaper suggested that "Canadians are justified in raising concerns as to whether this is a sign of Islamic fundamentalism in their own backyard," and went on to explain how some Muslims in Canada adhere to a dogmatic form of Islam that is in tension with Canadian liberal, democratic values.[12] Commentaries like these are symptoms of a broader suspicion of Muslims, who are feared to be fundamentalist and antidemocratic. The argument that Muslims' collective failure to separate themselves from the violence committed in the name of their culture exacerbates an already existing fear that Muslims are in fact not willing to separate themselves from these acts (this is a mistake, of course; the vast majority of Muslims living in Western democratic countries desire and are proud of their capacity to integrate).[13] Unfortunately, the perception, whether or not it is true, that minorities are sometimes unwilling to adopt the norms that characterize the host community's public culture makes it more difficult for the public culture to produce widespread trust relations.

The examples above are cases in which newcomers appear unwilling to accommodate to new norms and values, and I suggested that this unwillingness (whether mere perception or not) makes trust relations more difficult to sustain. Trust relations can also experience tension in diverse communities in which members of the receiving society are unwilling, or are perceived to be unwilling, to alter their own social norms to accommodate newcomers. This apparent unwillingness originally motivated members of ethnic minorities to mobilize against the lack of hospitality and acceptance demonstrated by the host communities within many Western liberal democracies. As thinkers including Kymlicka have argued, his mobilization motivated many important accommodations of ethnocultural diversity; the turban-wearing Mountie is such an example, as are permissions granted to Sikhs to carry the *kirpan* in public places and exemptions from so-called humane animal killing regulations for Muslim and Jewish butchers.

Nevertheless, the perception that host communities are unwilling to accommodate minorities is not gone, and for what seems like good reason.[14]

At the moment, among the most public examples of the pressures against accommodation are the attempts in European countries to increase the obstacles to attaining citizenship. In 2002, Britain announced plans to implement citizenship tests for new immigrants complete with citizenship classes that would teach British norms and culture in addition to the structure of British government.[15] As one commentator observes, however, the newest edition of the citizenship test preparation manual has been edited to remove information suggesting the tolerance of British society, and to instead offer a "you-will-need-to-toe-the-line-if-you-live-here approach."[16] This change, and others like it, is accompanied by an increase in anti-immigrant rhetoric across many diverse communities, an anti-immigrant rhetoric that declares the death of multiculturalism and therefore calls for reductions in accommodations offered to newcomers, as well as a reduction in the number of migrants admitted in the first place.[17] Although the increase in obstacles to naturalization are (in my view, rightly) criticized by those who believe they are an expression of anti-immigrant attitudes, they are obstacles that are faced by newcomers during a (relatively) short period (although the residency requirements necessary to achieve naturalization are rising).[18] State policy that affects ethnocultural minorities over the longer term can also reflect the unwillingness of a cultural majority to accommodate minority cultural practices and norms. The recent Swiss decision to ban the construction of minarets on mosques is one such example, as is the proposal in the Quebec national legislature to ban women from wearing full facial coverings in interactions with public institutions of any kind. These are bans that will have a longer-term effect on the building of trust relations across cultural groups, since they clearly signal the majority community's unwillingness to accommodate the religious and cultural beliefs of minority *citizens* (rather than simply potential citizens).

Let me summarize where we are. I suggested in chapter 4 that the shared norms and values that form part of a public culture are responsible for its capacity to build trust. In this section, I have tried to account for the ways in which the migration of citizens from cultures that are foreign to host societies can generate the belief (sometimes well founded and sometimes unfounded) that norms and values are no longer shared. The apparent (and real) threats to these norms can, in other words, be a source of weakened trust relations. The danger, however, is that the same phenomena that cause weakened trust relations, if left to fester, can also produce political action that, as I will describe in the next section, can exacerbate rather than ease the stress on trust relations.

Diversity, Political Representation, and Exclusion

As we saw in chapter 2, political representation in democratic communities functions best when citizens believe their representatives have their best interests in mind, and therefore trust them to behave accordingly. As I described earlier in this chapter, conditions of ethnocultural diversity may cause some members of the community to believe that those who operate the systems that govern their lives do not have their best interests in mind. They may come to believe that only members of their own group are concerned to promote their welfare; they may become suspicious of the political interests and motives of those they perceive to be outsiders. These beliefs are the product of weakened trust relations and often motivate political activities that serve further to undermine trust. Under conditions of diversity, these weakened trust relations can press in multiple directions: members of the majority group may turn to parties that they believe represent the best interests of their constituency, and members of minority groups may believe that representatives from within the majority group are unwilling or unable consider their interests.

The emergence of xenophobic political parties and actors across Europe, as well as the adoption by mainstream political parties of policies that make immigration (and integration) more difficult, is one increasingly frequent response to perceived threats to the public culture.[19] These parties and representatives claim to speak on behalf of the best interests of the community at large, in ways that serve ultimately to produce policies that exclude or discriminate against newcomers in pernicious ways. The British National Party is just one example among many of parties that have adopted an anti-immigrant attitude in the name of "us." As one British National Party supporter explains, for example, the party is "just for the people, that's all; English people," and not for those who arrive on English shores to destroy what Great Britain is all about.[20] The public expression of these attitudes serves to weaken trust relations across cultural and ethnic lines.[21]

This exclusionary attitude has, in part, motivated a series of policies recently adopted in Arizona to combat illegal migration into the state from Mexico; among other things they give police the right to ask for identification from any resident they have reasonable suspicion to believe may be living in the state illegally. Opponents of these policies argue that they are objectionable for multiple reasons including, especially, the negative effects they will have on legal migrants and Hispanic citizens in Arizona. The repeated demand of legal migrants and Hispanic citizens that they produce evidence of their right to be in Arizona only serves to signal to them that they are not welcome in their own country; the demand therefore foments distrust in legal migrants and Hispanic citizens in response to policies that are borne from an absence of trust in them.[22] Attempts to ban, and the banning of, full facial coverings in a range of public spaces demonstrate the same dynamic; they are policies that emerge from an absence of trust, borne from the (often mistaken view) that those who cover their faces do not share "our" norms and values—that they desire and intend to separate themselves from the community in which they live, and are therefore not worthy of trust. Such policies ultimately serve to produce and exacerbate distrust.[23]

Alternatively (and sometimes in response to what I have just described), we see calls from within minority groups for self-representation.[24] Insiders, or descriptive representatives, are believed to share with group members an understanding of the collective experiences that have shaped their vision of the world and their sense of what must be altered in order to improve their political and social status. They need not be members of political parties in order to take on the job of representing minority groups; descriptive representatives are often leaders of religious groups or advocacy organizations that claim to speak on behalf of marginalized groups. In particular, it is suggested that there may be a *special* trust relationship between representatives who emerge from within a marginalized group: "representatives and voters who share membership in a subordinate group can also forge bonds of trust based specifically on the shared experience of subordination."[25]

As an example of the latter situation, consider Melissa Williams's observations about the challenges connected to representing African Americans in the political sphere, which I introduced in chapter 3. As she explains, "the repeated betrayals of marginalized group interests through history produces a profound—and often quite reasonable and understandable—distrust of privileged groups."[26] During Reconstruction, for example, blacks had believed that their new access to equal citizenship would be protected and, in time, lead to substantive equality in American political society. As it became evident that this was not the case, their initial trust "yielded to a profound distrust of Whites in general"; the history of betrayed trust is thus offered as justification for descriptive representation.[27] As a consequence of these betrayals, we witness a gap in levels of trust felt by members of marginalized and dominant groups. As Barbara Arneil observes, again in the case of African Americans, it is not simply that decades of betrayed trust have resulted in African American distrust of whites; it has also resulted in lower trust expressed *in general* by African Americans in comparison to whites. Levels of trust displayed by members of a given community are, she observes, clearly shaped by collective experiences, and in the case of African Americans these experiences are of "betrayal or broken promises."[28] A history of broken trust generates a generalized disposition of distrust.

In most cases, as in the case of African Americans, the purpose of descriptive representation is to secure policies that foster integration, in large part by combating the discrimination that prevents it. Requests, for example, for what have been termed "cultural exemptions," exemptions from laws that religious or cultural minority groups may find onerous, are often framed in this way: the exempting of Sikhs and Muslim women from uniform requirements, the provision of political information and electoral ballots in multiple languages, the abandonment of Sunday closure laws, were all justified in terms of their capacity to *integrate* newcomers (in part because these accommodations signaled that newcomers are welcome).[29] Once these exemptions are secured, and integration can proceed, descriptive representation becomes superfluous; at its best, therefore, it will prove to be a temporary phenomenon that is abandoned once widespread trust emerges. At its worst, however, descriptive representation can generate segregation and isolation in the form of extensive support for policies that enable and encourage them both. The policies can also find support from well-meaning political parties, who encourage their adoption in an attempt to build trust where it is absent.

Rather than supporting mere cultural exemptions, for example, descriptive representatives can extend support to policies described as ethnically separatist or radically multicultural. These policies reach "far beyond mutual tolerance and the belief that each person should have equal political opportunities regardless of sex, class, race, etc., to the view that the very purpose of politics is to affirm group difference."[30] They are often attempts to protect cultural practices that ought to be sacrificed in the service of integrating into a larger political community, and they often demand that receiving societies tolerate cultural practices that a genuine liberal democracy must reject. The demand for these kinds of policies typically emerges from low levels of trust, and serves as well to build distrust in culturally and ethnically diverse societies.[31] There are many well-known examples, including extending support to communities that practice arranged marriages, in part by recognizing a formal distinction between arranged and forced marriages; or via publicly funded faith-based schools; or by permitting gender-segregated gym classes in public schools.[32] Until 2002, one such policy exempted Swedish girls who were members of certain ethnocultural minorities from the requirement that they wait until the age of eighteen to marry (they were permitted to marry at fifteen). This policy was *described* as multicultural and was adopted from concern to provide an environment in which ethnocultural minorities would be able to sustain the norms and values characterized by their own culture. Yet this policy, and others like it, weakened rather than built trust between native Swedes and immigrant newcomers by permitting minority communities to isolate themselves and to resist integration into the larger community.[33] In general these policies often permit isolation rather than demand integration, and thus fail to provide a basis on which trust can build. Those voices calling for the abandonment of a commitment to multiculturalism, in light of its alleged failure, typically point their finger only at policies that foster the segregation and exclusion of minorities.[34]

Underpinning the more general concern that minority groups will remain segregated rather than integrate is the fear that they are doing so to protect against accepting democratic and liberal norms.[35] That minority groups may be permitted, or even encouraged, to reject "our" values infuses debates about the justifiability of arranged marriages, or about separate educational environments for girls, or the acceptability of privatized family law, or whether women should be permitted to wear full facial coverings in public; at issue is whether these practices are compatible with a commitment to gender equality, and therefore whether permitting them discourages the group's adoption of the liberal and democratic norms that define "us."[36] In general terms, the situations described above inhibit the development of trust relations by discouraging the interaction and exchange of information from which trust can emerge.[37] When isolation and separation are permitted or encouraged, or when misperceptions of cultural norms and values are allowed to persist in the public sphere, weakened trust relations may also persist. I do not wish to make a judgment on these specific practices here; I only mean to point out that an agreement on shared political, democratic norms is one key element of a willingness to trust others to participate fairly in the political system, and there is a real danger that these practices will undermine the basis for trust.[38]

Cultural exemptions and radically multicultural policies thus have different trust-related sources and consequences, which are worth spelling out briefly by way of conclusion. Cultural exemptions are extended on the basis of a kind of *presumptive* trust, according to which newcomers are thought to be willing and able to adopt the norms and values that characterize their new home, if only certain obstacles to their social and political participation are removed. The ideal progression is, therefore, from the extension of presumptive trust to the development of real trust relations among citizens of a diverse society as the norms and values that describe the public culture come genuinely to be shared over time. The demand for radically multicultural policies, however, typically stems from an absence of trust that prompts newcomers to retreat from the public sphere; this absence of trust is a response to the hostility against newcomers that can persist over time and that is interpreted (by newcomers) as evidence that they are perceived to be threats to the public culture and therefore undeserving of trust. The isolation and segregation these policies enable serve to diminish opportunities for trust to emerge by eliminating (or reducing) the need for newcomers and members of the receiving society to interact in environments in which the shared norms and values that underpin trust relations might grow.

I have tried to illustrate that the norms that underpin trust in the political environment can be undermined by practices that accompany, or seem to accompany, increases in ethnocultural diversity. In the first case, I suggested that the danger that political representatives are seen as representing ethnically defined groups is that it can erode trust (both when the representatives appeal to members of the host community, to the exclusion of ethnocultural minorities, and vice versa). In the second case, I suggested that the perception that newcomers are choosing to participate in the political environment with the sole purpose of pressing for accommodation policies that permit their community to focus inward and reject integration can also pose a threat to widespread trust in the political environment. Both of these reasons can account for the decline in trust in ethnically diverse political communities.

Diversity, Redistribution, and Trust

In this section, my intention is to consider one among many alleged consequences of declines in trust in political and social environments: the alleged decline in support for welfare state policies. There are others, including declines in willingness to participate in public goods (such as collective efforts to reduce pollution) and more robust forms of democratic politics (such as those celebrated by deliberative democrats). The reasons to consider redistributive policies in particular are, first, the centrality of questions of social justice to political philosophy as a whole, and second, the recent focus on whether welfare states are at risk of losing widespread support as a result of increases in ethnocultural diversity. The point is there are many kinds of policies—among them those that aim at redistribution—that rely on widespread trust and will therefore suffer in its absence.

Redistributive policies have as their goal the transferring of material resources from those who can afford it to those who are needy. They come in various forms, including health care coverage, pension plans, welfare payments, unemployment insurance, child care subsidies, and so on. Some intend to provide protection from the risks inherent to life in modern, complex societies, and others are more overtly egalitarian in their objective and so aim at moving closer to material equality by redistributing wealth from wealthier to poorer citizens. What these policies share is their reliance on fairly extensive trust relations; the support that underpins social justice policies *depends* on trust relations.[39] In order to extend this support to social justice policies, citizens must trust in two directions: first, trust others in their community not to take advantage of available funds and to contribute to the collective funds, and this is social trust: Second, citizens must expect that those who implement the system do so fairly and impartially, and this is political trust.[40] Moreover, redistributive policies are public goods, in the sense that regardless of who contributes to them, no citizen is, as a matter of policy, excluded from the benefits they produce. In agreeing to participate, people recognize not only that their decision to participate will have a positive effect on the welfare of the group as a whole, but also that any one person's welfare (in times of need) depends on the contribution of others. We trust that others will help us in our times of need, and this trust motivates us to participate in redistributive policies as well.[41] Of course, redistribution policies can survive the ebb and flow of trust relations under conditions of diversity, at least in part because trust is not the only ingredient needed to underpin their political support (moreover, participation in many redistributive policies is legally mandated, and participation may be the result simply of fear of punishment). Yet in the withering or absence of trust, over time redistributive policies will fail to find support from within a population.[42]

In chapter 4, we saw that a public culture underpins any community characterized by trust relations. One observation that emerged from that discussion was this: to a considerable degree, the commitment to redistributive policies may well be in part determined by cultural values and norms.[43] In other words, some cultures or nations may be committed to redistribution as an aspect of their public culture—Canadians often define themselves by their commitment to universal access to health care, and do so to distinguish themselves from Americans, who often define themselves by their commitment to a kind of rugged individualism that eschews a strong commitment to welfare policies. If this is true—that a commitment to redistribution is culturally determined, or at least culturally influenced—then it would be in principle possible to explain away differences among states with respect to their commitment to redistribution in terms of culture rather than trust. This explanation, however, is plausible only if we take evidence at one moment in time. I shall soon suggest that there is considerable evidence taken *over time* that suggests an inverse relation between diversity within a population and the support it extends to redistributive policies. This evidence suggests that whatever the influence of culture in determining a community's level of commitment, this commitment is under threat in response to increases in diversity. Before I do so, however, I would like to consider a debate that may appear deeply connected to the argument I'm attempting to make here. This debate concerns the possible relationship between *multicultural policies* (not diversity per se) and support for redistributive policies.

Maybe It's the Multicultural Policies that Draw Attention to Diversity, Rather than Diversity Itself?

According to some scholars, we are witnessing a decline in support for redistributive policies, and this decline can be attributed to the increased salience of diversity as a result *of the adoption of multicultural policies*. Diversity is not an explanatory factor per se, on this view; multicultural policies serve to highlight differences between citizens. For example, Canadian social commentator Neil Bissoondath gained notoriety for arguing that the effect of the Canadian Multicultural Act has not, as many of its advocates contend, been the accommodation of difference. The act, which formally recognizes the contribution of ethnic minorities to the Canadian social fabric, and which explicitly acknowledges Canada as a multicultural society, has instead threatened Canadian social cohesion. He writes, "not only are differences highlighted, but individuals are defined by those differences . . . to accept the role of the ethnic is also to accept a gentle marginalization. It is to accept that one will never be just a part of the landscape but always a little apart from it, not quite belonging."[44] Mere tolerance, rather than solidarity, is encouraged by policies that purport to integrate ethnocultural groups by allowing them—

even encouraging them—to maintain many aspects of the cultural identity they ought to have left behind. Complete acceptance is critical for Bissoondath; we need to encourage acceptance of others as Canadian, and not as hyphenated Canadians or as people who are living here but are really from somewhere else.[45] We need therefore to prevent actively the implementation of multicultural policies, since they necessarily permit minorities to opt out of mainstream political and social interaction. Bissoondath doesn't worry about diversity itself; instead, he worries about the allegedly damaging effects of policies that highlight differences among Canadians along ethnocultural lines. On this view, then, it is the overemphasis on accommodating diversity rather than the fact of diversity itself that is problematic.

For many who express views like Bissoondath's, the particular worry is often that our focus on multiculturalism has dragged our attention away from what really matters, that is, economic inequality. Rather than focusing on how to make the poor less poor, socially conscious liberals have mistakenly turned their attention to issues that are considerably less pressing, that is, to issues of cultural politics that only (if anything) scratch the surface of inequalities facing contemporary democracies.[46] Brian Barry is perhaps the most well known among the critics who argue that multicultural politics is the wrong way to go. He writes that "nobody seems to care much about the increasing inequality of opportunity," a concern for which has been jettisoned in favor of managing and accommodating cultural difference.[47] Barry is not alone, moreover, in questioning whether the emphasis on cultural politics is misguided. Todd Gitlin writes, for example, that "the politics of identity is silent on the deepest sources of social misery: the devastation of cities, the draining of resources away from the public and into the private hands of the few. It does not organize to reduce the sickening inequality between rich and poor. Instead, it struggles to change the color of inequality."[48]

Keith Banting and his colleagues have attempted to respond to this complaint, namely, that *multicultural policies* are to blame for an apparent retrenchment of welfare state policies. In recent work, they have compared the types and numbers of multicultural policies implemented across a range of welfare states a systematic evaluation of the data they have collected suggests the absence of a correlation between the adoption of multicultural policies and the retrenchment of welfare state policies.[49] Analysis that fails to find a link between multicultural policies and a decline in support for redistributive policies is heartening, certainly, but somewhat tangential to the point raised here: the presence of diversity drives levels of both social and political trust down in ways that are not directly related to the presence or absence of multicultural policies. For example, Canada and Australia, the two countries that are, among the countries at issue, the most multicultural, have witnessed declines in trust among their populations; these declines pose a long-term risk to the redistributive policies to which egalitarians are committed, as I shall soon explain.[50]

There is considerable evidence that we should indeed worry about the effect of diversity on citizens' capacity to rely on one another in times of need. In one study of 152 countries—in which a range of factors including "public sector efficiency, quality of public good provision, government size, and political freedom" were assessed—researchers concluded that the quality of government performance in general correlated negatively with rates of ethnic diversity. In particular, they found that ethnically divided countries tend to choose against implementing redistributive policies.[51] This study thus suggests that we may indeed have cause to worry *specifically* about redistribution in ethnically divided communities; that is, redistribution is more difficult to effect because of the existence of ethnocultural diversity within a populace. Smaller-scale research provides further evidence that in diverse communities redistributive policies may be threatened by lack of support in the populace. In one study, researchers found that when comparing diverse and homogeneous communities, people living in diverse communities would *explicitly and deliberately* choose to divert tax revenues away from a range of public goods, including education, roads, and welfare programs, that seem to tax one ethnic or racial group for the benefit of another. Note that this is a comparative observation about the welfare-related *choices* made by citizens in diverse versus homogeneous communities. Moreover, diverse localities are more likely to be forced to rely on county or municipal governments to provide them with revenue to fund public education, since members of diverse communities are less willing to contribute their tax revenue to public education.[52]

Patterns indicate, moreover, that individuals alter their support for redistributive policies based on their assessment of who the aid recipients are likely to be. Evidence gathered in some American communities indicates that white citizens will reduce their support for welfare if they learn that the money will aid black citizens, and that black support for welfare programs declines if they are told that welfare revenue will likely aid whites. White support for welfare does not change in response to the information that the welfare revenue will aid other white citizens, nor does black support for welfare policies decline in response to the information that the revenue will aid other black citizens. Thus, as Erzo Luttmer writes, "if individuals prefer to redistribute to their own racial, ethnic, or religious group, they prefer less redistribution when members of their own group constitute a smaller share of beneficiaries. As demographic heterogeneity increases, on average, the share of beneficiaries belonging to one's own group declines. Thus average support for redistribution declines as heterogeneity increases."[53] This observation—that changes in commitment to redistributive policies of various kinds occur in response to *changes* in one's perception of the recipients—is relevant to discussions concerning how to handle increased rates of immigration, and we will return to this observation in the final chapter. In the long run, the goal is for all citizens, regardless of ethnic or cultural status, to share a public culture in such a way that these differences have no impact on support for, and willingness to contribute to, redistributive policies.

Earlier in the chapter, I provided the tools we need to understand why we might see declines in support for redistributive policies in ethnically diverse societies. If I am right that support for redistributive policies depends on trust, and if I am right that trust relations are stressed by the presence of diversity, then these arguments serve to explain why support for redistributive policies may erode in the presence of diversity. As we saw, citizens living in diverse communities may find that they are not guided by shared norms and values, the consequence of which is the failure of trust to emerge. In sum, the evidence that suggests a link between ethnocultural diversity and declines in trust produces good reason to worry about the ongoing support of redistributive policies in diverse communities.

Ethnocultural Diversity and the Weakening of Trust

This chapter has considered the extensive evidence that the presence of ethnocultural diversity in a community (rather than the presence of multicultural policies) decreases the likelihood that a public culture can facilitate the emergence of trust relations, makes democratic politics more difficult, and therefore generates difficulties for maintaining support for redistributive policies over the long term. Readers were asked to look at these familiar worries through the lens of trust (and distrust). These problems, I suggested, are mainly the result of damaged trust relations, that is, trust relations that are under strain because of the presence of ethnocultural diversity, as well as by the behavior of those who attempt to capitalize politically on the heightened sense of vulnerability that diversity generates (often, it must be admitted, this sense of vulnerability is deliberately manipulated by political actors who believe that they can gain from mobilizing a population against diversity). I traced a progression from the weakened trust relations that sometimes appear in the presence of new ethnocultural diversity, through the politicization of ethnicity, to the adoption of isolationist policies that permit distrust to emerge and persist over time.

Whatever benefits we expect from widespread trust relations—compliance with democratically determined law or, as I have considered in this chapter, a commitment to redistributive programs—are thereby at risk in communities characterized by (increasing rates of) ethnocultural diversity. A public culture facilitates the emergence of trust in part because of its role in providing a system of social sanctioning (both positive and negative), and it plays a role in generating shared expectations that underpin the extension and reciprocation of trust. In other words, a public culture provides its members with a sense of the behaviors and values that will garner approval and those that will not. Knowing that we share this value system—a value system that underpins the decisions we are likely to make—maintains trust among members who share it. For better or for worse, ethnocultural diversity signals (often mistakenly, as I have emphasized) a shift in the values among a population in such a way that they cannot necessarily be relied upon to underpin trust relations.

Additionally, in daily interactions with others, at both the political and social levels, we have *expectations* for how others behave, and these expectations (when they are met) underpin trust relations. The presence of ethnocultural diversity, however, can erode the expectations we have regarding how others will behave, in some cases because there are fewer opportunities to interact in a public environment together (for example, where minority groups choose to segregate rather than integrate), and in others because newcomers appear to participate in shared space in ways that seem alien to us, and therefore are taken to signal value differences (which may, or may not, exist). My main point, ultimately, is this: there is reason to believe that there is nothing *inherent* in ethnocultural diversity that causes it to erode trust relations. Rather, ethnocultural status serves as a proxy for value difference, as a result of which trust can be more difficult to achieve. There may therefore reason to believe that the ways in which ethnocultural diversity signals value difference (and so erodes the capacity of a public culture to serve as an effective sanctioning method), and the ways in which it shapes expectations, can effectively be overcome by public policy, and this possibility will occupy me in the final chapter.

The analysis I offered was intended to illustrate that trust weakens in response to *evidence* that a public culture is eroding; those who argue (rightly in my view) that the presence of diversity in a population is of considerable long-term *benefit* are sometimes loathe to acknowledge the challenges it can pose in the short term. My own view is that in many cases, those who have become less trusting in response to apparent evidence that the public culture is eroding are *misinterpreting* the evidence available (often with the aid of political actors who encourage this misinterpretation of evidence). It is, I argued, unfortunate that the mere presence of diversity (as well as the not infrequent attempts to capitalize politically on directing hostility toward new migrants, who represent a large proportion of this diversity) is correlated with weakened trust relations among members of a political community. Yet it is a mistake to ignore the importance of active and concerted attempts to counteract the (further) erosion of trust relations. I describe these attempts more fully in chapter 7 and suggest that it is the job of political actors to encourage better interpretation of the evidence, and therefore to reduce the likelihood that distrust emerges in situations where it is unwarranted.

It is, moreover, a mistake to simply accuse those who exhibit anxieties in response to the increased presence of diversity of intolerance; those who do may be failing to take seriously the dangers to trust posed by diversity, and therefore they may enable mistrust to flourish and, in the worst case scenario, translate into distrust. In other words, it is mistake to ignore the challenges that trust relations face in diverse environments; as we saw in chapter 4, those who object to our advocating a public culture do so on the grounds that it diminishes trust by imposing and enforcing homogenizing and static values and norms on newcomers (or those who otherwise reject those values). This view reflects an impoverished account of what the public culture intends to accomplish and how it does so: its goal is not to *impose* values and norms in common but rather to *reflect* them. This chapter has intended to illustrate how it is that ethnocultural diversity can inhibit the task we have assigned to a public culture, namely, its trust-building task. Is trust impossible under conditions of ethnocultural diversity? I don't believe so, even though I believe it is a mistake to ignore the challenges it poses; as I have indicated, these questions will occupy the final chapter. Before I consider trust-building mechanisms, however, let us first assess trust relations in societies that are more severely divided than those at issue in this chapter. The reason to do so is to some degree a warning: it serves to illustrate the dangers of permitting weakened trust relations to solidify into distrust. As we shall see, severely divided societies are characterized by rampant distrust, and they will therefore demand trust-building strategies that are different in form from those required in ethnoculturally diverse societies.

6

SEVERELY DIVIDED SOCIETIES, TRUST, AND THE STRUGGLE FOR DEMOCRACY

It is commonplace to argue that democracy is impossible to construct and maintain in severely divided societies. Some kind of shared commitment to a democratic polity, and the cooperation this implies, is required in order that democracy survives, and this commitment may not exist when ethnocultural divisions within a population run deep.[1] By way of example, consider the following assessments. Alvin Rabushka and Kenneth Shepsle write that "democracy—the free and open competition for people's vote—is simply not viable in an environment of intense ethnic preferences."[2] Similarly, Larry Diamond and Marc Plattner write that "ethnicity is the most difficult type of cleavage for a democracy to manage."[3] Arend Lijphart writes that "the deep social divisions and political differences within plural societies are held responsible for instability and breakdown in democracies."[4] The pessimism of these scholars emerges from a considered assessment of past and existing divided societies, and all offer (sometimes incompatible) institutional solutions that might prevent the dissolution of these kinds of communities.

In the previous chapter, I described the status of trust in ethnoculturally diverse societies in which the public culture is threatened, and therefore in which trust relations are threatened. In these multicultural societies, the thinning of the public culture heightens the sense of vulnerability associated with extending trust to others, and thereby reduces the likelihood that it will ultimately be extended. As a result, the opportunity to see one's trust rewarded diminishes over time. Severely divided societies, as we shall see, are instead characterized by a deep *distrust* along both social and political dimensions of the other ethnocultural group(s) that make up the polity, and therefore the trust that is at the core of even the most basic of democratic functions is weak or nonexistent. The vulnerability in extending trust is felt to be too high, at least across group boundaries, as a result of which trust is rarely extended and rewarded. The opportunities to build trust, even in cases where it is likely warranted, are vanishingly small. In the next and concluding chapter, I shall develop principles that can guide us in strengthening and rebuilding trust relations.

I begin this chapter by describing four features that define a severely divided society along ethnocultural lines,[5] so as to distinguish them from the multicultural societies that occupied my attention in chapter 5. Severely divided societies, I shall suggest, have great difficulty in sustaining a shared public culture, as a result of which levels of trust among citizens are low. I then turn to an assessment of the prospects for democracy in severely divided societies—these prospects are evidently dim in the absence of trust. In chapter 2 I described the three most basic features of democratic practice: the willingness of a governing party to give up power following an electoral loss, a commitment to the representative system, and the existence of reliable minority protection. I shall illustrate the difficulties severely divided societies face as they try to sustain a commitment to each of these three features of democratic practice in the absence of trust: parties are reluctant to give up power; the representative system fails to offer generalized representation, since citizens only extend trust to in-group representatives; and minority protection is not reliable. In sum, we shall see that there is a clear and "inherent difficulty . . . in maintaining the inclusiveness of a polity superimposed on an ethnically divided society."[6]

Defining Severely Divided Societies

Some severely divided societies are easy to identify—no one would dispute that Northern Ireland and Sri Lanka are severely divided along ethnocultural lines. What of other societies in which there are marked divisions that might not consistently dominate the politics of the central government? Is Spain a severely divided society, for example, or simply multicultural, or both? Is Canada a society divided between English and French, or perhaps between Aboriginals and non-Aboriginals, or is it a tossed salad of multiple ethnocultural groups? There are four central characteristics that generally define severely divided societies, all of which produce an environment in which distrust prevails, and that therefore distinguish them from the multicultural societies I described in the prior chapter.

First, a severely divided society is characterized by hostile and competitive ethnocultural groups. Each ethnocultural group is itself characterized by the belief that its members belong together, a belief that often emerges from a sense of common descent (a belief that is, as many scholars of nationalism note, often imagined or constructed by past social and political forces).[7] The competing groups likewise share a history, but in general the history is one of conflict and competition. To take an obvious example, we might say that the Palestinians and the Israelis are characterized internally by a sense that they belong together, a sense of loyalty to other members of their group (i.e., Palestinians belong with Palestinians and Israelis belong with Israelis). What serves to make Israel a divided society is that these two groups share a history with each other, a history that is conflictual, hostile, and often violent.

Second, in severely divided societies, ethnocultural divisions frame the vast majority of political conflicts. Not all political conflicts break down along ethnic or cultural lines: witness, by way of counterexample, the political parties in Northern Ireland or Israel, which on occasion make deliberate attempts to frame politics in other than ethnocultural terms, in general by framing their policy proposals in ways that could reasonably appeal to members of all groups. Nevertheless, a defining feature of severely divided societies is that political conflicts are perceived by those engaged in them in mainly ethnocultural terms. The claim that ethnocultural divisions frame political conflicts is not incompatible with the possibility that the groups in conflict will share some important norms and values: Sri Lanka, Nigeria, the former Yugoslavia, and Northern Ireland provide good examples of communities in which many norms are shared across groups, but where the existence of shared norms hasn't necessarily served to limit the severity of the conflict.

Third, the groups who make up a severely divided society perceive the divisions to be intractable. Most members of competing groups will characterize the conflict as ongoing, insoluble, and perhaps even inevitable given the apparently conflicting objectives of each group. Groups will present their demands as nonnegotiable, and others will take them as nonnegotiable and will feel no motivation to compromise in the face of the apparently invariable demands of others.

Fourth and finally, the existence of widespread hostility and more or less frequent outbreaks of violent conflict create an environment in which many citizens live under conditions of discrimination and insecurity. In some societies, fear of sectarian violence translates into segregated communities in which citizens in one group will feel physically insecure mainly when they enter areas in which another group lives (as is partly the case in present-day Northern Ireland and Israel). In other societies, they are more immediately present, and citizens feel constantly insecure as a result of ongoing and widespread violence, as was the case in post-invasion Iraq for example.

Severely Divided Societies, the Absence of Public Culture, and Trust

At least two observable consequences emerge as a result of the characteristics described above. Severely divided societies struggle to support a public culture and they are therefore characterized by an absence of trust between citizens of different ethnocultural groups. Paradoxically, and dangerously, they are instead often characterized by an unhealthy level of in-group cohesion and loyalty. As a result, severely divided societies face considerable difficulty in achieving genuine democratic politics.

There Is Little or No Public Culture in Severely Divided Societies

Severely divided societies struggle to produce an inclusive public culture. In most political communities, even the multicultural communities described in the previous chapter, political coalitions do not inevitably break down by ethnocultural group; instead, cross-cutting coalitions often emerge. One reason that these coalitions might form is that the community itself is underpinned by at least a thin public culture. Even if trust relations, both social and political, are under some tension in multicultural communities, there continues to be a recognizable public culture.[8] Citizens believe that some interests, values, and principles are shared by all (or most members), and so can be taken for granted in political negotiations. Citizens of these communities generally abide by the norms that these shared beliefs entail and are trusted to do so, whereas this is less likely in severely divided societies.

There is at least some reason to be skeptical of the claim that a public culture doesn't exist at all in a severely divided society. It is rarely true that *no* norms or values or principles are held in common among members of competing ethnocultural groups. Protestants and Catholics in Northern Ireland ostensibly share a number of values and norms—in general, both groups are committed to basic liberal values and to democratic procedures for resolving most political disagreements. Moreover, both Catholics and Protestants appear willing in the abstract to participate in shared institutions. What they appear to lack, however, is the belief that others are willing to do the same—they do not believe that "these ideas and principles *are* shared across society."[9] As we saw in chapter 4, there may be norms and values held in common, but they are insufficient to support democracy over the long term. I argued that to have a public culture in the sense that it is relevant for democracy means more than sharing some set of values and norms, and it means more than having certain cultural or normative features that might reasonably be characterized as shared. Recall that although Hungary is not a severely divided society, its public culture does not contain the two main features needed in order to generate trust, as a result of which its democratic capacity is compromised.[10] These are a willingness to cooperate (which is a source of social trust and political trust among citizens) and a commitment to shared institutions charged with effecting this cooperation (which is a source of political trust).

In severely divided societies often which members are unwilling to cooperate within shared institutions; in divided societies, "the path from acceptance of the principles of justice to overlapping consensus [on shared norms and values that underpin democratic politics] is disrupted by the mistrust that exists between" competing communities.[11] In other words, even if there are some shared norms and values across members of ethnocultural groups in a severely divided society, they often prove insufficient to provide the environment in which trust might develop, and so democracy remains under threat if it has taken hold at all.

In chapter 4 I merely stated that two features were missing from the Hungarian public culture that made it insufficient to the task of facilitating trust relations. Here I outline the evidence that can be marshaled to assess whether these features are present in a public culture. There are at least two separate methods we might employ to demonstrate that a public culture does not exist in severely divided societies: one focuses on the effectiveness of the institutions that govern the community, and a second focuses on the kinds of statements made or actions taken by members of competing ethnocultural groups. The former method emphasizes the number of functioning shared institutions and the nature of citizens' participation within these shared institutions. Does voting always break down along ethnocultural lines, for example? Do citizens evidently participate in shared institutions (say, national elections) *only* for the purpose of improving the lot of their own ethnocultural group?

The latter method relies on surveying citizens to ascertain their willingness to cooperate across groups, or it might focus on citizens' efforts to effect further separation than already exists. Do citizens demand access to separate school boards? Do citizens of one group frequently publicly proclaim the untrustworthiness of citizens from competing ethnocultural groups (or do they silently support discrimination against them)? Neither method will *prove* that there exists little willingness to cooperate between ethnocultural groups, but it should make it reasonable to claim that severely divided societies, by and large, are unlikely to have the public culture that is necessary to support democratic institutions over time.

Let me deploy the first method to offer a simplified account of Nigeria's recent political history by way of example. As I shall suggest, Nigeria is a severely divided society along all four of the criteria I outlined: it is characterized by hostile and competing ethnocultural groups, these divisions shape the political conflicts that the country faces, these divisions are perceived as intractable, and the existence of simmering hostility frequently produces violence.

Nigeria is composed of three main ethnocultural groups—the Yoruba (in the west), the Igbo (in the east), and the Hausa-Fulani (in the north)—and they are divided by (among other things) religion, language, and levels of wealth.[12] Social life is largely organized by ethnocultural group, and so to a considerable extent Nigerians are already displaying some unwillingness to commit to shared institutions. Religious and ethnic groups organize their members to compete for land, for educational opportunities, and for employment opportunities. Segregation exists across all of these domains: some groups are overrepresented in higher education and some are overrepresented in the ranks of the unemployed. Relative success in each of these domains breaks down by ethnocultural group: the Hausa-Fulani are the least likely to be educated and the most likely to be relocated because of environmental degradation, for example.[13] Additionally, ethnocultural groups, rather than the federal government, generally regulate basic social structures, including schools, police forces, and so on. A far too common recent occurrence of this, for example, is the current Nigerian federal administration's unwillingness (for various social and political reasons) to intervene to prevent the harsh application of Sharia law in Muslim states.[14] There is no widespread commitment to the shared democratic principles that are meant to regulate Nigerian democracy, but that are sometimes (though only in rare cases) in conflict with Sharia law.

Nigeria's social structures are not the only signal that there exists an unwillingness to submit to shared institutions for cooperation. Even more telling is the difficulty that Nigeria is having in effecting a balanced federation. Federalism is a system of governance that is often chosen to accommodate the fact of minorities or at least territorially concentrated ethnocultural groups, in particular when these groups are possessed of competing senses of how their political and social lives ought to be organized, but have some desire nevertheless to be united as a single polity.[15] Arguably, both Belgium and Spain chose federalism under these conditions. Yet the danger is that the institutional duplication that is associated with federalism—states or provinces may regulate their own educational institutions, their own health systems, and so on—can generate the belief that territories are largely self-governing and therefore support the belief that a deeper self-government is possible.[16] As the number of member units in the Nigerian federation has increased in response to demands for autonomy by more and more groups, one obvious consequence is an increase in the duplication of political institutions, in addition to the already duplicated social institutions (since social institutions are, in Nigeria, largely regulated by religious and ethnic groups already).[17] The claim is not that the number of autonomous regions in a federation is in any way a clear indication of a severely divided society (and *not* that every instance of an expanding number of member units in a federation indicates a general unwillingness to cooperate). Rather, it may be that the *increasing duplication* of institutions over time, especially in response to demands for further autonomy, signals a society that is not committed to remaining united under shared institutions.

The party politics in Nigeria give us further reason to suspect an unwillingness to cooperate among the competing ethnocultural groups. At present Nigerian political parties are subject to stringent rules that encourage them to appeal widely to Nigerians rather than merely to specific ethnocultural groups. The Independent National Electoral Commission's (INEC) newest rules for party registration and competition require, among other demands, that parties open membership to all Nigerians regardless of their ethnocultural or religious identity, and that parties must "maintain functional branches" in at least twenty-four of thirty-six federal states; furthermore, the party's "name, slogan, or motto and identifying symbols and colors shall not have any ethnic, religious, professional or sectional connotation or give the appearance that its activities are confined only to a part of Nigeria."[18] These demands are intended to counter the damaging effect of historically group-based party politics on democratic stability. Given Nigeria's history, writes one commentator in support of the stringent rules for political party formation, even if it is true that "sectional interests must be given their due weight, it is highly doubtful whether the expression of such interests in the form of political parties would promote stable democracy."[19]

Before these requirements were implemented, Nigerian political parties broke down by ethnocultural group: "During the nationalist struggles for independence and constitutional developments (1920s–1960), the three dominant ethnic groups . . . controlled their respective regions under the framework of ethnically/regionally based political parties."[20] The continual threat of state breakdown in Nigeria (for example in the civil wars of 1967 and 1970) was primarily a consequence of ethnically based agitations and violence encouraged and sponsored by competing ethnocultural groups.[21] At present there are three major political parties in Nigeria that have qualified to compete according to the new stringent rules of the INEC. Although all three parties have met the formal requirements, however, there is some preliminary evidence that the base support for two of them remains squarely within a region or cultural group. In the 1998 local election, for example, the All People's Party's electoral success (nine governorships) was only in the north, and the Alliance for Democracy's success (six governorships) was only in the southwest. The story is, obviously, more complicated than is reported here—as A. Sat Obiyan suggests, to assess the success of the new party registration rules solely in terms of governorships would be "myopic" (42). Nevertheless, evidence from Nigeria bolsters the claim that an unwillingness to participate in shared institutions—I am referring specifically to national rather than regional political parties—is a worry for democratic stability and ongoingness.

There Exists Little Trust Between Groups in a Severely Divided Society

As the discussion of Nigeria was meant to illustrate, Nigerians do not share a willingness to cooperate, nor do they share a willingness to submit to the shared institutions that would, in principle, be charged with effecting this cooperation. If I am right that severely divided societies are characterized by and large by the absence of a trust-supporting public culture, they will equally be characterized by distrust. In the face of an inability to trust people in general, ethnocultural groups in severely divided societies are instead often characterized by particularized (rather than generalized) trust. This particularized trust defines the often very strong trust relations that do in fact exist among members of ethnocultural groups in a divided society, and it is born under threat, or perceptions of threat, ranging from discrimination to material deprivation to physical insecurities of various kinds.[22] In this context, ethnocultural affiliations serve to provide "a sense of security in a divided society, as well as a source of trust, certainty, reciprocal help, and protection against neglect of one's interests by strangers."[23] There are at least three distinctions that can be made between generalized trust and the particularized trust and loyalty that can come to characterize ethnocultural groups under conditions of physical and political insecurity.

One way in which in-group trust or loyalty differs from generalized trust is true by definition: it extends more narrowly, only to those people who display a very select, *ethnoculturally based* set of characteristics. The perception of who belongs is therefore very tightly defined and membership is obviously exclusive. Another distinction between in-group trust and a more generalized trust is that the former, in addition to "in-group favoritism," is often accompanied by "out-group denigration," that is, "the tendency is to enhance one's own group by diminishing the performance of contending groups."[24] A final distinction is that in-group loyalty tends to be especially demanding, in two ways. First, the conditions of politics in severely divided societies are such that groups attain great importance, so that any member's success is highly contingent on the general success of the group; when the political leadership is dominated by members of a particular group, that group is more likely to find jobs in the public service, for example. Second, since the group offers a kind of protection and insurance for individuals, and the cost of leaving the group is often so high, members can feel restricted from expressing any kind of dissent or disagreement (even if they are not formally prevented from doing so).[25]

In-group trust or loyalty can secure at least minimum safety under highly insecure and volatile political conditions, and it is therefore not surprising that this kind of relation extends internally among members of competing groups. Yet the existence of in-group loyalty, combined with out-group denigration, not only causes rampant distrust between members of different ethnocultural groups, but it also precludes the kind of interaction that might plausibly serve to break down negative stereotypes. As I suggested in chapter 1, both trust and distrust are evidence resistant—once a judgment is formed about whether another person or group is trustworthy, this judgment is resistant to change even in the face of evidence to the contrary. In particular, the likely history of trust violations makes interactions that might require or lead to trust especially difficult.[26]

Trust, Severely Divided Societies, and Democracy

I suggested earlier that in a multicultural society, the trust that supports voluntary compliance in a democracy is endangered by apparent threats to the shared values and norms that compose a public culture, and that mistrust can and often does emerge. These challenges—to cooperation, to compliance, to trust—are exacerbated in severely divided societies. As Brian Barry explains: if "the group to which they belong [is] systematically discriminated against, treated as second-class citizens, denied cultural expression or communal organization, and generally not dealt with in terms of equal partnership," they will be inclined to "deny the legitimacy of a regime."[27] Here we shall see, by way of general examples, that the trust essential to supporting some or all of the basic features of democratic institutions is absent in severely divided societies often because of one community's willingness to violate (often repeatedly) that trust, the consequence of which is widespread unwillingness to comply voluntarily with the decisions made by the central government.

In general, political decision making can be perceived to treat citizens unequally in two ways: materially or symbolically. One source of disagreement is connected to the distribution of material resources—this is especially problematic where material resources are scarce, so that decisions about who gets what are always made with the knowledge that some people will not have enough.[28] Decisions about who controls which material resources, even when plentiful, are likely also fraught with tension in severely divided societies, since the group with control will be perceived (often rightly) to be concerned mainly with furthering the objectives of its own group. From the perspective of citizens whose well being is tied tightly to membership in an ethnocultural group, the likelihood that resource distribution will be conducted in an impartial or unbiased way is low: the perception, whatever the decision, will often be that one ethnocultural group wins at the expense of another (or many other) ethnocultural group(s).

The present Israeli approach to water distribution and the funding of local politics illustrates this observation. Israelis and Palestinians share the main sources of water. One (particularly contentious) source is an aquifer underneath the West Bank, which came under Israeli control after the war in 1967. Israel declared the aquifer public property and has since relied on its water to provide for Israelis and Palestinians living in the West Bank. If all citizens had equal access to water, this decision and others like it would not be as problematic (even if unjust for other reasons). But empirical work shows the deeply unequal accessibility to and distribution of water enjoyed by Palestinians and Israelis. Israeli settlers in the West Bank pay approximately one-third of what Palestinians pay for water, and just under 30 percent of Palestinian households have no connection whatsoever to piped water (virtually all Israeli settlers do have such connections).[29] It is no surprise, then, that one might describe the situation as follows: "the water crisis is not one of insufficient supply, but of uneven and inequitable distribution."[30] In divided societies, the position of one's ethnocultural group in relation to others will often determine who is granted and who is denied access to material resources.

Second, the question of recognition or symbolism is a source of disagreement within a supposedly shared polity. Even if many ethnocultural conflicts in a democratic polity manifest themselves around the fair distribution of material resources, these kinds of conflicts, if limited to tensions around fair distribution, "may sometimes be resolved through conventional kinds of bargaining." However, while most ethnocultural conflicts involve tensions around issues of distribution, they often also "revolve around exclusive symbols and conceptions of legitimacy. They are characterized by competing demands that cannot easily be broken down into bargainable increments."[31] Manifestations of this sort of difficulty are reflected, for example, in debates about language policy, about the protection of minority rights, about national holidays, and so on. No one doubts that attempts to restrict the use of minority languages in public spaces—say, Kurdish in Turkey—is an attempt to deny public recognition of the minority in question.[32]

When the state is no longer able or willing to provide goods on an equal basis, either materially or symbolically, the legitimacy of political decisions will over time diminish in the eyes of those subject to them. The consequence of this increasing illegitimacy is a decrease in the voluntary compliance that underpins the effectiveness of democratic politics in general. Below, we shall see the specific loci at which trust is missing.

Majority Rule, Minority Protection, and Trust

In chapter 2 I elaborated the role that the majority principle plays in democratic decision making, the principle that the majority, by virtue of being the majority, ought to dictate which party forms the government and what policy choices are made.[33] For any given decision, obviously, some people's preferences will not be reflected. How many depends both on how a given society defines the term "majority" and the choice of electoral system (whether majoritarian or consensual, for example). The reason why members of the minority voluntarily comply with decisions in which their preferences aren't reflected can partially be explained by the perceived legitimacy of democratic procedures. Majority rule is generally acceptable on two conditions. First, there is a reasonable expectation that the makeup of the minority will change over time (any person who finds herself in the minority on any given decision can reasonably expect to find herself in the majority on other decisions). Second, there exists some form of formal protection for those in the minority. Minority leaders must be allowed the freedom to take up the role of opposition without fear of persecution or harassment, and the rights of those citizens who have supported the minority must be formally protected. In stable democracies that are not fraught with severe divisions, these two conditions are easily fulfilled—citizens understand that they will find themselves in the minority and the majority at different times,[34] and minority supporters are secure in the knowledge that their rights will not be violated as a result of their political position or because of their minority status more generally.

The standard application of the majority principle is more difficult in divided societies. Since the relative size of each constituency is known in advance, and since voting typically breaks down along ethnocultural lines, the results of apparently democratic decision making will likewise be known in advance. Indeed, evidence from divided societies indicates that there is very little voting across ethnocultural lines, and that winners can ultimately be predicted by assessing the total populations of each ethnocultural group. For example, research conducted in the 1970s in Northern Ireland showed that there was "very little inclination among Ulstermen to cross religious lines in their voting. Ninety-five percent of Unionist supporters are Protestant, and ninety-nine percent of Nationalist supporters are Catholic."[36] Statistical data taken of more recent elections indicate roughly consistent trends. In 1997, unionist parties received 50 percent of the vote (57 percent of the electorate is Protestant), and nationalist parties received 41 percent of the vote (40 percent of the electorate is Catholic).[37] The main worry therefore about decisions made by the majority principle in divided societies is that the conclusion will be foregone. One ethnocultural group or coalition of ethnocultural groups will win "by its sheer demographic weight," the consequence of which is that "others see themselves as losing all, excluded not only from the government but also from the larger political community."[38]

In Northern Ireland, the application of the majority principle guarantees electoral victory to the Protestants; in Israel, the application of the majority principle guarantees victory to Israeli Jews; in Sri Lanka, the application of the majority principle guarantees victory to the Sinhalese.[39] The worry extends to societies divided into more than two groups: in Iraq, the majority principle guarantees victory to the Shiites, for example, and in India, the principle favors the Hindu majority. The worry is the same whatever the social divisions; namely, the belief that electoral loss translates into virtual exclusion from government and institutional ostracism in the form of discrimination, hostility, and often violence. This belief, moreover, has good empirical grounding. The decision in 1956 to make Sinhala the only official language of Sri Lanka is often cited as the origin of the (until recently) violent conflict between the Tamils and the Sinhalese; the Sinhalese were a clear electoral majority and the Tamils had no legal recourse once the decision was made. Without formal protections against these kinds of decisions, minorities will be unwilling and indeed unable to trust that the application of the majority principle will treat them fairly.[40]

These failures of protection motivate ethnocultural groups to violate the trust that is central to the democratic process—for example, to take matters of crime and punishment into their own hands rather than to leave them to state law enforcement agencies. It is a vicious circle of sorts: the belief that others are not trustworthy permits and encourages people to behave in untrustworthy ways.

Trust and Electoral Legitimacy

One consequence of the failure to adopt, or respect, minority rights protection legislation is that the stakes associated with winning versus losing at the ballot are felt as particularly high—the winning group will be able to attain control of state resources, for example—and therefore there exists an increased willingness to violate the trust that is central to securing the legitimacy of an electoral outcome to begin with. Recall that there are a number of individual features of any electoral system that require trust so that in general individuals accept the outcome. One danger in a severely divided society is that one party—sometimes the majority party and other times the minority party—will manipulate the electoral system to secure dominance artificially or to secure more power than their numbers would legitimately permit. The examples I shall give of possible ways to manipulate the electoral system are certainly not exhaustive; instead, they show that there is a range of ways in which communities can violate the trust that is central to the legitimacy of electoral outcomes. Violations of this trust transpire both during the election, when those running the election engage in electoral fraud, and prior to the election, when the community attempting to maintain control of the political apparatus rigs certain portions of the system in such a way as to (illegitimately) secure its victory.

First, a community with a slim majority may manipulate the system in such a way as to ensure their dominance. In Fiji, for example, indigenous Fijians make up 51 percent of the population and Indo-Fijians 43 percent. The 1990 constitution mandated that of the seventy seats in the House of Representatives, thirty-seven would be guaranteed to indigenous Fijians, thus securing for them a permanent majority regardless of electoral performance.[41] A second way to secure dominance artificially is to structure voting requirements in such a way that they exclude members of the minority from voting. For example, in Northern Ireland in the 1960s and 1970s, property requirements for voting prevented the relatively poorer Catholics from voting, so that Protestants were able to govern over predominantly Catholic towns.[42] This method of fixing electoral outcomes is not restricted to communities in which one group is only a slight majority. Some communities with a substantial majority may nevertheless worry about the political strength of a substantial minority, and so manipulate an electoral process in such a way as to further minimize any strength the minority might be able to exert. For example, one of the first steps taken by the newly independent Sri Lankan (then, Ceylonese) government was to strip Indian Tamils of their citizenship (Tamils make up 25 percent of the Sri Lankan population, and approximately half of them are Indian Tamils). This decision, which was made possible by the substantially greater size of the Sinhalese population, muted the political strength of an already marginalized Tamil community by reducing its politically effective population by half. In preventing certain members of the population from voting, the trust required to secure the legitimacy of the outcome is violated. Third, a minority community may attempt to secure electoral dominance by disenfranchising entirely a majority community. This, obviously, is what transpired in South Africa's apartheid era, where the black population (which made up almost 75 percent of the population) was disenfranchised and oppressed by a white minority, which wielded complete and exclusive political control over the country for decades.[43] It goes nearly without saying that these actions violate the trust that is central to securing the legitimacy of an electoral outcome.

Trust and Representation

As I articulated in chapter 2, the relation between trust and representation in stable and relatively homogeneous political communities is as follows: we trust legislators to act in the national interest (broadly conceived) and legislators trust one another to play by the rules, namely, to be willing to give up power in the face of electoral loss. Citizens trust their leaders and representatives to do the same. There is a different dynamic at work in severely divided societies, however, with respect to the relation between trust and representation.

Group leaders in divided societies are just that: leaders who are charged with negotiating on behalf of specific groups. Recall that representatives can be described in two ways: as a delegate and as a trustee. The former "carries the mandate of a constituency which he or she advocates" and the latter "exercises independent judgment about the right thing to do under these political circumstances."[44] In general, most representatives act as both delegate and trustee: representatives are authorized to make decisions that bind the behavior of their constituents and so act as trustees, and representatives must engage in constant processes of authorization to ensure that their mandate to act is renewed on a regular basis, and in this sense they act as delegates. A representative thus both expresses the view of the group—she is mandated to do so via various electoral and consultative processes—and in negotiating on their behalf is ideally open to the possibility of altering her group's positions. Her openness to genuine negotiation derives from her belief that she is trusted by her constituents, and so can negotiate on their behalf knowing they will comply with her decisions.[45] Yet in severely divided societies, group leaders are more like advocates or delegates than are representatives in societies that do not suffer from severe divisions, and they are often charged with negotiating zealously on behalf of their constituents.

Representation therefore is a source of struggle in severely divided societies. The main (trust-related) cause of the difficulties associated with political negotiating arises from the belief that the group being represented is necessarily uniform in its views.[46] Yet even when a group's members have collectively extended a mandate to negotiate on behalf of the group to one person or one set of people, it is likely not granted by a unified group. Rather, it is more likely that some number of group members agree to a mandate, which other nonagreeing members accept out of loyalty to the group or perhaps out of a commitment to the decision-making procedures adopted to choose the mandate. Further, in many severely divided societies—Israel or Northern Ireland for example—group representatives lead groups that contain within them extremists who are more reluctant than others to negotiate with the apparent enemy.[47] Thus, when Yasser Arafat negotiated on behalf the Palestinians, there was some question about whether he was able to control members of Hamas and Islamic Jihad. When Gerry Adams negotiated on behalf of Catholic nationalists, there was some question about whether he had been granted the authority necessary to negotiate on behalf of members and supporters of the IRA. Consequently, trust between representatives at the negotiating table is precarious. If group leaders are unable or unwilling to exert control over their (ostensible) constituents, negotiations in which leaders are asked to make concessions on behalf of their constituents are made difficult. Not only do group leaders have little leeway to negotiate, but their counterparts can also never be sure that decisions made will elicit sufficient voluntary compliance.

There are two intertwined trust-related reasons why group members may only feel comfortable extending their leaders limited room to maneuver. It is often the case that trust is more difficult to extend, and is extended in a more tenuous way, to representatives within severely divided societies. The general explanation for why trust is more difficult to extend in those societies, even when group leaders are perceived to be trustworthy, is in large part because of the nature of the issues at stake. Initial politicking in severely divided societies concern high-stakes issues: who is entitled to participate in government, how opposition members ought to be treated, which kinds of concessions ought to be made by which groups. Should the oil-rich states of Nigeria be forced to redistribute their revenues to poorer provinces? Should minority populations be guaranteed representation in governmental bodies, and, if so, to what extent and on what issues should minorities be able to exert their

influence? On these and similarly basic issues, it is not surprising that compromise is perceived as difficult, if not impossible. As a result there is considerable reluctance to authorize representatives to make concessions, for fear
that their preconcession advantages will be permanently lost.

Trust is extended in a limited way, however, on the basis of the view that
leaders can be trusted to negotiate effectively with leaders of reviled groups.
The danger exists that group members will misunderstand the activities
of their leaders as they negotiate with leaders of opposing groups, and so accuse them of disloyalty (and consequently withdraw their support, the dangers of which are outlined above). Leaders must constantly work to persuade
their own group to remain loyal to its cause, while working with others who
are reviled as untrustworthy. It is inherent in the nature of politics in severely
divided societies that political conflicts are, or at least seem to be, intractable.
As a consequence, the disposition of group members toward members of other
groups is already distrustful, and this is so even if most members of conflicting
groups agree that the present state of affairs (i.e., conflict-ridden, acrimonious,
and perhaps even violent) is undesirable. The knowledge that compromise is
necessary in order to live together is often overridden by the deep distrust that
pervades the relations between the communities in question.

Conclusions

Whereas the trust relations that support democratic politics are under threat
in multicultural communities, the analysis here illustrates the additional
struggles that severely divided societies face in creating and securing a commitment to shared democratic institutions over time. We have good reason
to think that many severely divided societies do not share a public culture;
given the absence of a public culture, and so the absence of trust, it is virtually impossible to support democratic institutions in severely divided societies. The political (and often physical) insecurity that pervades severely
divided societies heightens the vulnerability citizens feel in interacting with
others, and therefore diminishes their willingness to extend trust. The analysis here bears on a question raised earlier against the public culture argument. In chapter 4 we saw that one objection to the public culture argument
is that it is unnecessary to insist that democracies are underpinned by anything more than a commitment to shared values; on this view; shared values,
which can be instantiated in democratic institutions, are sufficient to secure

ongoing support for democratic institutions. Yet as we saw here, citizens of severely divided societies frequently *do* share values, often democratic values, even as they continue to resist participating in democratic institutions in common. More is needed in order to secure the *trust* that underpins democratic political activity, and it is provided by a public culture, the content of which is defined by norms and (ideally democratic) values. As one scholar observes, "politics relies not only on agreement over the principles of justice, but on the networks of trust required for engagement to take place"; in severely divided societies, "public institutions are unstable" because the expectation that trust will be rewarded "simply does not exist."[48] Although severely divided societies struggle more obviously than do democratic communities divided by ethnocultural diversity of the kind described in chapter 5, the analysis here was meant to illustrate that the struggles are of the same *kind* even if they are deeper; whereas multicultural societies often struggle with mistrust, severely divided societies are plagued with distrust. Can we do something about these struggles? In the next and final chapter, I consider how to rebuild trust in the societies I've described here, and how we might go about strengthening the weakened trust relations that are present in the multicultural polities I described in chapter 5.

7

GUIDING TRUST BUILDING IN DEMOCRACIES

Attempts to rebuild trust in divided societies take many forms with which we are familiar. For example, Northern Ireland has invested in integrated schools (which are in high demand and not yet widely available), schools in which students from both Catholic and Protestant backgrounds learn and work together daily. Nongovernmental organizations worked for years in the many divided communities of the former Yugoslavia to organize cross-cultural construction projects in which citizens from hostile ethnocultural groups worked together to rebuild homes destroyed during the conflict. Summer camps explicitly aim to attract children from across divided societies to play and work together for many weeks in an attempt to break down negative stereotypes and build lasting cross-cultural friendships.

In this chapter, I offer a set of principles that can guide trust-building projects in general. These principles are intended to guide trust-building in multicultural environments, where the goal is both to prevent weakened trust relations from degenerating into distrust and to build conditions in which trust can emerge, and in severely divided societies, where the goal is to move from distrust to trust. Here I shall suggest that the key to sustaining and building trust is cooperation, and that we should therefore focus our trust-building efforts on developing the conditions under which cooperation can and does lead to generalized trust among citizens.

I begin by revisiting the public culture argument to illustrate that when it is under pressure its capacity to minimize vulnerability is reduced, and therefore its trust-generating role is constrained. I then turn to an explicit focus on cooperation and its connection to trust. I suggest that in order for cooperation to proceed absent trust, we need to adopt three generalized strategies: we need to generate cooperative environments in which we can secure monitoring, impose sanctions, and commit to participatory rule generation. These strategies aim to create an environment that can stand in for a public culture; that is, they mimic the mechanisms by which a public culture produces trust, in particular by minimizing the vulnerability connected to extending trust. I examine deliberation in some depth as a prototypical trust-building exercise, in particular to describe how the three strategies I listed can be implemented in the deliberative arena. Deliberation is a good test case, since all three strategies can easily be implemented to ensure that it can build trust. I conclude the chapter by pointing to the ways in which multicultural policies more generally can aid the trust-building project.

Pressures on the Public Culture

As I described earlier, a public culture is ideally defined by its refusal to demand complete homogeneity of values and norms, its commitment to public access, and its fluidity. It is of course the case that no public culture is ideal, in the sense that access to the environments that shape it is near-perfectly equal. Equally, the extent to which the defining norms and features of a public culture are embraced by its members ebbs and flows over time—in times of transition, for example, members will display varying levels of commitments to principles and norms that are said to define their public culture. So, for example, Australians continue to discuss whether they ought to retain a commitment to British royalty, or whether they ought to instead embrace a republican Australia. Americans continue to discuss the present-day implications of being a land of immigrants, a label that most Americans agree describes their public culture; some believe that borders should be opened to admit many newcomers, and others believe it is time to close borders to potential migrants. Although public cultures are fluid, they are often resistant to changes of various kinds and give way slowly, cautiously, and often with some public displays of regret.

As I suggested in the previous chapters, ethnocultural diversity, both the kind that increasingly describes multicultural democratic communities and the kind that characterizes severely divided societies, can stress the public culture along the three dimensions listed above. In order to understand the implications of this stress, we need to examine in more detail what it means to say that each of these of these features is under pressure.

Nonhomogeneity Under Pressure

To say that a public culture meets the nonhomogeneity requirement is to say that it displays a kind of cultural easygoingness with respect to society's central values and norms; under stress, however, this relaxed attitude may be lost. When there is an increase in publicly made demands for express commitment to *all* or to perceived essential elements of the public culture, then the nonhomogeneity component of a public culture is under threat. The demand that Muslims publicly proclaim their commitment to European norms following terrorist actions allegedly carried out in their name provides an example. The desire to impose fixed cultural standards was in evidence in the Netherlands after the murder of film director Theo van Gogh by a Muslim fundamentalist. Many (non-Muslim) Dutch citizens felt it essential that "all Muslim immigrants take a stand with regard to their appreciation of liberal-democratic citizenship."[1] As I described in the introduction, in order to guard against the influx of further nondemocratic illiberal immigrants, immigration services in the Netherlands developed a deeply controversial citizenship education video, intended to convey Dutch norms to newcomers, that depicts gay men kissing and a topless woman emerging from the sea onto a beach. Potential immigrants to the Netherlands are required to purchase the video and to show knowledge of the content in their citizenship test. The video was intended, in the words of one report, to be a "test of their readiness to participate in the liberal Dutch culture. If they can't stomach it, no need to apply."[2] This case, and others like it, illustrates a concern to establish a consensus regarding the content of the public culture, a consensus that will ultimately be impossible to achieve. The healthy nonhomogeneous overlap and crisscross of norms and values that will, as a matter of course, characterize a public culture is at risk in the kinds of situations described above, in which attempts are made to determine what is *required* of all citizens by way of norms and values.

Publicity Under Pressure

At their best, the environments in which the public culture is shaped are truly *public*. These include the political arena, the media, and so on. The history of Western democratic governments is replete with attempts to restrict entry to these kinds of environments, for all kinds of reasons. For example, immigrants to the United States in the early twentieth century were victims of a range of discriminatory government policies, and various institutional barriers prevented them from entering the public arena on fair terms. Italians were subject to ongoing surveillance during World War II (they were suspected of disloyalty until Italy surrendered), and again afterward when they were accused of sourcing organized crime in the United States. Jews and other immigrant groups were excluded from Ivy League universities and professional schools for a time. Japanese Americans were interned during World War II, and immigrants from Asian countries in general were prevented from entering in the first place or admitted in very small numbers and subject to tremendous discrimination upon arrival.[3] In general members of a public culture under threat may attempt—both formally and informally—to shield the environments in which a public culture is shaped from the input and suggestions put forward by newcomers: they will engage in a kind of cultural preservation that attempts to secure the public culture against change.[4]

For example, a recent public debate in Ontario concluded with the closing of debate that revealed a hostility to change. In 2005 it came to public attention that Muslims were deploying the provincial Arbitration Act to give authority to imams to resolve Muslim family disputes. Although intended to speed up minor contractual disputes that had been clogging the provincial courts, the Arbitration Act had also allowed religious groups to choose a figure to resolve a certain set of disputes (mainly familial), in which the resolution was viewed as legally binding. The public knowledge that Muslims were using the act in this way opened a debate with respect to whether Ontarians were comfortable with permitting religious groups to resolve their own familial disputes in general.[5] Yet before public debate was permitted to proceed, the premier of Ontario declared peremptorily that there would be no Sharia law in Ontario, thus closing debate before it began in earnest concerning whether religious groups should be permitted to resolve their family disputes internally. The premier's response illustrated his worry that the norms and values that define Ontario were threatened, and his conviction that the proper course of action was to close debate about norms and values rather than open it for free and open negotiation in a way that might have served to build trust among diverse citizens.[6] Instead, his response signaled a public culture closed to the voices of Muslim citizens.

Fluidity Under Pressure

Public cultures change organically over time in response to external and internal pressures. What matters is that there is continuity among some of the core values and norms that define a public culture over time and at any given time, not that change is prevented from transpiring. Thus, to say that the fluidity of a public culture is under pressure as a result of ethnocultural diversity is to observe a heightened sense of vulnerability, and therefore a decrease in trust among members of the host community in response to pressures to alter their norms and values. To be sure, the underlying political position—that political communities are entitled to control some elements of the immigration process so as to secure the continuity of the public culture—is frequently deployed to argue for limiting (too greatly) rates of immigration. But its central intuition—that increases in the proportion of ethnocultural diversity as a result of increased immigration can sometimes appear to members as though they are too much to absorb at once—seems plausible at least.[7] The changes associated with incorporating large numbers of migrants will not in this case appear organic and natural, as they would do if they transpired slowly over time; rather, they appear unnatural and are felt as taking place under unwanted pressure. This is the worry of Dutch citizens with respect to the putative impact of increased Muslim migration on Dutch cultural identity. They worry that "their culture is being threatened," and this manifests itself as a worry that "people are no longer willing to conform to established rules and standards."[8]

Trust, Cooperation, and the Public Culture

Each of these three features of the public culture—its fluidity, its nonhomogeneity, and its commitment to publicity—plays an essential role in its capacity to work as a trust builder (or sustainer); in particular, the capacity of a public culture to reduce vulnerability hinges on these three features. When the three defining features of a public culture are at risk, so too is its capacity to act as a source of trust.

This is not the whole story. In order for a public culture to sustain trust relations over time, it must additionally be characterized by a willingness to cooperate and to abide by the rules produced by the institutions that facilitate cooperation on a large scale. Let me now make the connection among these central features clearer: a public culture's fluidity, nonhomogeneity, and commitment to publicity together illustrate a commitment to cooperation or to facilitate cooperation. An acceptance of the natural fluidity of the public culture's content enables cooperation among newcomers and members of the receiving society by indicating a willingness to allow negotiations over changes in that content. An acceptance of nonhomogeneity equally facilitates cooperation by recognizing that the process of becoming a citizen is a long-term project, such that adopting a commitment to the shared norms and principles of a society takes time and effort by newcomers (and the provision of resources by the receiving society). A commitment to publicity suggests a willingness to cooperate with newcomers to define and redefine the content of a public culture. Taken together, these features are essential to the public culture's capacity to generate trust among citizens because they serve to underpin the larger cooperative project that defines democracies in general.

Although these defining features work together to generate the capacity of a public culture to serve as a trust builder, it will prove helpful to recall the additional two features that occupy a special role in securing a public culture's capacity to act as a source of trust: a willingness to cooperate and to submit to shared institutions that facilitate this cooperation. Although these two features *reinforce* each other when they interact, there is no *necessary* connection between them: this is in part what makes trust building a messy and imperfect business.

However, that these features are mutually reinforcing suggests that as trust builders we have at minimum two strategies that we can employ to build trust: we can focus on the shared norms and values that frequently underpin trusting relationships, since these relationships serve to sustain the cooperation that is essential to democratic politics, or we can encourage cooperation in the hope that shared norms and values will *emerge* from this cooperation over time, and so reinforce cooperation and over time produce trust. In actual cases, it will often prove difficult to separate these strategies, since many aim to do both at the same time. Yet analytically, it will serve us to consider them separately. In order for these two strategies to make sense, it is essential that cooperation is able to proceed without trust relations in the first place, and it is to this issue that I now turn.

Cooperation Without Trust

When a group of people works together to achieve a goal, where completing this task requires the effort of all or most members of the group, they are cooperating. All around us, cooperation transpires on a regular basis—construction workers build a house, lawyers build a case, children construct snow forts, friends cook a meal, and so on. These are examples of cooperation among people on a relatively small scale. Cooperation can also transpire on relatively large scales, and so we describe the collective willingness of members of a political community to contribute to public goods in terms of cooperation. The availability of public goods—environmental cleanliness, national defense, legal stability, and so on—depends on the willingness of all (or most) individuals in a political community to do their part to produce the good in question. The public good is provided only when most people choose against free riding and rely on the willing compliance of others; few political communities can afford the resources essential to enforce compliance in the production of many (or most) public goods.

One might interpret such examples of cooperation in terms of trust—certainly, trust frequently underpins cooperative activities of the kind that I have described—but trust is not essential to achieve these cooperative tasks. In all of these examples (with the likely exception of friends cooperating to prepare a meal), those who are cooperating could be doing so for self-interested reasons alone, and they could impute others' willingness to cooperate to self-interested reasons as well. If this were the case, we would say that participants' willingness to cooperate is based on an assessment of others' self-interested reasons to do so.[9] On reflection, it seems that there are many situations in which people cooperate for mutual benefit, or in which they believe that others have strong incentives to refrain from defecting, in which trust is manifestly not present: as long as people "share the knowledge that they can individually benefit from following the same pattern of behavior, cooperation can in principle be sustained" even when they don't trust each other, or "value the pattern of behavior to the same degree or in the same way."[10] Two distrustful political adversaries can team up to prevent the victory of a third equally distrusted adversary, for example. The Kurds and Sunni Arabs in Iraq are by no means trusted allies, but they had shown some willingness to work together to delay the (first) Iraqi elections and to include minority protections in the eventual Iraqi constitution. The *New York Times* further speculated that the Kurds and Shiites are equally "united on some issues, including their intense distrust of Sunni Arabs, a minority group that ruled the country for decades . . . they are likely to work together to revamp the security forces" that until now have been run by Sunni Arabs.[11] In spite of this example, and others like it, trust is frequently a key component of cooperative activities.

As I noted earlier, the decision to trust is in part based in past experience— citizens decide whether to trust at least in part by assessing the reliability of others in the past.[12] In some cases, negative feelings emerge from a perception of value or norm incompatibility of the kind described over the course of this book, which can translate into conflicts over a range of political and social issues. In others, geographical segregation is so high that opportunities for trust across ethnocultural lines are low;[13] people who have never experienced the untrustworthiness of others believe that those others are unreliable via reports from others.[14] In distrusting environments, citizens decide repeatedly against trusting in response to evidence, either personally collected or via word of mouth, that they believe demonstrates the untrustworthiness of others.[15] In order to build trust, we will need to focus on creating opportunities for positive, cooperative interactions—note that the claim is not that we want to create trust as much as it is that we want to create space in which trust can grow. Providing sufficient evidence that others can be trusted, in the face of what is perceived to be substantial evidence that others are not deserving of trust, is made more difficult, however, by its evidence resistance: recall that trust and distrust are both evidence resistant, and decisions to trust (or not) are frequently made in the face of clear evidence that we ought to make a different decision.[16] In the cases that are discussed here, distrust's evidence resistance is a significant obstacle to building trust in its place: when trust has been repeatedly violated (or when it remains untested because trust violations appear to be the only result of extending trust), people will be unwilling to place themselves in the positions of vulnerability that trusting necessarily demands.

In order for cooperation to erase the effect of past negative experiences it must extend over time. The importance of securing ongoing cooperation should be clear enough; since distrust is persistently resistant to evidence, the need is for cooperation that extends over a considerable period of time. If we are hoping for generalized trust to emerge, we will first need a firm basis of successful cooperation in one situation. The need is for a sufficient (if such a thing exists) number of successful cooperative ventures to erase, or at least ease, the painful memories (or reports) of past trust violations. As a result, we have good reason to create situations that allow for repeated interactions among distrusting individuals, and, ideally, interactions designed to accomplish the same task over and over again. Trust can pertain solely to one task or one set of tasks—it is possible to trust A with task B and only with task B. At first this may not appear to meet the goal of generalizing trust, but there is a certain logic to this strategy. If we are in conditions of distrust, and we are hoping to build trust, we are wise to start small with one task alone. If I can learn to trust someone with one task, it may then prove easier to develop trust in her with regard to some other task. We have good reason to hope that by starting small with one repeated cooperative interaction, we can initiate a process that will slowly and over time lead to a more generalized trust between previously distrusting individuals. The hope that repeated positive trusting interactions at the small scale can over time translate into larger scale trust is, for example, the motivating principle underpinning integrated schools in Northern Ireland. If Catholic and Protestant schoolchildren learn to work together in a safe and nurturing educational environment, they may be able to carry the trust relationships they have developed with them into the larger political and social environment.[17] The mechanisms by which this translation transpires are complicated, but they include at a minimum the development of cross-community friendships that persist outside of the educational environment; the willingness to live and interact in integrated rather than segregated neighborhoods; the public displaying of a willingness to trust and reciprocate trust across community barriers, which serve by example to encourage others to do the same; and so on.

Mitigating Vulnerability

I described trust as part attitude and part behavior, where the behavior demanded a willingness to put oneself in a position of vulnerability to another's expected good will (or lack of ill will). In trusting others, we accept a kind of vulnerability, even if we don't recognize that we are doing so; when it functions smoothly, trust obscures the vulnerability that defines it, since trusters do not find themselves actively considering the vulnerability that their behaviors entail. That trusting is defined by a position of vulnerability, however, emerges especially when trust is betrayed—once our trust is betrayed or disappointed, we realize in retrospect the vulnerability connected to our having extended trust. In personal relationships it is sometimes difficult to be specific with respect to what enables or encourages our trust in others: we trust our friends, our relatives, our neighbors, our colleagues, and so on after having observed them and engaged with them in a variety of environments and situations in which trust is extended and rewarded repeatedly. These personal experiences provide the epistemic conditions under which trust flourishes over time.

It is the existence of a public culture that provides the social and political conditions under which trust can flourish across communities between people who have not necessarily met and interacted personally. So long as the public culture is believed to be shared, trust among members of communities can proceed without attention being drawn to the vulnerability connected with doing so. However, when citizens become concerned that the public culture is no longer shared, their attention is drawn to the vulnerability inherent in trust, and the likelihood that they extend trust as a matter of course declines. The connection between trust and perceived vulnerability tells us to focus on developing cooperative environments that reduce the *vulnerability* connected to extending and rewarding trust.

The objective is to create cooperative engagements that engender a transformation from distrust, or simply weakened trust relations, to robust and widespread trust. Under conditions of widespread trust we will cooperate not only when it is in our *immediate* best interest, but also when it is in our long-term best interest, or because we prefer to be people who cooperate with others, or more generally because ours is a community defined by cooperation.

Before trust emerges, however, we need to rely on other mechanisms to encourage cooperation. Distrusters perceive cooperation to be a risky and uncertain activity: the unwillingness to cooperate emerges because the costs associated with failed cooperation are believed to be high. It may seem paradoxical that the *key* feature of trust is the vulnerability that is inherent to extending and receiving it, and that in order to develop cooperative engagements from which trust can emerge we will need to focus on minimizing the vulnerability associated with the cooperative task at issue. However, our goal will be to minimize the vulnerability connected to cooperation, not to erase it entirely: since vulnerability is at the core of trust, if we erase it entirely there will be no opportunity to build trust.

There is plenty of evidence to indicate that most people, in the best of times, are what can be described as "conditional" cooperators. If the conditions are right, people will cooperate; we have good reasons to think that these conditions are especially stringent when deep distrust characterizes the relations between potential cooperators.[18] There are at least three general ways in which we can ease the sense of vulnerability associated with cooperating with distrusted others, so that we can create the conditions under which cooperation might reasonably transpire without trust: we can implement monitoring mechanisms, we can introduce sanctions that reward cooperative behavior and punish uncooperative behavior, and we can include distrusting cooperators in generating the conditions under which cooperation will take place. Careful readers will have observed that these are the roles played by a public culture that enable it to be a source of trust; it is no mistake that the objective is to mimic the various roles played by a public culture that enable it to produce trust.

Monitoring

One way to encourage cooperation is to ensure that some form of *monitoring* exists. For one thing, it is well known from experimental economics that the mere knowledge that one is being monitored can have a direct and positive influence on cooperative behavior. Additionally, formal monitoring mechanisms can reassure cooperators that in addition to their own behaviors, the behaviors of others are being monitored. Monitors are a regular part of democratic life; for example, traffic officers monitor our observance of traffic laws, subway staff monitor our payment of fares, and elections are formally monitored by outside parties. The existence of monitors thus ensures that whether we cooperate will be made *public*. There are, obviously, more or less explicit methods to monitor others' behaviors—in some cases, it is sufficient to allow citizens to monitor each other, and in others there is a need for a more formal (and impartial) monitoring mechanism.[19] In relatively small-scale trust-building environments, monitoring is often provided in the form of a figure called the "mediator" or "facilitator" or "moderator," who is responsible for making sure that the information that participants need to cooperate without being taken advantage of is made available. In larger scale political environments, this monitoring role is facilitated by transparency mechanisms; they may, for example, permit citizens to access information about political decisions, information that can be used to "hold institutions, experts and officials to account."[20] As Onora O'Neill explains, "the expectation that one's (non-) performance will be subject to scrutiny can be expected to have a galvanising effect, and to reduce tendencies and temptations to deceive."[21]

Monitoring mechanisms thus play a crucial role with respect to gathering information, and they therefore facilitate the evaluation of the trustworthiness of others. If these mechanisms are reliable, those who worry that others will defect can be reassured that they will be informed if others fail to hold up their end of the bargain. In this way all cooperators will know, rather than suspect (and so perhaps wrongly retract their own cooperative behaviors), that others are or are not cooperating, and adjust their behaviors accordingly. In this way they not only avoid being suckers, but they also avoid worrying about whether they are being suckered.[22]

Sanctions

Both positive and negative sanctions serve to mitigate the vulnerability associated with cooperating with those whom we distrust. Potential cooperators must know that their cooperative moves will be praised and that their failure or unwillingness to cooperate will be punished. Sanctions, imposed by citizens on one another or by a more formal and impartial mechanism, play a role similar to that of monitoring mechanisms. Whereas monitoring mechanisms offer potential cooperators the knowledge they need to assess whether they are being taken advantage of, sanctioning mechanisms offer potential cooperators the knowledge that there are burdens and benefits associated with defecting and cooperating (in addition to whatever benefit is meant to emerge from the cooperative endeavor in question). Sanctions punish and reward defectors and cooperators, respectively, and in so doing, they ensure that cooperation is likely to continue, by controlling the nature of the rewards and punishments associated with cooperating or otherwise.

In particular, distrusters are likely to be motivated to cooperate when the payoffs for successful cooperation are large. Note the analogy here to the voluntary compliance with large-scale public goods in trusting communities. In both cases, the payoffs are high and the cost of choosing against participation is low; the difference is that the attention being paid to whether one participates is high in the low trust community and low in the high trust community. In distrusting environments, the benefits ought to be genuinely appealing to potential cooperators to avoid their thinking the risk isn't worth it. In addition to creating a cooperative enterprise in which cooperation gives rise to clear and desirable benefits, there are good reasons to construct these interactions in such a way that the costs of failed cooperation are not equivalently great; rather, the costs of failed cooperation ought to be relatively small. In constructing cooperative interactions in this way, we acknowledge both the distrusters' self-interest and the depth of their dis-

trust. We structure the cooperation in such a way that, first, whatever benefits are associated with cooperating appear to be worth the risk and, second,
in such a way that the costs of failed cooperation do not have (much) impact
on the distrusters' risk assessment. Both conditions are intended to allow the
possibility of trying again if the cooperation fails in the first instance. The
costs of failing to accomplish any one of the cooperative tasks are low; the
benefits of cooperating over a range of tasks are high.

The punishments for those who renege on their promises to cooperate
need not be extensive. As Elinor Ostrom suggests, "the initial sanction needs
to be considered more as information both to the person who is 'caught' and
to others in the community."[23] The information being provided is such that
it prevents people from cooperating with others who may well fail to carry
out their end of the bargain. The danger, however, is that the failure of one
party to cooperate will generate a kind of downward spiral: not only does
failure to cooperate make it less likely that further attempts at cooperation
will be made, but it is also clear enough that unreciprocated cooperation
serves to reduce rather than build trust relations.[24] The point of ensuring that
any initial punishment for reneging on cooperation is minor is to encourage
cooperators to try again. In the ideal, those who cooperated in the first place
will be willing to continue to cooperate, at least for a time, as a way to signal
that their commitment to the larger project has not waned (significantly) in
the face of a lone defector.

Participatory Rule Generation

Third and finally, potential cooperators must *either* have some say in the
rules associated with cooperation or, at the very least, the opportunity to
change the rules once they are in place. In some environments this may include the choice of monitoring mechanism in the first place. In distrustful
environments potential cooperators will clearly need to be strongly encouraged to cooperate—either by the offer of substantial rewards or by the threat of
punishments. But having agreed to cooperate, they will need to feel that they
have some way to participate in how this cooperation takes place. They will
need to feel that they are participating in institutions or policies of their own
creation, at least to some extent—that they are, in effect, governing themselves. This strategy was deployed in the housing reconstruction program in
the former Yugoslavia that I described in the introduction to this chapter.
Villagers were told that the reconstruction of homes destroyed by the war

would be funded so long as the construction team was made up of both Serbs and Croats and the list of homes requiring reconstruction was agreed to by a committee made of members from both communities.[25]

It is widely known that cooperation between rivals is virtually impossible to achieve without their willing participation; they need to feel that the institutions that regulate their cooperation are internally and willingly imposed, that is, that they are (by and large) subject to self-imposed restrictions on their behaviors.[26] (This suggestion is not unlike the Rawlsian insight that political stability is best achieved when citizens have internalized the principles of justice and so accept them as their own principles for action.) When distrusters participate in cooperative engagements where they are in large part responsible for the rules of cooperation, "more individuals are willing to abide by these rules because they are participants in their design."[27]

Trust-building mechanisms aim to build generalized trust in two senses: trust should generalize to beyond those who have participated in the trust-building exercise, and it should generalize to activities that are other than the trust-building exercise. In building trust, we can rely on cooperation: cooperation itself doesn't necessarily rely on trust, but successful cooperation can serve to facilitate the emergence of trust. In order to persuade distrusters to cooperate, we need to remove a key element of trust, that is, the vulnerability associated with it. As trust builders, we therefore need to concern ourselves with creating the conditions under which vulnerability, or risk, is perceived to be low. We can do so in three ways: by creating effective monitoring mechanisms, by creating both positive inducements to cooperate and negative inducements to defect from cooperating, and by including the participants themselves in the process of rule creation. In the ideal, all three of these principles will be adopted in projects that aim to build trust; in practice, each will individually contribute to building conditions under which trust can emerge. The deeper the distrust, the more important a commitment to all three of these principles will be to building trust. The objective is to mimic the role played by the public culture in producing widespread trust; in creating mechanisms by which vulnerability is reduced, trust may slowly emerge.

Deliberation, Cooperation, and Trust

In the literature concerned with the declining levels of trust among democratic citizens in Western liberal countries, many of which are characterized by high levels of ethnocultural diversity, deliberation is frequently proposed as a remedy.[28] Deliberative accounts of democracy suggest, both implicitly and explicitly, that deliberation will serve to ease the often deep value differences that impede the proper functioning of democracy, or, at least, that it will serve to generate a spirit of compromise that will lead to agreement on practicable solutions in environments where moral agreement is difficult or unlikely to be found: "deliberative democracy has recently come to the fore as one of the most promising ways to address protracted cultural conflict."[29] For example, ongoing attempts in Canada to resolve constitutional disagreements are often described as deliberative attempts to build trust among Canadians.[30] Although deliberative democrats disagree along many dimensions—they disagree with respect to the proper scope of deliberation, the proper objectives of deliberation, and the sorts of reasons that can legitimately be deployed in the deliberative arena[31]—they generally do agree that the commitment to deliberate in the first place is a "manifestation of an agreement among the parties to work through their problems together through dialogue."[32] The adoption of dialogue as a mechanism by which to build trust between minorities and majorities is increasingly frequent.[33]

Trust Facilitates Deliberation

There is a two-way relation between deliberation and trust: first, trust "complements and supports deliberative resolutions of political conflict," and second, "deliberative approaches to political conflict can generate trust, both among individuals and between individuals and institutions."[34] On the one hand, that trust facilitates deliberation seems clear enough. Deliberation's objective is to develop agreed resolutions to tension-filled conflicts, and so it seems eminently plausible to suggest that trust facilitates deliberation. Deliberation is, after all, a technique employed specifically when disagreement arises or when there exists uncertainty over what policies to pursue; it is a technique employed to resolve disagreement in such a way that widespread agreement with respect to policy, and sometimes even with respect to principles and values, can emerge. Trust is deeply implicated in deliberation, in particular in securing a commitment to the sincerity that is central to its effective functioning as a trust builder. Under conditions of trust we anticipate the sincerity of others as a matter of course. We take it on trust that what others say roughly corresponds to what they believe and intend for us to believe: a "disposition of sincerity" is concerned with "sustaining and developing relations with others that involve different kinds and degrees of trust.[35] If I trust you, even if we are presently on opposite sides of a heated and tension-filled debate, I am more likely to believe you are abiding by the (ideally, agreed in advance) conditions. It is, after all, difficult to *prove* that one's view is sincere; trust will make it so that the burden of proof is lower.[36] On the other hand, in the absence of trust, deliberation will prove challenging: "straightforward engagement in deliberation is not a feasible alternative because one or both sides lack sufficient trust to accept the vulnerability that good faith deliberation entails."[37]

Not only does the motivation to speak sincerely over the course of deliberations rest on trust relations, so too does citizens' willingness to moderate views in order to compromise with others. My willingness to moderate my views in this instance depends on my view that you, too, will at some point in the future be willing to do the same. I must *trust* that my compromise here will encourage your compromise in some unspecified future disagreement. Trust is what prevents my thinking that my willingness to reciprocate is mere gullibility, that is, that you are not merely free riding on my credulity without the full intention of reciprocating, in some future instance, my present sacrifice. Since trust facilitates the willingness to reciprocate and a commitment to sincerity—and since both of these features are essential to deliberation—deliberation itself will be more likely to succeed under conditions of trust.[38]

Deliberation Builds Trust

Although it is relatively clear that trust enables deliberation, it may be less clear that deliberation can be a source of trust. Advocates of deliberative democracy frequently point to its transformative effects: at the very least, deliberation can generate agreement, and at the most, it can transform hostile political environments into friendly ones. This transformation requires, on the one hand, that each "participant [is willing] to give up important human defenses that define her or his own identity as it contrasts to the identity of the 'other' and, on the other, that they give up ideas of the 'others' as an unconditional enemy: deliberators must recognize that others have legitimate interests," which they may have previously "flatly dismissed . . . as unworthy of respect."[39] In its ideal, deliberation is able to "transform contested terrain into social ground which individuals can take for granted and which they are likely to experience as relatively predictable and secure."[40] Skeptics might ask, however, whether these transformative effects of deliberation can be achieved in multicultural or severely divided societies.

We saw that building trust proceeds via effectively structured cooperation among hostile parties. In order for deliberation to serve as a trust builder, we will need to transform deliberation into a form of cooperation. Is this a plausible transformation? There are at least three reasons to think so. First, cooperation is generally characterized by *willingness* among cooperators to work jointly to fulfill some task, in general, some task that is difficult or impossible to fulfill by any one person. Deliberation likewise will ideally be characterized by a set of deliberators who are willing to work jointly to fulfill a task, namely, to resolve a conflict. Second, in agreeing to cooperate, cooperators are more or less explicitly thought to be giving up overt competition: cooperation is only effective when cooperators agree that competition is a less successful method to achieve a set of objectives than is cooperation.[41] In order for deliberation to be effective, the same must be true: deliberators must agree that a compromise in which concessions are made is a better outcome than an ongoing competitive and hostile environment. We might, alternatively, think of deliberation as providing an environment in which competition is now worked out via dialogue. Third, cooperators tend to have an agreed objective of some kind, an objective they pursue under (previously) agreed rules or methods; likewise, deliberation ought to have an agreed objective, along with a set of rules or methods by which it is agreed this objective—conflict resolution—will be sought. In other words, in agreeing on the rules in advance, deliberators generate a kind of second-order trust in the process itself, even if not in the other deliberators per se.

In order for deliberation to be an effective form of cooperation, we must implement the three elements that are essential to minimizing the vulnerability that makes effective cooperation—in this case, effective deliberation—possible in the first place. We need to secure an effective monitoring system, we need to implement a set of effective sanctions (both positive and negative), and we need to provide room for deliberators to set some of their own, collectively agreed, rules. If these conditions are secured, deliberation is indeed genuinely cooperation; in particular, it is cooperation of the kind that might plausibly facilitate the emergence of (the background conditions that might produce) trust relations in both multicultural and severely divided societies.

First, we need an effective way to monitor or moderate deliberation. Remember that the cooperation—in this case, the deliberation—must be, in an important sense, public. Participants must engage with others (or perhaps via a moderator) in such a way that they are largely aware of the negotiating stances, and changes, made by those with whom they are deliberating.[42] In situations of tension and hostility, the chance that a member of a deliberating group is concerned about being taken advantage of is high. A study cited earlier in this chapter presents evidence that trust violations that are accompanied by deception are impossible to repair fully. We should take heed of this observation here. One way to mitigate the concern that deliberators may be actively deceived is to make sure that the content of the participants' positions, and the content of their subsequent suggested compromises, are made public. The publicity condition allays worries that some participants are free riding on the compromises of others. Transparency, in other words, allays suspicion of deception.

A moderator in such a deliberative forum will be able to secure the publicity condition. As a result, a well-trained moderator may make compromise among hostile groups a genuine possibility: although moderators "have no authority to impose a settlement," they can "play a fundamental role in the generation of the conditions required for a successful dispute resolution process."[43] In order for a moderator to play this role, she must be trusted to be fair. Extensive research into the ways in which the moderator can influence the outcome of deliberations suggests that those who are believed to be partisans of one side of the dispute have a more difficult time being perceived as impartial between the partisans, even when they adjudicate the dispute in an even-handed way.[44]

A moderator has at least four obvious roles to play in facilitating deliberation. First, she must monitor the content and format of the discussion: a moderator "advocates and defends a particular type of process," without advocating a particular position or pressing deliberators toward a particular resolution.[45] Certain kinds of speech, including hate speech and incitements to violence, will make compromise unlikely if not impossible—"incitement to use [violence] will impair the democratic procedure"[46]—and a moderator's job is in part to curb this kind of speech. Second, a moderator may be called on to provide information about the facts of the matter (if there are any) about which deliberators may disagree. Although the product of moderated deliberation is "a mutually agreeable solution [agreed] under the aegis of a third party," the moderator is not tasked with supporting one side or the other. She may, however, "provide a conduit for initial communication among the actors, [and] disseminate pertinent information to all sides."[47] Third, a moderator must be concerned with exclusion: "it is unacceptable in a liberal democracy to call for the exclusion of citizens from the body politic," and the same is true of the deliberative arena.[48] There is plenty of research (that I'll not go into here) elaborating the dynamics of deliberative groups that indicates that—if unmoderated—some participants will contribute more than others and that others will feel intimidated in a deliberative forum and choose against contributing unless pressed to do so.[49] Finally, a moderator is charged with ensuring that the rules previously agreed upon—a condition for effective deliberation that I describe below—are secured.

Second, we need a mechanism by which to sanction members, and this too is a role that may usefully be played by a moderator. Sanctions are used in order to create an environment in which participants are praised for cooperation and blamed for their efforts at stalling of otherwise hindering the process of deliberation, and in which the benefits associated with cooperation are high, even when the costs of failed deliberation are low. Sanctioning is best provided by a third party rather than by the members themselves, and the moderator is perhaps the best person for the job. The third strategy by which deliberation can act as a form of trust-building cooperation suggests engaging deliberators in the process of rule formation; once these rules are established, members can be held accountable (by each other) for upholding them.[50]

Third, regulative norms are most likely to arise when "members identify with the deliberative forum as a special sort of body,"[51] and this condition is best met by involving deliberators in the process by which the rules of deliberation are established. One benefit of deliberation is its "morally provisional" nature; it allows for the open discussion of all kinds of ideas and principles and policies that have in the past been taken for granted.[52] To a considerable extent this is a benefit in conflict situations in particular, since participants are coming to the deliberative forum with the specific intention of altering an existing but unsatisfactory arrangement. But we need also to consider one merit of deliberation, namely, that in including as decision makers many among those who are affected by its outcomes, the legitimacy of the outcome is enhanced.[53] By extension, we can see that not only will deliberators value being participants in the decision-making process, but that they will also value taking a role in creating the rules by which these decisions are made.

Of course, deliberation is not a panacea for broken or battered trust relations, nor is any other trust-building strategy we might devise. Yet, in its ideal, the process of deliberating can generate the background conditions that give rise to trust: over time, deliberation can produce a set of "authoritative background commitments and beliefs that both sustain and contain democratic challenges."[54] Put differently, deliberation can produce a shared sense that the features of a public culture—norms, values, and so on—are held in common, and can therefore serve as a basis for trust relations. More generally, the examination of deliberation through the lens of trust illustrated, I hope, that cooperative activities can—under the right conditions—serve to build trust. They will do so by mimicking the role, as best as possible, that the public culture plays in producing trust.

Multicultural Policies and Building Trust

Especially in multicultural communities, most policies that aim to build trust will not be as comprehensively focused on trust building as are deliberation or dialogue. The purpose of highlighting dialogue specifically is to illustrate the multiple ways in which policies can aid in trust building, especially when trust building isn't their sole objective. In chapter 5 I described the large range of policies that are termed "multicultural." They ranged from policies that permit modifying uniforms to accommodate religious practices (to permit the wearing of headscarves or the *salwar kameez*), to those that require that public schools provide kosher and halal food at lunchtime, to those that allow employees to take short breaks during the workday to pray, to those that support ethnically based community centers that provide political information and legal support, to the efforts made to quickly recognize foreign professional credentials, to permitting and supporting faith-based (or race-based) schools, and so on. For the defenders of multiculturalism, the purpose of adopting these policies is to facilitate the full inclusion of minorities whose cultural and religious practices may otherwise make their full inclusion into the social and political community unnecessarily difficult. The successful adoption of integrative multicultural policies thus serves to reduce the vulnerability of minorities by easing their integration into the trust-building public culture that defines the political community in which they are members.

In light of recent proclamations of the death of multiculturalism, asking whether multicultural policies serve to reduce or heighten vulnerability for both minorities and nonminorities is important. These proclamations, which have grown in strength over the past decade, have in part motivated the debates that frame the observations in this book. The critics of multiculturalism argue that, contrary to what may have been intended, multicultural policies in fact facilitate the isolation of minority groups, who are legally permitted and sometimes encouraged to live parallel lives. To declare that multiculturalism has failed is thus to declare that contrary to its alleged integrative purpose, it has produced isolation, exclusion, and alienation among minority groups, who remain external to the public culture that defines a political community.[55] In part, the declaration has emerged in response to perceptions that certain cultural practices are objectionable; these practices are alleged to be incompatible with liberal democratic norms, and therefore are believed to signal an absence of integration and an absence of a desire to integrate. The desire to sustain some of these practices is taken to signal an absence of trustworthiness on the part of minorities, an absence of trustworthiness that stems from the apparent failure of immigrants and minorities to adopt the shared values and norms that characterize a public culture. And, say their critics, multicultural policies are often intended to allow cultural practices to persist over time; since these practices signal an inability or an unwillingness to adapt to a public culture, and since a public culture is the primary source of trust in a democratic political community, multicultural policies that enable the continuation of these practices serve to erode rather than build trust.

In most cases this chain of reasoning is flawed, however. As I suggested in chapter 5, the desire to retain minority cultural or religious practices is infrequently a signal of a desire to remain distinct and therefore to refuse to adapt to, or integrate into, the public culture that defines a political community. The demands for the adoption of multicultural policies by minority groups are nearly always justified by the contribution they will make to facilitating the integration that their members desire and seek.[56]

Let me conclude this chapter by making some observations about the conditions under which we can describe a multicultural policy as trust building, and how we should think of these policies as related to trust. In general terms multicultural policies can serve to build trust when they aim to respond to, and in particular reduce, the vulnerability felt by minorities as they participate in the social and political environment. Consider some examples. Multicultural policies often permit minorities to maintain practices—to cover their heads in public, to maintain a particular prayer schedule, to display symbols of their religious or cultural commitment, to retain dietary commitments—the abandonment of which is felt as so strongly disorienting that forcing them to do so will increase their sense of vulnerability in relation to members of the majority community. They often permit culturally specific organizations to provide political and legal information to their members that will enable minorities to participate actively in the larger political life of the community in which they reside. They frequently focus on language education to ensure that minorities possess the language skills necessary to participate in, and thereby reduce the likelihood of their exclusion from, political decision making. In pursuing all of these policies, the barriers for minorities to extend trust to members of the majority are lowered.

Taken together, these policies reduce and mitigate the frequent intolerance toward distinctive cultural practices to which minorities are subject upon arrival, an intolerance that often translates into discrimination against minorities and thereby prevents easy integration. Multicultural policies, especially those that self-consciously aim to integrate minorities, therefore target the specific vulnerabilities that minorities experience in relation to a sometimes hostile and sometimes intolerant host community, and thus enable them to integrate into the public culture and therefore to display the signals typically associated with trustworthiness.

Conclusion

The challenge of building trust in multicultural and severely divided societies is difficult to meet, and this chapter has sought to take some important steps toward spelling out the general principles according to which it can be done. The public culture that ideally prevails in democratic societies typically underpins the trust that supports large-scale cooperative activities in a political community; these trust-building principles intend to *mimic* the role played by the public culture, until such time as a public culture can emerge in a previously distrusting, or mistrusting, community. The key, I suggested, is to focus on cooperation. Although cooperation proceeds best under conditions of trust, it can proceed absent trust so long as the right conditions are in place. These conditions are threefold: cooperative activities must be *monitored;* cooperative and anticooperative behaviors must be *rewarded or punished,* respectively; and cooperators must have the opportunity to *participate* in the generation of the rules that govern the cooperation in question. The

focus on deliberation suggested how, by implementing these three principles, it can serve as a trust builder in a distrusting political environment. All
of these efforts are directed toward reducing the vulnerability that is inherently connected to trusting others; if this vulnerability isn't effectively mini-
mized, distrusting adversaries will not be able to begin the baby steps essential
to cooperation and, in time, the development of trust.

CONCLUSION:
THE CHALLENGES OF MULTICULTURALISM?

This book began with an account of cultural and ethnic tensions in which, I alleged, the central issue was the trust relations, or the absence thereof, among citizens. I pointed to the debates in Europe about whether to implement citizenship tests for newcomers to establish that they had adopted, or were at least aware of, the norms that are said to define the receiving community's public culture. I pointed to anti-Hispanic policies in the United States, many of which ostensibly aim to make the life of illegal migrants more difficult, but which have a tremendously negative impact on Hispanic citizens as well. I pointed to requests made my newcomers to have their children exempted from coed gym classes, and sometimes also music classes, on cultural and religious grounds. I pointed to the disdain directed more generally toward the norms and values that immigrants bring along with them that apparently threaten the "way we do things around here."

I argued these tensions can best be understood by looking at them through the lens of trust, and the book has attempted to justify and account for these initial claims. If we focus our attention on the trust relations at stake, we can see that ethnocultural diversity often does stress trust relations among citizens. The reason we should care about this stress is a democratic one: widespread trust is essential to supporting democratic practice. Without trust, democratic practice is stunted at best and impossible at worst. Moreover, it will prove immensely challenging, if not impossible, to sustain support for the kinds of policies that liberal egalitarians value if trust is not first in place among citizens of a democratic community. I argued that the voluntary compliance on which democracy relies is founded on trust relations, trust relations that extend in two directions: between citizens and their political representatives and among citizens themselves. Citizens must engage with one another both as political actors and more generally as active participants in a range of social environments. Democracies function only when citizens are willing to comply with rules and regulations without being actively coerced to do so; democracies typically choose to divert their resources away from enforcement and toward providing the benefits that flourishing democracies are able, and expected, to provide.

The primary source of trust in democratic political communities is an inclusive public culture composed of the shared values and norms that come over time to define it. The concept is controversial, and it is worth revisiting this controversy by way of conclusion. One central worry about emphasizing the importance of a public culture has to do with the extent to which its content is, in fact, a matter of ongoing debate; recognizing that this is the case is essential to avoiding the worst case scenario, that is, a situation in which a majority culture is imposed on a minority who views the norms and values in question as alienating and marginalizing. I argued that we must emphasize that the public culture in question is, after all, *public:* its content is determined by all members of the community, and it is our job to ensure that all members are willing and able to contribute. This is considerably easier said than done— but until this condition is met, we cannot be sure that a public culture is genuinely shared. To say that public culture is shared is not to say that all members of the community ascribe to its content in equal measure. Rather, a public culture is characterized by citizens who hold values and norms in common, but to varying degrees (and some will reject them entirely). A public culture that operates as I have described is protected from its critics, since it proves able to produce the trust among community members that enables democratic practice to function smoothly in a nonhomogenizing and nonexclusive way.

The calls we now witness for the better integration of minorities—many of whom are minorities—and correspondingly the claim that minorities fail to integrate, are fundamentally anxieties about the decline of the force of a shared public culture and therefore about the decline of widespread trust.[1] These calls for better integration are accompanied by proclamations of the death of multiculturalism, which are increasingly widespread. German chancellor Angela Merkel recently declared that attempts to build a truly multicultural community in Germany have "utterly failed," and British prime minister David Cameron joined her in reporting that British attempts at multiculturalism have poorly served its minorities. Multiculturalism in Britain, he said, should be abandoned for its role in encouraging the separation and isolation of minority communities: British society has apparently "tolerated segregated communities behaving in ways that run counter to our values."[2] Multiculturalism has, say its critics, worked to make the integration of minorities into the trust-building public cultures that define democratic communities more difficult. Whereas I fundamentally disagree that multicultural policies are responsible in any simple, causal, way for the declines in trust that often accompany diversity, it seems clear enough that we will be irresponsible if we fail to pay attention to the anxieties that critics of multiculturalism are highlighting. It is important to recognize that a true acknowledgement of ethnocultural diversity and the benefits it so clearly brings can coexist with the recognition that, on the ground, it can and does generate stresses with which we must be concerned. By proclaiming that those who worry about the integrity of a public culture in response to high rates of immigration are silly or discriminatory or racist, we fail to acknowledge the realities of multiculturalism as individuals often feel them.

For these critics of multiculturalism, trust is under threat—or at least is perceived to be under threat—in contemporary multicultural communities as well as in severely divided societies. The second part of the book considered these threats in some detail. The objective of this analysis was manifestly not to argue against an embrace of the diversity that increasingly characterizes Western democratic communities. Rather, my objective has been to offer a sober look at the dangers to trust that increasing ethnocultural diversity does present to democracies, with a view to moving away from the simplistic claims that multiculturalism is either dead or living to an explanation of how we should think about the dilemmas that we face as increasingly diverse communities. We are living in an era of super diversity—where the number of religions, races, ethnicities, and cultures living together and participating in and governed by shared political institutions is on the rise, and where political communities are now composed of citizens who genuinely hail from around the world—and the failure to construct public policy to cope with it is a failure of democracy.[3] If I am right that the source of stress is the perception that the shared values and norms that define a public culture are, after all, no longer relevantly shared, or no longer perceived to be shared—then we must focus on building trust through a revitalized public culture, the revitalization of which should be pursued via the principles I outlined in the final chapter.

The final part of the book has covered a wide range of issues connected to building trust in multicultural democracies. Its main thrust was that trust-building in multicultural democracies and severely divided societies must focus on the reduction of vulnerability connected to extending and reciprocating trust. I took a lead here from the literature devoted to conflict resolution in severely divided societies, a literature that highlights the role that highly controlled cooperation can play in constructing the conditions under which trust can emerge. Distrusters ought to be encouraged to cooperate as a means to build trust among them; yet, as that chapter suggested, cooperation will not *necessarily* yield trust. Rather, the cooperative environment must be organized in such a way that it is able to do so: monitoring, sanctioning, and participant involvement in rule making are essential features of trust-building cooperative ventures. These features all serve to reduce (but not erase) the vulnerability felt in particular by minorities as they attempt to integrate into the larger public culture, and they serve to reduce the belief that the public culture is vulnerable to erosion as a result of the introduction of new norms and values that migrants often bring with them. I spent some time considering the deliberation or dialogue that is increasingly being called for or deployed in multicultural communities as a trust-building mechanism and suggested that properly structured it could source to build trust. I pointed to the multiple strategies by which deliberation can reduce the vulnerability of all those who participate in the conversation. More generally, multicultural policies can serve to alleviate vulnerability even when they do not display all of these features; the best multicultural policies serve in some part to reduce the vulnerability of minorities, who are then better able to integrate into the trust-generating public culture.

As this book has gone through the stages of publication, there have been more examples of the cultural and ethnic tension (in my analysis, distrust) in democratic communities that have motivated this work. Roma citizens across Europe are the subject of ongoing state-sponsored discrimination, highlighted most recently in the form of forced deportations from France. European countries continue to struggle with whether, and in what environments, women should be required to uncover their heads and faces to signal their commitment to the norms of gender equality that are among the formal commitments of democracies. Across democratic states we see struggles with whether to allow familial disputes, over marriage and divorce, for example, and over the education of children, to be regulated by religious or cultural groups rather than state institutions. More and more American states are introducing legislation allegedly directed at limiting the spread of Islamic influence in the United States. As migration across borders continues, and as Western democratic communities continue to encourage it, we will only see more examples of these kinds of conflicts. It is a mistake, I believe, to focus our efforts on chastising those who are threatened by, and so distrust, newcomers; rather, as this book has advocated, we should look at the relations among citizens through the lens of trust. This lens allows us to better see what is needed to secure the commitment to the shared democratic institutions that we desire.

NOTES

Introduction

1. See, respectively, Goodhart, "Too Diverse?"; Sniderman and Hagendoorn, *When Ways of Life Collide*; and Zimmerman, "The English-Only Movement."

2. Montpetit, "Quebec Martial Arts Team."

3. Walker, "Muslim Woman Jailed."

4. Bennhold, "Veil Closes France's Door."

5. See, for example, Cesari and McLoughlin, *European Muslims*; Klausen, *The Islamic Challenge*; Laborde, "Secular Philosophy"; Laborde, *Critical Republicanism*; and Modood, Triandafyllidou, and Zapata-Barrero, *Multiculturalism, Muslims, and Citizenship*.

6. Hamilton, "Welcome!"; "No Stoning" (BBC News).

7. "No Stoning."

8. Franks, "Obscure Object of Concern."

9. Kiwan, "Journey to Citizenship"; Lowenheim and Gazit, "Power and Examination"; and Osler, "Testing Citizenship and Allegiance."

10. Associated Press, "Film Exposes Immigrants."

11. Hundley, "Dutch to Muslims."

12. The power of this example is only somewhat muted by the fact that the offending images were, apparently, almost immediately censored for Muslim viewers. See Joppke, "Immigrants and Civic Integration," 342.

13. Hamilton, "Welcome!"

14. Mackey, "Arizona Law." See also Medrano, "Ethnic Studies Classes Illegal"; and Santa-Cruz, "Arizona Bill." Additional anti-Hispanic laws are in effect or are being considered in Arizona, among them a ban on teachers who speak with a foreign accent. See Jordan, "Arizona Grades Teachers."

15. Navarrette, "Commentary." The worry that the Anglo-Saxon heritage of the United States is threatened as a result of Hispanic immigrants is spelled out in considerable detail in Huntington, *Who Are We?*

16. D'Emilio, "Speak Our Language"; Goodman, "Integration Requirements"; and Goodman, "Controlling Immigration."

17. Although many of the issues that are at stake in this book are a result of immigration that produces new and more diversity, my observations will also touch on the challenges posed by the presence of long-term cultural minorities, some of whom desire separation from the mainstream (e.g., Amish communities) and others who desire integration (e.g., Hispanic Americans).

18. For discussions, see Modood, "Is Multiculturalism Dead?," and Vertovec and Wessendorf, *Assessing the Backlash*.

19. Rawls, *Political Liberalism*, 36.

20. Weinstock, "Problem of Civic Education," 112.

21. Of course, victims of injustice and inequality, who are often in the minority, will feel a strong motivation to fight for justice and equality.

22. As I shall observe, there are important exceptions, including O'Neill, *Question of Trust*; Pettit, "Cunning of Trust"; Warren, "Democratic Theory and Trust"; and M. Williams, *Voice, Trust, and Memory*.

23. Hobbes, *Leviathan*, 202. For two additional accounts of the treatment of trust in the history of political theory, see Hollis, *Trust Within Reason*, and Maloy, "Two Concepts of Trust."

24. Allen, *Talking to Strangers*, 97.

25. Locke, *Second Treatise on Government*, 70.

26. For a contemporary account of Burke's theory of representation, see M. Williams, *Voice, Trust, and Memory*.

27. Uslaner, *Moral Foundations*; and Uslaner and Brown, "Inequality, Trust, and Civic Engagement." See also Labonne, Biller, and Chase, "Inequality and Relative Wealth."

28. Warren, "What Does Corruption Mean?," and Warren, "Political Corruption."

29. Some scholars refer to a "shared public culture." Here, as a matter of definition, a public culture is *shared*. If it is not shared, it is not a public culture.

30. Levy, *Multiculturalism of Fear*, 5–6.

31. Deveaux, *Gender and Justice*; and Phillips, *Multiculturalism Without Culture*.

32. Quoted in Delacourt, "More Ethnic Diversity." See also Putnam, "E Pluribus Unum."

Chapter 1

1. Hardin, "Street-Level Epistemology of Trust," 36.

2. Poole, "Arnie the Governor."

3. For evidence of the decline, see, for example, Chanley, Rudolph, and Rahn, "Origins and Consequences"; Hetherington, *Why Trust Matters*; and Holmberg, "Down and Down."

4. This is not to deny that institutions are sometimes more than the sum of their parts. It is simply to acknowledge that institutions function effectively or not as a result of the people who operate them effectively or not.

5. For discussions of generalized trust, see Bjørnskov, "Determinants of Generalized Trust"; Marschall and Stolle, "Race and the City"; and Warren, "Introduction."

6. Baier, *Moral Prejudices*, chap. 7.

7. Gambetta, "Can We Trust Trust?," 218.

8. Ibid., 218–19.

9. Jones, "Trust," 15. As Jane Mansbridge observes, however, Jones acknowledges that it is possible to cultivate an attitude of trust ("Altruistic Trust," 294).

10. Though, as Zofia Stemplowska pointed out to me, taking responsibility in and of itself does not show that we had a choice, it only shows that we believe we had one.

11. Or see the distinction between cognitive and noncognitive trust as described in Becker, "Trust as Noncognitive Security."

12. The basic trust game has a distinct pedigree that is related in Camerer, *Behavioral Game Theory*, 83–100. I am describing only one variant.

13. The recipients, too, are separated into two categories—trustworthy and untrustworthy—which are defined by the amount they choose to return to the sender. If they choose to return all or more of the original amount, they are designated as trustworthy, that is, they choose against making the sender worse off than she was before sending the money.

14. There is extensive research that discusses and illustrates these observations. See, for example, Engle-Warnick and Slonim, "Evolution of Strategies"; and McCabe, Rigdon, and Smith, "Positive Reciprocity."

15. Russell Hardin is perhaps best known for offering an account of trust as self-interest. See, among his voluminous writings, "Trusting Persons" and "Street-Level Epistemology of Trust."

16. Hardin, *Trust and Trustworthiness*, 13.

17. Baier, *Moral Prejudices*, chap. 7.

18. Jones, "Trust," 8.

19. Baier, *Moral Prejudices*, 104–5.

20. Dawes, van de Kragt, and Orbell, "Cooperation," 99.

21. The promise condition is a variation on the Bert-Dickhaut-McCabe trust game, as outlined in Glaeser et al., "Measuring Trust," 821.

22. See Uslaner, *Moral Foundations*, 15–16.

23. See Warren, "Introduction," 9. Warren's account draws on Eric Uslaner's work. For my own critical assessment of Uslaner's terminology, see Lenard, "Decline of Trust." For another helpful account of the distinction between generalized and particularized trust, see Jean Cohen, "Trust." Simone Chambers and Jeffrey Kopstein make a similar distinction between "particularist civility," which obtains "only between members of a particular group," and "democratic civility," which "extends the goods learned in participation to all citizens regardless of group membership" ("Bad Civil Society," 841).

24. Two surveys in particular are of note, since they generate most of the information with which researchers make conclusions about the general trust attitudes that pervade various communities. The *General Social Survey* has polled between fifteen hundred and two thousand Americans on a range of issues annually since 1972. The *World Values Survey* now surveys people living in seventy-nine countries (which the organizers boast accounts for 85 percent of the world's population) on a range of issues, including trust. For more on the *General Social Survey*, see http://www.norc.uchicago.edu/projects/gensoc1.asp. For more about the *World Values Survey*, see http://www.worldvaluessurvey.org/.

25. There are also well-known concerns with the value of data collected by surveys more generally, which I don't discuss here. For one thing, survey questions rarely offer respondents the option of reflecting and giving a nuanced opinion as they answer questions. Also, it is frequently observed that the specific wording of the question may have a tremendous impact on how people respond.

26. There is a small but growing movement in the trust literature to develop trust scales to deal with issues of nuance in trust attitudes. See Couch and Jones, "Measuring Levels of Trust."

27. Uslaner, *Moral Foundations*, 4.

28. In case it's not obvious from the questions, respondents were undergraduate university students. See Glaeser et al., "Measuring Trust," 819. To be clear, these questions weren't posed to large numbers of people, but the suggestion in the article is that questions like these ought to be included in the *General Social Survey* as a more reliable indicator of trust within a community than the questions that currently feature there.

29. As Natalia Letki pointed out to me, it is not clear who responders think counts as "most people" when they answer the question. Do they answer the question thinking about the people with whom they interact daily? Or do they answer the question thinking about the people with whom they share a political community, but whom they will never have a chance to meet? Or do they think about their impression of all the people in the world?

30. Soroka, Johnston, and Banting, "Ethnicity," 39.

31. This component is referred to by the authors as the strategic element of trust. They suggest that "considerations about whether to trust someone in a particular situation" might be "strategic" rather than moral (ibid., 40). I agree that by asking about particular situations, the authors are better able to capture the behavioral element of trust. It's not obvious, however, that the behavioral element of trust is strategic. If I have a generally trusting attitude, and so I determine that in this situation I will trust a specific other to do a specific thing, it's not obvious that we should describe this action as strategic.

32. Putnam, "E Pluribus Unum," 137.

33. Stolle, "Sources of Social Capital."

34. Putnam, *Making Democracy Work*.

35. Stolle, "Sources of Social Capital," 25.

36. Ibid. This evidence—that there is an element of self-selection going on—is reproduced in many of the studies in the volume of which Stolle's essay is a part.

37. A variation on this argument acknowledges that participation in civil society organizations does provide an opportunity to learn some of the skills that are essential to participating in politics. In this way, they are properly described as schools of democracy. See, for example, Letki, "Does Diversity Erode Social Cohesion?"

38. Putnam, "E Pluribus Unum," 143.

39. This argument is made by Chambers and Kopstein, "Bad Civil Society."

40. Baker, "Trust and Rationality," 4.

41. See, ibid., 5.

42. Gambetta, "Can We Trust Trust?," 230.

43. Ibid., 233.

44. McGeer, "Developing Trust," 28.

45. Psychologists refer to this phenomenon as "confirmatory bias." I thank Rebecca Stone and Jonathan Quong for pointing me to the relevant literature as a way to understand this element of trust.

46. Baker, "Trust and Rationality," 6.

47. Hardin, *Trust and Trustworthiness*, chap. 1.

48. Trustworthiness, or at least the perception of trustworthiness, may be morally objectionable. We can imagine a situation in which someone is insulted in response to being perceived as trustworthy (Why would she trust me to do *that*? I would never do that!), as well as a situation in which a belief that another person is trustworthy is a signal that something has gone wrong. Of the latter case, imagine a situation in which slaves trust their masters to do what is in the best interests of the slaves. In this case, masters are perceived to be trustworthy, but the extension of trust might be thought objectionable along some dimensions. Barbara Arneil makes this point in a discussion of the ongoing discrimination directed at African Americans: "trust is inappropriate in a situation of untrustworthiness" (*Diverse Communities*, 141).

49. There is plenty of research available that could be cited here. Some examples include: Fehr and Gächter, "Cooperation and Punishment"; Gunnthorsdottira, Houserb, and McCabe, "Disposition"; and Offerman, Sonnemans, and Schram, "Value Orientations."

50. To be clear, participants were told only that their task "was to decide how many chips to give to their partner. No reference was made to possible strategies for maximizing joint outcomes or maximizing personal outcomes." See De Cremer, Snyder, and Dewitte, "The Less I Trust," 97. For a general explanation of the public-good dilemma and the games used to explore it, see Komorita and Parks, *Social Dilemmas*, chap. 3.

Chapter 2

1. As David Miller writes, for example, in a democracy, "much state activity involves the furthering of goals which cannot be achieved without the voluntary cooperation of citizens" (*On Nationality*, 91–92). Additionally, it is perhaps worth noting that some forms of democracy will be more trust dependent than others. Mark Warren and Matthew Festenstein, for example, both argue for the centrality of trust to *deliberative* democracy. They argue that deliberation is trust dependent. Festenstein, *Negotiating Diversity*; Warren, "Democratic Theory and Trust."

2. Tyler, "Trust and Democratic Governance," 271. Note, therefore, that my claim is not that the *only* reason people abide by democratically made laws is because they trust others. There is at least one further reason: people are afraid of incurring penalties if they violate laws. The claim I'm making here is only that in the long term, democracies will come to rely on trust as a key part of widespread obedience to laws. Thanks to Nicholas Cheeseman for forcing elaboration here.

3. Miller, *On Nationality*, 91–92.

4. My claim here should *not* be interpreted to mean that complying and free riding are dependent *solely* on the perception that others are doing the same. For a review of the reasons for choosing for or against free riding, see Komorita and Parks, *Social Dilemmas,* 55–79.

5. Diamond, *Developing Democracy,* 208.

6. Elections are not the *sole* method for securing the legitimacy of the governing party, but it is nevertheless the main one in operation in contemporary democratic systems.

7. Anderson et al., *Losers' Consent.*

8. I am only referring here to one aspect of representation. For more on the concept of political representation, see, for example, Manin, *Principles of Representative Government;* Pitkin, *Concept of Representation;* Saward, *Representative Claim;* Shapiro et al., *Political Representation;* Urbinati and Warren, "Concept of Representation."

9. Urbinati and Warren, "Concept of Representation," 391.

10. Burke, "Speech to the Electors."

11. Brown, "Survey Article," 217.

12. Burke, "Speech to the Electors."

13. Ibid.

14. There is some evidence that attempts to deploy direct democracy enhance distrust. See Dyck, "Initiated Distrust."

15. Hardin, "Street-Level Epistemology of Trust."

16. For more on trust and the media, see O'Neill, *Autonomy and Trust,* chap. 8.

17. Warren, "Democracy and Deceit," 167. As Warren points out, what is at stake is the capacity of citizens to make autonomous judgments. If citizens are expected to make decisions on the basis of information provided to them by legislators, then false information effectively serves to disempower citizens, who are deliberately denied access to the information they need in order to make autonomous decisions.

18. Ibid., 172. Indeed, for Warren, "when people lose confidence that public decisions are taken for reasons that are publicly available and justifiable, they often become cynical about public speech and deliberation.... When people are mistrustful of government, they are also cynical about their own capacities to act on public goods ... corruption in this way diminishes the horizons of collective actions and in so doing shrinks the domain of democracy" ("What Does Corruption Mean?," 328–29).

19. Admittedly, this is considerably easier said than done. Also, there is plenty of evidence that citizens who supported the winners are more likely to report satisfaction with, and trust in, the policy decisions than are the losers. See Anderson et al., *Losers' Consent.*

20. It may also be a signal that the commitment to protecting minorities has never been stable and that the political circumstances in which challenging these protections is possible has only recently emerged.

21. The system for electing the French president can involve two rounds of votes to ensure that the winning candidate secures a majority. If no candidate wins a majority in the first round, the two highest polling candidates participate in a run-off election to determine the president.

22. Mill, "On Representative Government," 228.

23. For more elaboration of ways to distinguish between social and political trust, see Newton, "Social and Political Trust."

Chapter 3

1. Alesina and Wacziarg, "Economics of Civic Trust," 149–50; Lenard, "Decline of Trust"; Uslaner, *Moral Foundations.*

2. Nye and Zelikow, "Conclusion," 276. It is not my intention to probe why, in general, we've witnessed a decline in positive responses to questions inquiring into whether one's government

and fellow citizens are trustworthy. For speculation about the reasons, see the contributions to *Why People Don't Trust Government* (in particular, Bok, "Measuring the Performance," 55–60).

3. Hardin, *Trust and Trustworthiness*, 96.

4. Nye, Zelikow, and King, *Why People Don't Trust Government*, 277.

5. At times, the evidence that people use to justify a distrustful attitude is not good evidence—for example, some people distrust others on the basis of mere prejudice, which is based on poor evidence.

6. Govier, "Distrust," 56.

7. Banfield, *Moral Basis*, 101. Montegrano is a pseudonym for the town in which Banfield conducted his studies. Banfield's wife, Laura Fasano Banfield, interviewed the members of Montegrano on Banfield's behalf since he did not speak Italian at the time.

8. Gambetta, "Can We Trust Trust?," 234.

9. Govier, "Distrust," 56.

10. Hobbes, *Leviathan*, 186–87.

11. For an elaboration of how conditions of insecurity breed active distrust, see Ross, Mirowsky, and Pribesh, "Powerlessness," 568–69.

12. Gambetta, "Can We Trust Trust?," 234.

13. Weinstock, "Building Trust," 299–305.

14. One common argument is that people in positions of material disadvantage are more likely to err on the side of caution and distrust others. This is because the cost of misplaced trust is often, it is alleged, greater for them. On this view, the central role for a democratic state concerned to revitalize trust relations is economic redistribution. This argument features in Ross, Mirowsky, and Pribesh, "Powerlessness," and Uslaner, *Moral Foundations*. I think there is a considerable degree of truth to this claim, even though it is not central to the arguments of this book.

15. Patterson, "Liberty," 190.

16. M. Williams, *Voice, Trust, and Memory*, 162–63. The struggle to secure trust in heterogeneous communities more generally is the subject of chapter 5.

17. Crepaz, *Trust Beyond Borders*; Dalton, *Democratic Challenges*; Hetherington, *Why Trust Matters*.

18. Assessing whether the distrust that has emerged is proportional or disproportional is evidently easier said than done.

19. See, for example, Statistics Canada, "Ethnic Diversity Survey," 19.

20. For an account of the ways in which rational choice calculations advise distrust in which irrational-seeming risk taking may very well serve to build trust, see Murighan, Malhotra, and Weber, "Paradoxes of Trust."

21. Kramer, "Collective Paranoia," 138, and Larson, "Distrust," 43, respectively.

22. Hewstone et al., "Intergroup Contact"; Trew, "Catholic-Protestant Contact."

23. Dickason, *Canada's First Nations*, 284.

24. Deveaux, *Gender and Justice*, chap. 5.

25. Hart, *Distrust and Democracy*, 208.

26. Skinner, "Paradoxes of Political Liberty," 37.

27. Skinner, "Republican Ideal of Political Liberty," 303.

28. Pettit, *Republicanism*, 263.

29. Ibid., 251.

30. Locke, "Second Treatise on Government," para. 136. For an assessment of the role of trust in Locke's work, see Dunn, *History of Political Philosophy*, and Parry, "Trust, Distrust, and Consensus," 130–34.

31. Parry, "Trust, Distrust, and Consensus," 137.

32. Hart, *Distrust and Democracy*, xi.

33. Maloy, "Two Concepts of Trust," 501. Similarly, Peter Johnson notes that the attention we place on accountability mechanisms stems from "an attempt to develop a notion of trust appropriate to the complexity of modern democratic politics" (*Frames of Deceit*, 18).

34. Johnson, *Frames of Deceit*, 18.

35. Ibid., 170–71.

36. Rosanvallon, *Counter-Democracy*, 280.

37. O'Neill, *Autonomy and Trust*, 234.

38. Rosanvallon, *Counter-Democracy*, 24.

39. O'Neill, *Autonomy and Trust*, 130.

40. Or in Rosanvallon's way of explaining the danger, these "counter-democratic" strategies, which protect us from the dangers of democratic rule, have a "dark side," which he terms "the unpolitical." He writes that "this depoliticization has given rise to a vague but persistent feeling of malaise" (*Counter-Democracy*, 306).

41. These explanations are not meant to account for the recent drops in levels of trust. Rather, they are intended to counter the claim that distrust is somehow inherent or central to democracy.

42. Warren, "Democratic Theory and Trust," 310.

43. This section may seem reminiscent of a distinction that Philip Pettit makes between having trust and expressing trust. The former corresponds to the attitude we have toward others and authorities and the latter refers to the consequent behaviors. It is possible, in Pettit's view, that we have trust in our legislators while we nevertheless express distrust toward them. We should, moreover, equate expressing distrust with vigilance. We are being vigilant when we insist that our legislators submit to constraints on their actions, and we can do so even if by and large we have a trusting attitude toward them. Pettit writes, "there is no inconsistency in having personal trust in the authorities while expressing personal distrust" toward them in the form of constraining their actions (*Republicanism*, 265). I disagree with this conceptualization for two reasons. First, this sort of conceptualization puts Pettit (and citizens) in the awkward situation of having to find ways to signal to our legislators that we trust them in spite of our seemingly distrustful behaviors toward them. Onora O'Neill explains why it is that this sort of reasoning fails (*Autonomy and Trust*, chap. 6). Second, distrust (like trust) is part attitude and part behavior, and, it seems to me, these two aspects cannot be separated in a way that makes conceptual sense. Either we are distrustful and behave that way, or we are trusting and behave that way.

44. In other words, institutions do relieve *some* of the burden associated with monitoring legislators. Contemporary republican theory simply rejects the claim that institutional protections against abuses of power are sufficient to protect citizens.

45. Mill, "On Representative Government," 245.

46. They may also hope that others will do the right thing on their behalf, without trusting them to do so. I may believe that they are unlikely to do so, but that there is nevertheless a slim chance that they will have reason to try. In this case, I cannot be described as trusting them.

47. My comments here draw in part on a discussion of civility in Pettit, *Republicanism*. He writes that we need civility to support shared laws, that we need civility in order to have vigilance, and that trust is a component of civility (chap. 8). We can assume, therefore, that a relation between trust and vigilance exists within his work. My attempt here is to make the relation explicit.

Chapter 4

1. Miller, *On Nationality*, 26. For a discussion of Miller's account of the public culture argument, see Lenard, "Shared Public Culture." For a discussion of my view and Miller's, see Festenstein, "National Identity."

2. Fukuyama, *Trust,* 34–41. I am reluctant to rely further on Fukuyama's work on trust; although we appear to agree that culture is a source of trust, Fukuyama also appears to believe that the only cultures that successfully produce trust are those that have extensive histories with more or less stable memberships. The implication that changing cultures, with changing memberships, will simply be unable to produce trust strikes me as dangerous and implausible. For an objection to Fukuyama's argument along these lines, see Warren, "Democratic Theory and Trust," 322–24. For an account of Fukuyama's anxiety about the effect of diversity, see Fukuyama, "Identity and Migration."

3. Miller, *On Nationality,* 41.

4. Ibid., 22.

5. Ibid., 41.

6. Ibid., 85.

7. I mean deliberation in the broadest sense, including political deliberation and public engagement and interactions that are facilitated by media outlets, and so on.

8. Miller, *On Nationality,* 68, 70.

9. Ibid., 40. See also Deveaux, *Gender and Justice,* chap. 8.

10. As I indicated in chapter 4, it is critical that minority groups are included in the formation of the public culture. It is part of the *meaning* of the word *public* that minorities are included. For an account of the importance of including minorities, see Deveaux, *Gender and Justice,* chap. 4.

11. Miller, *On Nationality,* 87.

12. Ibid., 32. The argument that communication technologies are an essential component of modern nation-states is most famously made in Anderson, *Imagined Communities.* Thus, as media sources continue to fragment along ideological lines, even formally universally available material may fail in its capacity to transmit widely held beliefs.

13. Scheffler, "Immigration," 107. Scheffler is critical of this view, and writes that "it fails to recognize that change is essential to culture and to cultural survival, so that to prevent a culture from changing, if such a thing were possible, would not be to preserve the culture but rather to destroy it."

14. One might quibble with the description of both the United States and South Africa as fully integrated for a variety of reasons, but that doesn't change the fact that each of the features described occupies a significant space in their respective public cultures.

15. Arneil, *Diverse Communities,* 140. This variation on the critique will be explored more fully in chapter 5 in the context of ethnocultural diversity and its effect on trust relations in a democratic community.

16. Brighouse, "Against Nationalism," 389.

17. Mason, *Community, Solidarity, and Belonging,* 117.

18. Weinstock, "Four Kinds," 65.

19. The accuracy of this analysis is largely undermined by Belgium's ongoing constitutional crisis, though.

20. Their support may depend to some extent, however, on the alternatives available—if there is no alternative, and they remain unhappy, their support for these institutions will likely be only lukewarm.

21. This point is made in Deveaux, *Gender and Justice,* chap. 8.

22. Miller, *On Nationality,* 92.

23. These examples are both taken from Abizadeh, "Liberal Democracy."

24. The example of an Iranian who would extend trust to a German judge illustrates, equally, that a public culture is not essential for all forms of trust; I do not deny that trust emerges from sources other than a public culture. Moreover, the example of the Iranian journalist may in fact illustrate something else entirely—for example, knowledge that freedom of speech is protected in Germany and not in Iran.

25. Citizens were responding to the standard trust question as outlined in chapter 1. I say "continued" suspicion of others because Communist regimes are well known to have created conditions under which most citizens came to be suspicious, and generally distrustful, of others. David Lovell writes, "even the deep trust we might expect in close personal relations was put at risk by the extent of secret police surveillance" ("Trust," 33). It may be that as post-Communist countries develop a firmer commitment to democratic institutions, the levels of trust will rise. For more on trust (and the lack thereof) in post-Communist societies, see Marková, *Trust and Democratic Transition*, and Rose, "Postcommunism." For more recent discussions, see the contributions to Lewandowski, *Trust and Transitions*.

26. Baier, *Moral Prejudices*, 99.

27. Careful readers may worry that this claim is tautological—I shall respond to this worry shortly. Tyler and Degoey, "Trust in Organizational Authorities." These studies further indicate that the attribution of positive motives is correlated more strongly with imputations of trustworthiness than is competence or evidence of past good decisions.

28. For a general account, see Coleman, *Foundations of Social Theory*.

29. I did not win this prize!

30. Certain sanctions are imposed by community law and so are enforced more rigorously; I mean, however, to signal the informal sanctions at work. The sanctions work, I believe, because of the expectations they place on members. Recall from chapter 1 that people are motivated to behave in trustworthy ways in part because they believe others expect them to do so.

31. Knack and Kropf, "For Shame!" See also Shang and Croson, "Field Experiment."

32. Hooghe, "Social Capital," 717–18.

33. De Cremer and Van Vugt, "Social Identification Effects," 872.

34. This study, and variations on it that come to comparable conclusions, is reported in De Cremer and Van Vugt, "Social Identification Effects." For a review of social dilemma experiments in which the result is confirmed, see Brewer and Schneider, "Social Identity."

35. Dawes, van de Kragt, and Orbell, "Cooperation"; Mansbridge, "Relation of Altruism," 139.

36. There is considerable confusion in the literature between the terms "identity" and "belonging"; I prefer to emphasize the latter term, since there is so much controversy surrounding questions of identity. I believe we need to focus on indicators of *belonging* rather than *identity*, and that attempts to focus on identity are inevitably misleading and divisive. Political theorists in the past have been concerned with identity—preoccupied, for example, with whether identity is merely a content-free label that can serve to bind us in spite of an absence of shared norms and values, or whether identity claims are necessarily founded in shared norms and values, or whether individuals can (and should) possess one dominant identity, or whether identities are nested, or whether people can possess multiple meaningful identities at any one time. These debates have encouraged the demand that immigrants be prepared to abandon one identity for another, and evidence that identity shifts are slow to transpire in new migrants has prompted much anxiety and hand-wringing. In my view, the term "identity" is a red herring. Identities are necessarily fluid and multiple, and they shift over time and depend on all kinds of factors that we cannot control. Instead, I believe we should be concerned with inclusion and belonging, that is, with whether immigrants are welcomed as members, are valued as contributors to the political and social community they have joined, and so on. The demand that they abandon identities that are inevitably meaningful is futile, and measuring their integration by whether they self-describe as "hyphenated" is misleading. It is a sense of *belonging* and the concomitant commitment to participating in and contributing to their new home that we must seek to encourage, and which so frequently demands the implementation of policies described as "multicultural." The trust on which democracies rely depends on people feeling included, that is, as though they belong.

37. Note that, at least as far as the first reason is concerned, it does not matter whether these motivations are positive or negative; the simple provision of information enables us to trust (or otherwise) more easily, that is, in the absence of a conscious awareness of our vulnerability.

38. For discussions of the various possible relations between cooperation and trust, see, among others: Cook and Cooper, "Experimental Studies of Cooperation," and Gambetta, *Trust*. I consider the relation between cooperation and trust more deeply in chapter 7.

39. I must repeat that my claim is not that trust doesn't have a positive effect on cooperation. Not only is it well known that high trusters are more willing than low trusters to cooperate, but the perceived risks associated with cooperation are also evidently mitigated when trust exists. The claim here is only that cooperation does not *require* trust. For ample evidence that high trusters are more likely to cooperate, see, for example, the review of these studies in Cook and Cooper, "Experimental Studies of Cooperation."

40. Lovell, "Trust"; Marková, *Trust and Democratic Transition*; Tworzecki, "Disaffected New Democracy?"

41. Indeed, the history of political thought since the English Revolution of 1688 is largely focused on why—and under what conditions—citizens ought to be willing to succumb to common governance.

42. Mill, "On Representative Government," 257–58.

Chapter 5

1. Cecile Laborde refers to the tendency to attribute values to individuals based on their ethnic or cultural identity as "ethnicization." See Laborde, *Critical Republicanism*. I discuss this process in more detail in "What Can Multicultural Theory Tell Us."

2. This distinction is analogous to one made by Robert Putnam, who distinguishes between bridging and bonding trust, where the former refers to a broad inclusive trust and the latter refers to in-group trust that doesn't extend to the population at large. See Putnam, "E Pluribus Unum." For discussion, see Forbes, "Is Bridging Not Bonding?"

3. Pennant, "Diversity, Trust." This study shows no clear correlation between ethnic diversity and participation in civil society associations or volunteer organizations.

4. See Costa and Kahn, "Civic Engagement," 106–8. This study suggests that as a community becomes more diverse, citizens (of the majority) are more likely to use referenda to produce policies that are disadvantageous to minority communities. It should be noted that these decreased rates of trust are *in addition to* the more generally decreasing levels of trust across Western democratic communities that I described in chapter 2. See also Tolbert and Hero, "Dealing with Diversity," 578.

5. What counts as "large enough to be noticed" will, of course, depend on the community itself.

6. Gamm, "Hispanic Council."

7. And, of course, controversies concerning appropriate dress in a liberal democratic community continue, as many countries consider whether to ban various forms of head and facial coverings in a range of social and political environments. I say a bit more about this later.

8. For an account of this debate, see Kymlicka, *Finding Our Way*.

9. The question of whether Sikhs should be exempt from motorcycle helmet laws has proved more controversial because the cost of treating citizens injured in motorcycle accidents is borne by the community at large.

10. Brink, "Imagining Civic Relations," 357.

11. Ali, "Islam's Silent Moderates."

12. Fatah and Hassan, "Deadly Face." The article itself *opposes* a monolithic view of Islam in which these values are ascribed to all Muslims, and argues that Muslims must stand up against radical and violent interpretations of Islam.

13. Elsewhere I argue that the requirement that Muslim citizens proclaim their allegiance to democratic and liberal values each time we witness a terrorist incident carried out by Muslims is objectionable. See Lenard, "What Can Multicultural Theory Tell Us."

14. For a recent account of the view that policies that unfairly burden members of immigrant groups are related to increases in mistrust, see Knight, "Social Norms," 363–64.

15. For two different views on the effects of the citizenship test in the United Kingdom, see Kiwan, "Journey to Citizenship," and Osler, "Testing Citizenship and Allegiance."

16. Osler, "Testing Citizenship and Allegiance," 66.

17. For an analysis in Europe, see Vertovec and Wessendorf, "Assessing the Backlash."

18. Canada and the United States have long relied on citizenship tests as part of the naturalization process. It is the *context* in which these tests are implemented, as well as their content, that tells us whether to interpret them as obstacles to naturalization.

19. On the rise of xenophobic political parties across Europe, see, for example, Boomgaarden and Vliegenthart, "Explaining the Rise," and M. H. Williams, "Can Leopards Change Their Spots?"

20. Miles, "Denial." The BNP is well known for its nationalist, anti-immigrant stance.

21. The public acceptability of anti-immigrant statements is rising, in my view. For an account of the dangerous effects of this trend as it pertains to Muslims in Europe, see Lenard, "What Can Multicultural Theory Tell Us."

22. The absence of trust stems in large part from the view that illegal migrants are free riding and are therefore costly to the economy.

23. For discussions of various decisions European countries have made in relation to Muslim head and face coverings see Joppke, *The Veil.*

24. M. Williams, *Voice, Trust, and Memory,* 163.

25. Mansbridge, "Should Blacks Represent Blacks," 641.

26. M. Williams, *Voice, Trust, and Memory,* 149.

27. Ibid., 151, 62–63. As Barbara Arneil observes, moreover, given the ongoing failures of white American political representatives to act in the best interests of African Americans, African Americans are *correct* to distrust their white representatives. She of course agrees that distrust is generally bad for democracies, but observes that in this case it would be far worse if African Americans continued to extend trust to representatives who consistently failed to represent them adequately. In this case, she argues, the distrust may well be productive rather than destructive. Arneil, *Diverse Communities,* chap. 5.

28. Arneil, *Diverse Communities,* 145.

29. Eisenberg, *Reasons of Identity;* Quong, "Cultural Exemptions"; Shorten, "Cultural Exemptions."

30. Miller, *On Nationality,* 132. Margaret Moore refers to these policies as "strong" multicultural policies and contrasts them with weak multicultural policies, which look more like the cultural exemptions I described earlier. See Moore, *Ethics of Nationalism,* 107.

31. Wikan, "Deadly Distrust," 195. For more on toleration and its connection to trust, see Dees, *Trust and Toleration.*

32. Quong, "Cultural Exemptions," and Shorten, "Cultural Exemptions."

33. These kinds of policies weakened trust for at least two reasons. First, the girls who had been required to marry may have been isolated—from regular forums of interaction for young girls, for example—by this practice. Second, and more important, practices that are radically divergent from the norm often have the effect of isolating the community as a whole as the community turns inward to protect them from erosion and themselves from wider social derision. Wikan, "Deadly Distrust." For more discussion, see Hellgren and Hobson, "Cultural Dialogues."

34. See, for example, Fukuyama, "Identity and Migration."

35. Wikan, "Deadly Distrust," 195.

36. For more on the arranged marriage debate, see Phillips and Dustin, "UK Initiatives." See also Deveaux, *Gender and Justice*, chap. 6.

37. Readers familiar with the social science literature will note the analogy to the contact hypothesis, which originally suggested that mere contact was sufficient to overcome group animosity. More recent accounts of the contact hypothesis specify the conditions under which the contact hypothesis holds true. I shall say more about the principles that should guide trust-building contact in chapter 7.

38. For more in general on the tensions between cultural claims and gender equality, see Chambers, *Sex, Culture, and Justice.*

39. Soroka, Johnston, and Banting, "Ethnicity, Trust," 50. Or as Avigail Eisenberg writes, "Trust might well enhance cooperative relations of the sort that drive redistribution programs" ("Equality, Trust, and Multiculturalism," 84–85).

40. Miller, *On Nationality*, 90–91.

41. Eisenberg, "Equality, Trust, and Multiculturalism," 84–85.

42. For a more sustained argument on this point, see Lenard, "Rebuilding Trust."

43. See, for example, Luttmer and Singhal, "Culture, Context."

44. Bissoondath, "No Place Like Home," 1.

45. Indeed, there is evidence that Canadians who describe themselves in hyphenated terms are less trusting of others. Reitz et al., *Multiculturalism and Social Cohesion*; Soroka, Helliwell, and Johnston, "Measuring and Modelling Trust," 107.

46. This worry is expressed, for example, in Phillips, *Which Equalities Matter?*

47. Barry, *Culture and Equality*, 64.

48. Gitlin, *Twilight of Common Dreams*, 237. Anne Phillips offers a nuanced account of this worry in *Which Equalities Matter?*

49. Banting et al., "Do Multiculturalism Policies Erode," 81.

50. Crepaz, "If You Are My Brother," 111.

51. La Porta, et al., "The Quality of Government," 265. This study revealed more than what I'm reporting here, of course. At first glance, ethnically divided countries seem to fare, on average, less well: they *seem* to experience more corruption, inferior quality of public service provision, lower government efficiency, and so on. But as the researchers are quick to observe, many divided countries are extremely poor, and if they control for poverty, it turns out that "fractionalized countries do not have especially bad governments." The exception as I reported above was with respect to support for redistributive policies. For some evidence that questions the link between ethnic diversity and declining support for public goods, see Baldwin and Huber, "Economic Versus Cultural Differences."

52. Alesina, Baqir, and Easterly, "Public Goods"; Miguel and Gugerty, "Ethnic Diversity." For example, educational spending at the local level was almost $2,000 lower per student in significantly heterogeneous communities (described as communities in which there is at least a 50 percent chance that another citizen is of a different ethnic group).

53. Luttmer, "Group Loyalty," 519. See also Hopkins, "Diversity Discount."

Chapter 6

1. I use the term "ethnocultural" to signal that groups can be divided by ethnic and cultural (including religious) lines, and often both. In the case of many conflicts, it may also be better to describe the conflicts as sectarian.

2. Rabushka and Shepsle, *Politics in Plural Societies*, 86.

3. Diamond and Plattner, *Nationalism, Ethnic Conflict*, xviii.

4. Lijphart, *Democracy in Plural Societies*, 1.

5. Ethnocultural divisions are certainly not the only divisions that contemporary political communities face. Class divisions are also often prevalent in ways that stress trust relations, for example. See Labonne, Biller, and Chase, "Inequality and Relative Wealth," and Uslaner and Brown, "Inequality, Trust, and Civic Engagement."

6. Horowitz, "Democracy in Divided Societies," 25.

7. Abizadeh, "Historical Truth, National Myths."

8. Weinstock, "Towards a Normative Theory."

9. O'Kelly, "Public Institutions," 564. For an evaluation of the norms and values of Catholics and Protestants in Northern Ireland, as well as in Ireland more generally, see Fahey, Hayes, and Sinnott, *Conflict and Consensus*. For evidence that trust continues to be low even though the conflict is less acute, see Gormley-Heenan and Devine, "The 'Us' in Trust."

10. Recall that my claim is not that democracy will immediately fail in the face of weakened trust relations; rather, the claim is that democracy may struggle and limp along in the absence of trust relations. The same is true in the case of Northern Ireland; although democracy has not broken down entirely, the struggles it has faced in sustaining shared democratic institutions through the 1990s and 2000s can be traced to an ongoing absence of trust across the sectarian divide. See Gormley-Heenan and Devine, "The 'Us' in Trust."

11. O'Kelly, "Public Institutions," 565. O'Kelly's concern is with Northern Ireland, but this observation can be generalized across severely divided communities.

12. There are estimated to be a further 250 ethnocultural groups that don't belong to any of the dominant ethnocultural groups that play major roles in the Nigerian federation, most of which would not be able to survive independently of the Nigerian federation. The basic facts about Nigerian politics are taken from Ejobowah, *Competing Claims to Recognition*.

13. Kamel, "Beyond Miss World."

14. We have seen this played out as courts in the mainly Muslim north of Nigeria have imposed (or refused to appeal) sentences of death by stoning on women accused of adultery, and the challenges that the central Nigerian government has faced in objecting to these sentences.

15. Weinstock, "Towards a Normative Theory."

16. Some researchers therefore suggest that federalism is a step toward state breakup. Whether this is the case is a source of debate among many of the contributors to Lehning, *Theories of Secession*, and Moore, *National Self-Determination and Secession*.

17. The Igbo in the east of Nigeria have certainly launched secessionist movements over the last fifty years, all of which transpired after the implementation of federal structures; this is, however, insufficient to impute causality from federalism to likely secession.

18. Obiyan, "Political Parties," 42.

19. Ibid.

20. Abukabar, "Ethnic Identity," 33.

21. For an extensive account of violent conflict in Nigeria that has been sponsored by ethnically based political parties, see Suberu and Diamond, "Institutional Design," 406–10.

22. Hewstone, Rubin, and Willis, "Intergroup Bias," 575–604.

23. Horowitz, "Democracy in Divided Societies," 32.

24. Blake and Mouton, "Comprehension," 305. See also Hewstone, Rubin, and Willis, "Intergroup Bias," 579–80. Some would argue that even inclusive national identity groups are successful only insofar as they denigrate outsiders to some extent; I don't believe, however, that inclusive national groups *necessarily* are bound by a commitment to the inferiority of outsiders, even if they are bound by a set of values and norms that they believe distinguish them from outsiders.

25. Levine and Moreland, "Group Reactions."

26. Weinstock, "Building Trust."

27. Barry, "Is Democracy Special?," 53.

28. Diamond and Plattner, *Nationalism, Ethnic Conflict,* viii.

29. Zureik, Moughrabi, and Sacco, "Perception of Legal Inequality," 27.

30. Isaac, *Core Issues,* 2.

31. Diamond and Plattner, *Nationalism, Ethnic Conflict,* xviii–xiv.

32. Turkey probably does not merit being described as a severely divided society more generally, however.

33. Brian Barry refers to the term "majority principle" (as distinct from the principle of majority rule) and I follow him. He articulates the principle as follows: "By something akin to the principle of insufficient reason, it seems difficult to say why the decisions should go in the way wanted by the minority rather than in the way of the majority" ("Is Democracy Special?," 27).

34. Even in stable democracies, political losers tend to display less satisfaction with the democratic process more generally. Democratic political systems *rely* on the consent of losers, whose compliance is essential to securing the ongoing legitimacy of democratic policies. See Anderson et al., *Losers' Consent.*

35. Horowitz, "Democracy in Divided Societies," 18.

36. Rabushka and Shepsle, *Politics in Plural Societies,* 147.

37. Data collected and published by the European Centre for Minority Issues, 1997.

38. Diamond and Plattner, *Nationalism, Ethnic Conflict,* xix.

39. Although in the first two cases, it is possible that over time demographic changes will alter the direction of the majority-minority relation.

40. This issue is of heightened importance since the Sri Lankan government has recently defeated the Tamil freedom fighters. One big question now is whether the government will be willing to institute and defend protections for the Tamil minority (something it has generally been disinclined to do).

41. Lal, "Constitutional Engineering," 274–75. For an overview of the Fijian constitutional crisis, see Carens, *Culture, Citizenship, and Community,* chap. 9.

42. According to voting requirements in the late 1960s and 1970s in Northern Ireland, "an elector must be the owner or tenant of a dwelling house of rateable value of ten pounds or over for three months prior to the election." Rabushka and Shepsle, *Politics in Plural Societies,* 154.

43. Ibid., chap. 5.

44. Young, *Inclusion and Democracy,* 128.

45. Ibid., 128–33.

46. In chapter 4, I rejected the claim often heard that public cultures are necessarily homogenizing, and therefore that they demand that citizens adopt a unified set of values and norms. Similarly, ethnocultural groups in divided societies are often wrongly viewed as having unified values and norms.

47. This is a broader question that representation theorists consider at great length, namely, whether groups that demand representation are, after all, internally heterogeneous. There is no *single* view or set of views that a group can be said, definitely, to hold.

48. O'Kelly, "Public Institutions," 567.

Chapter 7

1. Brink, "Imagining Civic Relations," 351.

2. Associated Press, "Film Exposes Immigrants."

3. Foner and Alba, "Second Generation."

4. Scheffler describes the kind of "strong cultural preservationism" that communities sometimes attempt to implement, and suggests that this sort of project necessary fails given the centrality of change to culture in general. See Scheffler, "Immigration."

5. For more on this debate, see Korteweg, "Sharia Debate in Ontario"; and Shachar, "Privatizing Diversity."

6. The provincial government then asked Attorney General Marion Boyd to evaluate the use of arbitration in familial disputes, with particular attention to its effects on vulnerable members of the community. Boyd recommended that arbitration be permitted to continue under certain legal constraints. The government ignored her recommendations. See Boyd, *Dispute Resolution.*

7. David Miller argues this way. See "Immigration." What counts as too much to absorb at once is a central question, the answer to which will likely depend on the context of the state in question.

8. Sniderman and Hagendoorn, *When Ways of Life Collide,* 105.

9. This is Russell Hardin's account of trust. See "Street-Level Epistemology of Trust."

10. Knight, "Social Norms," 258. See, more generally, Cook, Hardin, and Levi, *Cooperation Without Trust?*

11. Worth, "Iraq's New President."

12. See, for example, Schweitzer, Hershey, and Bradlow, "Promises and Lies." The authors of this article argue that trust never fully recovers when deception is associated with trust violations.

13. Hewstone et al., "Intergroup Contact," 101–2; Uslaner, "Segregation, Mistrust, and Minorities."

14. See, for example, Hardin, *Trust and Trustworthiness,* 139–40.

15. Adler, "Testimony, Trust, Knowing."

16. Weinstock, "Building Trust."

17. See, for example, McGlynn, "Integrated Education." The focus on children is important because the hope is that they will grow up without developing the distrustful attitudes toward members of the other sectarian group in the first place.

18. Fischbacher, Gachter, and Fehr, "Are People Conditionally Cooperative?," and Ostrom, "Collective Actions."

19. For examples of communities in which intergroup monitoring proved sufficient to secure ongoing cooperation, see the examples recounted in Ostrom, *Governing the Commons.* The examples, however, do not explicitly consider transitions from distrusting to trusting environments.

20. O'Neill, *Autonomy and Trust,* 135.

21. Ibid.

22. Fischbacher, Gachter, and Fehr, "Are People Conditionally Cooperative?"

23. Ostrom, "Collective Actions," 151.

24. Mansbridge, "Relation of Altruism," 136.

25. For a discussion of the best procedure to follow in pursuing post-conflict reconstruction, see Barakat, *Housing Reconstruction.*

26. This is well observed in recent efforts made by international organizations to build peace in societies recovering from civil war. Horowitz, "Some Realism About Peacemaking," and Werner, "Precarious Nature of Peace."

27. Ostrom, "Collective Actions," 150. This point is obviously familiar to deliberative democrats: legitimacy derives from the process of deliberation in the first place. See, for example, Joshua Cohen, "Deliberation and Democratic Legitimacy."

28. For example, see Dryzek, "Deliberative Democracy"; Noël, "Democratic Deliberation"; O'Flynn, *Deliberative Democracy and Divided Societies;* and Valadez, *Deliberative Democracy.*

29. Gutmann and Thompson, *Democracy and Disagreement;* Laborde, *Critical Republicanism,* 163.

30. Noël, "Democratic Deliberation."

31. There are surely additional dimensions to the disagreements among deliberative democrats, but these are the central ones. Some of the central texts in deliberative democratic theory include: Bohman and Rehg, *Deliberative Democracy;* Dryzek, *Deliberative Democracy and Beyond;* Elster, *Deliberative Democracy;* and Fishkin and Laslett, *Debating Deliberative Democracy.*

32. Laden, "Negotiation, Deliberation," 199.

33. For discussion of dialogue in the British context, see Council of Europe, *White Paper;* and McGhee, *End of Multiculturalism?,* chap. 4.

34. Warren, "Democratic Theory and Trust," 337.

35. B. Williams, *Truth and Truthfulness,* 121.

36. For more on the status of sincerity in deliberation and its relation to trust, see Adler, "Sticks and Stones"; Lenard, "Deliberating Sincerely"; Markovits, "Trouble with Being Earnest"; and Warren, "What Should and Should Not Be Said."

37. Laden, "Negotiation, Deliberation," 211.

38. Miller, *On Nationality,* 93–97.

39. Saunders, *Public Peace Process,* 84–85.

40. Warren, "Deliberative Democracy and Authority," 47.

41. There is a prior question here, which is how we get hostile parties to the table in the first place. The question is far beyond the scope of the present work.

42. I say largely because there are some moments in deliberation when members of a group may need to regroup and discuss possible compromises before making them public. Since no deliberating group is homogeneous, and there may be many members of the group at the table, it seems acceptable that group members have opportunities to discuss among themselves.

43. Smith, *Deliberative Democracy,* 81.

44. Carnavale, "Partisanship Effects."

45. Smith, *Deliberative Democracy,* 84.

46. Fennema and Maussen, "Dealing with Extremists," 383.

47. Dryzek, *Discursive Democracy,* 45–46.

48. Fennema and Maussen, "Dealing with Extremists," 383.

49. Sanders, "Against Deliberation."

50. McDonnell and Weatherford, *State Standards-Setting,* 20.

51. Ibid., 22.

52. The morally provisional nature of deliberation is discussed in Gutmann and Thompson, *Democracy and Disagreement,* 171.

53. This observation is made by many advocates of deliberative democracy, including Joshua Cohen, "Deliberation and Democratic Legitimacy." As critics of deliberation observe, the issue of whether an outcome is legitimate is independent to some extent of its moral justifiability. As Monique Deveaux observes, moreover, including stakeholders in the decision-making process can have the effect of producing *illiberal* outcomes that are, nevertheless, acceptable to those who are subject to them. In large part, this acceptance is connected to the revisability of these decisions over time. See Deveaux, *Gender and Justice.*

54. Warren, "Deliberative Democracy and Authority," 47.

55. For many examples of this debate, see Bauböck, "Farewell to Multiculturalism?"; Bertossi, "Mistaken Models of Integration?"; the article "Strike Multiculturalism"; and Vertovec and Wessendorf, *Assessing the Backlash.*

56. Kymlicka, *Finding Our Way;* and Kymlicka, "Rise and Fall."

Conclusion

1. For example, see McLaren, "Immigration and Trust."

2. Burns, "Cameron Criticizes 'Multiculturalism.'"

3. Vertovec, "Towards Post-Multiculturalism?"

BIBLIOGRAPHY

Abizadeh, Arash. "Does Liberal Democracy Presuppose a Cultural Nation? Four Arguments." *American Political Science Review* 96, no. 3 (2002): 495–509.

———. "Historical Truth, National Myths, and Liberal Democracy: On the Coherence of Liberal Nationalism." *Journal of Political Philosophy* 12, no. 3 (2004): 291–313.

Abukabar, Dauda. "Ethnic Identity, Democratization, and the Future of the African State: Lessons from Nigeria." *African Issues* 29, nos. 1–2 (2001): 31–36.

Adler, Jonathan. "Sticks and Stones: A Reply to Warren." *Journal of Social Philosophy* 39, no. 4 (2008): 639–55.

———. "Testimony, Trust, Knowing." *Journal of Philosophy* 91, no. 5 (1994): 264–75.

Alesina, Alberto, Reza Baqir, and William Easterly. "Public Goods and Ethnic Divisions." *Quarterly Journal of Economics* 114, no. 4 (1999): 1243–84.

Alesina, Alberto, and Romain Wacziarg. "The Economics of Civic Trust." In *Disaffected Democracies,* edited by Susan Pharr and Robert Putnam, 149–70. Princeton: Princeton University Press, 2000.

Ali, Ayaan Hirsi. "Islam's Silent Moderates." *New York Times,* December 7, 2007.

Allen, Danielle. *Talking to Strangers: Anxieties of Citizenship Since Brown v. Board of Education.* Chicago: University of Chicago Press, 2004.

Anderson, Benedict. *Imagined Communities: Reflections on the Origin and Spread of Nationalism.* New York: Verso, 1991.

Anderson, Christopher J., André Blais, Shaun Bowler, Todd Donovan, and Ola Listhaug. *Losers' Consent: Elections and Democratic Legitimacy.* Oxford: Oxford University Press, 2005.

Arneil, Barbara. *Diverse Communities: The Problem with Social Capital.* Cambridge: Cambridge University Press, 2006.

Arneil, Barbara, Monique Deveaux, Rita Dhamoon, and Avigail Eisenberg, eds. *Sexual Justice/Cultural Justice.* London: Routledge, 2007.

Associated Press. "Film Exposes Immigrants to Dutch Liberalism." *MSNBC.com,* March 16, 2006. http://www.msnbc.com/id/11842116/ns/world_news-europe/t/film-exposes-immigrants-dutch-liberalism/.

Baier, Annette. *Moral Prejudices: Essays on Ethics.* Cambridge: Harvard University Press, 1995.

Baker, Judith. "Trust and Rationality." *Pacific Philosophical Quarterly* 68 (1987): 1–13.

Baldwin, Kate, and John D. Huber. "Economic Versus Cultural Differences: Forms of Ethnic Diversity and Public Goods Provision." *American Political Science Review* 104, no. 4 (2010): 644–62.

Banfield, Edward C. *The Moral Basis of a Backward Society.* Chicago: The Free Press, 1958.

Banting, Keith, Richard Johnston, Will Kymlicka, and Stuart Soroka. "Do Multiculturalism Policies Erode the Welfare State? An Empirical Analysis." In Banting and Kymlicka, *Multiculturalism and the Welfare State,* 49–91.

Banting, Keith, and Will Kymlicka, eds. *Multiculturalism and the Welfare State: Recognition and Redistribution in Contemporary Democracies.* Oxford: Oxford University Press, 2006.

Barakat, Sultan. *Housing Reconstruction After Conflict and Disaster.* London: Humanitarian Practice Network, 2003.

Barry, Brian. *Culture and Equality: An Egalitarian Critique of Multiculturalism.* Cambridge: Harvard University Press, 2001.

———. *Democracy, Power, and Justice.* Oxford: Clarendon Press, 1989.

———. "Is Democracy Special?" In Barry, *Democracy, Power, and Justice,* 24–60.

Bauböck, Rainer. "Farewell to Multiculturalism? Sharing Values and Identities in Societies of Immigration." *Journal of International Migration and Integration* 3, no. 1 (2002): 1–16.

Becker, Lawrence C. "Trust as Noncognitive Security About Motives." *Ethics* 107 (1996): 43–61.

Bennhold, Katrin. "A Veil Closes France's Door to Citizenship." *New York Times,* July 19, 2008.

Bertossi, Christophe. "Mistaken Models of Integration? A Critical Perspective on the Crisis of Multiculturalism in Europe." In *European Multiculturalism Revisited,* edited by Alessandro Silj, 235–51. New York: Zed, 2010.

Bissoondath, Neil. "No Place Like Home." *New Internationalist,* September 5, 1998.

Bjørnskov, Christian. "Determinants of Generalized Trust: A Cross-Country Comparison." *Public Choice* 130, nos. 1–2 (2007): 1–21.

Blake, Roger R., and Jane Srygley Mouton. "Comprehension of Own and of Outgroup Positions Under Intergroup Competition." *Journal of Conflict Resolution* 5, no. 3 (1961): 304–10.

Bohman, James, and William Rehg, eds. *Deliberative Democracy: Essays on Reason and Politics.* Cambridge: MIT Press, 1997.

Bok, Derek. "Measuring the Performance of Government." In Nye, Zelikow, and King, *Why People Don't Trust Government,* 55–76.

Boomgaarden, Hajo G., and Rens Vliegenthart. "Explaining the Rise of Anti-Immigrant Parties: The Role of News Media Content." *Electoral Studies* 26, no. 2 (2007): 404–17.

Boyd, Marion. *Dispute Resolution in Family Law: Protecting Choice, Promoting Inclusion.* Toronto: Ministry of the Attorney General, 2004.

Brewer, Marilynn B., and Sherry K. Schneider. "Social Identity and Social Dilemmas: A Double-Edged Sword." In *Social Identity Theory: Constructive and Critical Advances,* edited by Dominic Abrams and Michael A. Hogg, 169–84. New York: Harvester Wheatsheaf, 1990.

Brighouse, Harry. "Against Nationalism." In *Rethinking Nationalism,* edited by Jocelyne Couture, Kai Nielsen, and Michel Seymour, 365–405. Calgary: University of Calgary Press, 1998.

Brink, Bert van den. "Imagining Civic Relations in the Moment of Their Breakdown: A Crisis of Civic Integrity in the Netherlands." In Laden and Owen, *Multiculturalism and Political Theory,* 350–72.

Brown, Mark B. "Survey Article: Citizen Panels and the Concept of Representation." *Journal of Political Philosophy* 14, no. 2 (2006): 203–25.

Burke, Edmund. "Speech to the Electors of Bristol." *The Online Library of Liberty* http://oll .libertyfund.org/?option=com_staticxt&staticfile=show.php%3Ftitle=659&chapter= 20392&layout=html&Itemid=27 (accessed May 23, 2011).

Burns, John F. "Cameron Criticizes 'Multiculturalism' in Britain." *New York Times,* February 5, 2011.

Camerer, Colin F. *Behavioral Game Theory: Experiments in Strategic Interaction.* Princeton: Princeton University Press, 2003.

Carens, Joseph. *Culture, Community, and Citizenship: A Contextual Exploration of Justice as Evenhandedness.* Oxford: Oxford University Press, 2000.

Carnavale, Sharon Chad, and Peter Carnavale. "Partisanship Effects in Judgments of Fairness and Trust in Third Parties in the Palestinian-Israeli Conflict." *Journal of Conflict Resolution* 38, no. 3 (1994): 423–51.

Cesari, Jocelyne, and Seán McLoughlin, eds. *European Muslims and the Secular State*. Surrey: Ashgate, 2005.

Chambers, Clare. *Sex, Culture, and Justice: The Limits of Choice*. University Park: The Pennsylvania State University Press, 2007.

Chambers, Simone, and Jeffrey Kopstein. "Bad Civil Society." *Political Theory* 29, no. 6 (2001): 837–65.

Chanley, Virginia A., Thomas J. Rudolph, and Wendy M. Rahn. "The Origins and Consequences of Public Trust in Government: A Time Series Analysis." *Public Opinion Quarterly* 64 (2000): 239–56.

Cohen, Jean. "Trust, Voluntary Association, and Workable Democracy: The Contemporary American Discourse of Civil Society." In Warren, *Democracy and Trust*, 208–48.

Cohen, Joshua. "Deliberation and Democratic Legitimacy." In Bohman and Rehg, *Deliberative Democracy*, 67–92.

Coleman, James. *Foundations of Social Theory*. Cambridge: Belknap Press, 1998.

Cook, Karen S., and Robin M. Cooper. "Experimental Studies of Cooperation, Trust, and Social Exchange." In *Trust and Reciprocity*, edited by Elinor Ostrom and James Walker, 209–44. New York: Russell Sage Foundation, 2003.

Cook, Karen S., Russell Hardin, and Margaret Levi. *Cooperation Without Trust?* New York: Russell Sage Foundation, 2005.

Costa, Dora L., and Matthew E. Kahn. "Civic Engagement and Community Heterogeneity: An Economist's Perspective." *Perspectives on Politics* 1, no. 1 (2003): 103–11.

Couch, Laurie L., and Warren H. Jones. "Measuring Levels of Trust." *Journal of Research in Personality* 31, no. 3 (1997): 319–36.

Council of Europe. *White Paper on Intercultural Dialogue: Living Together as Equals in Dignity*. Strasbourg: Council of Europe, 2008.

Crepaz, Markus. "If You Are My Brother, I May Give You a Dime! Public Opinion on Multiculturalism, Trust, and the Welfare State." In Banting and Kymlicka, *Multiculturalism and the Welfare State*, 92–120.

———. *Trust Beyond Borders: Immigration, the Welfare State, and Identity in Modern Societies*. Ann Arbor: University of Michigan Press, 2007.

Dalton, Russell. *Democratic Challenges, Democratic Choices: The Erosion of Political Support in Advanced Industrial Democracies*. Oxford: Oxford University Press, 2007.

Dawes, Robyn M., Alphons J. C. van de Kragt, and John M. Orbell. "Cooperation for the Benefit of Us—Not Me or My Conscience." In Mansbridge, *Beyond Self-Interest*, 97–110.

De Cremer, David, Mark Snyder, and Siegfried Dewitte. "The Less I Trust, the Less I Contribute (or Not)? The Effects of Trust, Accountability, and Self-Monitoring in Social Dilemmas." *European Journal of Social Psychology* 31, no. 1 (2001): 93–107.

De Cremer, David, and Mark Van Vugt. "Social Identification Effects in Social Dilemmas: A Transformation of Motives." *European Journal of Social Psychology* 29 (1999): 871–93.

Dees, Richard. *Trust and Toleration*. London: Routledge, 2004.

Delacourt, Susan. "More Ethnic Diversity Means Less Trust." *Ottawa Citizen*, December 6, 2001.

D'Emilio, Frances. "Speak Our Language or Leave: Europe Tightens the Linguistic Screws on Immigrants." *The Associated Press*, March 5, 2011.

Deveaux, Monique. *Gender and Justice in Multicultural Liberal States*. Oxford: Oxford University Press, 2007.

Diamond, Larry. *Developing Democracy: Toward Consolidation*. Baltimore: Johns Hopkins University Press, 1998.

Diamond, Larry, and Marc F. Plattner, eds. *Nationalism, Ethnic Conflict, and Democracy*. Baltimore: Johns Hopkins University Press, 1994.

Dickason, Olive P. *Canada's First Nations: A History of Founding Peoples from Earliest Times.* Toronto: McClelland & Stewart, 1992.

Dryzek, John. *Deliberative Democracy and Beyond: Liberals, Critics, Contestations.* Oxford: Oxford University Press, 2000.

———. "Deliberative Democracy in Divided Societies." *Political Theory* 33, no. 2 (2005): 218–42.

———. *Discursive Democracy.* Cambridge: Cambridge University Press, 1990.

Dunn, John. *The History of Political Philosophy.* Cambridge: Cambridge University Press, 1995.

Dyck, Joshua J. "Initiated Distrust." *American Politics Research* 37, no. 4 (2009): 539–68.

Eisenberg, Avigail. "Equality, Trust, and Multiculturalism." In Kay and Johnston, *Social Capital, Diversity, and the Welfare State,* 67–92.

———. *Reasons of Identity: A Normative Guide to the Political and Legal Assessment of Identity Claims.* Oxford: Oxford University Press, 2009.

Ejobowah, John Boye. *Competing Claims to Recognition in the Nigerian Public Sphere: A Liberal Argument About Justice in Plural Societies.* Maryland: Lexington, 2001.

Elster, Jon, ed. *Deliberative Democracy.* Cambridge: Cambridge University Press, 1998.

Engle-Warnick, Jim, and Robert Slonim. "The Evolution of Strategies in a Repeated Trust Game." *Journal of Economic Behavior & Organization* 55, no. 4 (2004): 553–73.

Fahey, Tony, Bernadette C. Hayes, and Richard Sinnott. *Conflict and Consensus: A Study of Values and Attitudes in the Republic of Ireland and Northern Ireland.* Dublin: Institute of Public Administration, 2005.

Fatah, Tareh, and Farzana Hassan. "The Deadly Face of Muslim Extremism." *The National Post,* December 12, 2007.

Fehr, Ernst, and Simon Gächter. "Cooperation and Punishment in Public Goods Experiments." *The American Economic Review* 90, no. 4 (2000): 980–94.

Fennema, Meindert, and Marcel Maussen. "Dealing with Extremists in Public Discussion: Front National and The 'Republican Front' In France." *Journal of Political Philosophy* 8, no. 3 (2000): 379–400.

Festenstein, Mathew. "National Identity, Political Trust, and the Public Realm." *Critical Review of International Social and Political Philosophy* 12, no. 2 (2009): 279–96.

———. *Negotiating Diversity: Culture, Deliberation, Trust.* Cambridge: Polity, 2005.

Fischbacher, Urs, Simon Gachter, and Ernst Fehr. "Are People Conditionally Cooperative? Evidence from a Public Goods Experiment." *Economic Letters* 71 (2001): 397–404.

Fishkin, James S., and Peter Laslett, eds. *Debating Deliberative Democracy.* Oxford: Blackwell, 2003.

Foner, Nancy, and Richard Alba. "The Second Generation from the Last Great Wave of Immigration: Setting the Record Straight." *Migration Information Source,* October 2006. http://www.migrationinformation.org/feature/display.cfm?ID=439.

Forbes, Hugh Donald. "Is Bridging Not Bonding? Social Capital and Ethnic Conflict." Paper presented to the European Research Centre on Migration and Ethnic Relations, Utrecht University, 2009.

Franks, Mary Anne. "That Obscure Object of Concern: Selective Feminism and the Rise of Anti-Sharia Laws." *Concurring Opinions,* February 16, 2011.

Fukuyama, Francis. "Identity and Migration." *Prospect Magazine,* February 25, 2007.

———. *Trust: The Social Virtues and the Creation of Prosperity.* New York: Free Press, 1995.

Gambetta, Diego. "Can We Trust Trust?" In Gambetta, *Trust,* 213–37.

———, ed. *Trust: Making and Breaking Cooperative Relations.* Oxford: Blackwell, 1988.

Gamm, Joe. "Hispanic Council Aids Cultural Integration." *The Daily Astorian,* May 27, 2009.

Gitlin, Todd. *Twilight of Common Dreams.* New York: Henry Holt, 1995.

Glaeser, Edward L., David I. Laibson, José A. Scheinkman, and Christine L. Soutter. "Measuring Trust." *The Quarterly Journal of Economics* 115, no. 3 (2000): 811–46.

Goodhart, David. "Too Diverse?" *Prospect Magazine,* February 2004.

Goodman, Sara Wallace. "Controlling Immigration Through Language and Country Knowledge Requirements." *West European Politics* 34, no. 2 (2011): 235–55.

———. "Integration Requirements for Integration's Sake? Identifying, Categorising and Comparing Civic Integration Policies." *Journal of Ethnic and Migration Studies* 36, no. 5 (2010): 753–72.

Gormley-Heenan, Cathy, and Paula Devine. "The 'Us' in Trust: Who Trusts Northern Ireland's Political Institutions and Actors?" *Government and Opposition* 45, no. 2 (2010): 143–65.

Govier, Trudy. "Distrust as a Practical Problem." *Journal of Social Philosophy* 23, no. 1 (1992): 52–63.

Gunnthorsdottira, Anna, Daniel Houserb, and Kevin McCabe. "Disposition, History, and Contributions in Public Goods Experiments." *Journal of Economic Behavior & Organization* 62, no. 2 (2007): 304–15.

Gutmann, Amy, and Dennis Thompson. *Democracy and Disagreement.* Cambridge: Harvard University Press, 1996.

Hamilton, Graeme. "Welcome! Leave Your Customs at the Door." *National Post,* January 30, 2007.

Hardin, Russell, ed. *Distrust.* New York: Russell Sage Foundation, 2004.

———. "Street-Level Epistemology and Democratic Participation." *Journal of Political Philosophy* 10, no. 2 (2002): 212–29.

———. "The Street-Level Epistemology of Trust." In *Organizational Trust: A Reader,* edited by Roderick M. Kramer, 21–47. Oxford: Oxford University Press, 2006.

———. *Trust.* Cambridge: Polity, 2006.

———. *Trust and Trustworthiness.* New York: Russell Sage Foundation, 2002.

———. "Trusting Persons, Trusting Institutions." In *Strategy and Choice,* edited by R. Zechauser, 185–209. Cambridge: MIT Press, 1991.

Hart, Vivien. *Distrust and Democracy: Political Distrust in Britain and America.* Cambridge: Cambridge University Press, 1978.

Hellgren, Zenia, and Barbara Hobson. "Cultural Dialogues in the Good Society: The Case of Honour Killings in Sweden." *Ethnicities* 8, no. 3 (2008): 385–404.

Hetherington, Mark J. *Why Trust Matters: Declining Political Trust and the Demise of American Liberalism.* Princeton: Princeton University Press, 2005.

Hewstone, Miles, Ed Cairns, Alberto Voci, Juergen Hamberger, and Ulrike Niens. "Intergroup Contact, Forgiveness, and Experience Of 'The Troubles' In Northern Ireland." *Journal of Social Issues* 62, no. 1 (2006): 99–120.

Hewstone, Miles, Mark Rubin, and Hazel Willis. "Intergroup Bias." *Annual Review of Psychology* 53 (2002): 575–604.

Hobbes, Thomas. *Leviathan.* Edited and with an introduction by C. B. Macpherson. New York: Penguin, 1981 [first published 1651].

Hollis, Martin. *Trust Within Reason.* Cambridge: Cambridge University Press, 1998.

Holmberg, Sören. "Down and Down We Go: Political Trust in Sweden." In *Critical Citizens: Global Support for Democratic Government,* edited by Pippa Norris, 103–23. Oxford: Oxford University Press, 1999.

Hooghe, Marc. "Social Capital and Diversity, Generalized Trust, Social Cohesion, and Regimes of Diversity." *Canadian Journal of Political Science* 40, no. 03 (2007): 709–32.

———. "Voluntary Associations and Democratic Attitudes: Value Congruence as a Causal Mechanism." In Hooghe and Stolle, *Generating Social Capital,* 89–112.

Hooghe, Marc, and Dietlind Stolle, eds. *Generating Social Capital: Civil Society and Institutions in Comparative Perspective.* New York: Palgrave Macmillan, 2003.

Hopkins, Daniel J. "The Diversity Discount: When Increasing Ethnic and Racial Diversity Prevents Tax Increases." *The Journal of Politics* 71, no. 1 (2009): 160–77.

Horowitz, Donald L. "Democracy in Divided Societies." *Journal of Democracy* 4, no. 4 (1993): 18–38.

———. "Some Realism About Peacemaking." Paper presented to the conference on Facing Ethnic Conflict: Perspectives from Research and Policy Making. Organized by the Center for Development Research. Bonn, Germany, December 14–16, 2000.

Hundley, Tom. "Dutch to Muslims: Do You Really Want to Settle Here?" *The Chicago Tribune*, April 9, 2006.

Huntington, Samuel. *Who Are We? Challenges to America's National Identity.* New York: Simon & Schuster, 2004.

Isaac, Jad. *Core Issues of the Palestinian-Israeli Water Dispute.* Jerusalem: Applies Research Institute, 1996.

Johnson, Peter. *Frames of Deceit: A Study of the Loss and Recovery of Public and Private Trust.* Cambridge: Cambridge University Press, 1993.

Jones, Karen. "Trust as an Affective Attitude." *Ethics* 107, no. 1 (1996): 4–25.

Joppke, Christian. "Immigrants and Civic Integration in Western Europe." In *Belong? Diversity, Recognition, and Shared Citizenship in Canada,* edited by Keith Banting, Thomas J. Courchene, and F. Leslie Seidle, 321–50. Montreal: Institute for Research on Public Policy, 2007.

———. *The Veil: Mirror of Identity.* Cambridge: Polity, 2009.

Jordan, Miriam. "Arizona Grades Teachers on Fluency." *The Wall Street Journal,* April 30, 2010.

Kamel, Kareem M. "Beyond Miss World: Muslim Protest in Nigeria." *OnIslam,* February 6, 2003. http://www.onislam.net/english/politics/atrica/414453.html.

Kay, Fiona M., and Richard Johnston. *Social Capital, Diversity, and the Welfare State.* Vancouver: University of British Columbia Press, 2007.

Kiwan, Dina. "A Journey to Citizenship in the United Kingdom." *International Journal on Multicultural Societies* 10, no. 1 (2008): 60–65.

Klausen, Jytte. *The Islamic Challenge: Politics and Religion in Western Europe.* Oxford: Oxford University Press, 2005.

Knack, Stephen. "Civic Norms, Social Sanctions, and Turnout." *Rationality and Society* 4, no. 2 (1992): 133–52.

Knack, Stephen, and Martha E. Kropf. "For Shame! The Effect of Community Cooperative Context on the Probability of Voting." *Political Psychology* 19, no. 3 (1998): 585–99.

Knight, Jack. "Social Norms and the Rule of Law: Fostering Trust in a Socially Diverse Society." In *Trust and Society,* edited by Karen Cook, 354–73. New York: Russell Sage Foundation, 2001.

Komorita, Samuel E., and Craig D. Parks. *Social Dilemmas.* Wisconsin: Brown & Benchmark, 1994.

Korteweg, Anna C. "The Sharia Debate in Ontario: Gender, Islam, and Representations of Muslim Women's Agency." *Gender & Society* 22, no. 4 (2008): 434–54.

Kramer, Roderick M. "Collective Paranoia: Distrust Between Social Groups." In Hardin, *Distrust,* 136–66.

Kymlicka, Will. *Finding Our Way: Rethinking Ethnocultural Relations in Canada.* Oxford: Oxford University Press, 1998.

———. "The Rise and Fall of Multiculturalism? New Debates on Inclusion and Accommodation in Diverse Societies." In Vertovec, *The Multiculturalism Backlash,* 32–49.

Labonne, Julien, Dan Biller, and Rob Chase. "Inequality and Relative Wealth: Do They Matter for Trust? Evidence from Poor Communities in the Philippines." *Social Development Papers. Community Driven Development,* no. 103 (March 2007). The Social Development

Department Working Papers Series, edited by the Social Development Department of the Sustainable Development Network of the World Bank.

Laborde, Cecile. *Critical Republicanism: The Hijab Controversy and Political Philosophy.* Oxford: Oxford University Press, 2008.

———. "Secular Philosophy and Muslim Headscarves." *Journal of Political Philosophy* 13, no. 5 (2005): 305–29.

Laden, Anthony Simon. "Negotiation, Deliberation, and the Claims of Politics." In Laden and Owen, *Multiculturalism and Political Theory*, 198–218.

Laden, Anthony Simon, and David Owen, eds. *Multiculturalism and Political Theory.* Cambridge: Cambridge University Press, 2007.

Lal, Brij V. "Constitutional Engineering in Fiji." In Reynolds, *The Architecture of Democracy*, 267–93.

La Porta, Rafael, Florencio Lopez-De-Silanes, Andrei Shleifer, and Robert Vishny. "The Quality of Government." *Journal of Law, Economics, and Organization* 15, no. 1 (1999): 222–79.

Larson, Deborah Welsh. "Distrust: Prudent, If Not Always Wise." In Hardin, *Distrust*, 34–59.

Lehning, Percy, ed. *Theories of Secession.* London: Routledge, 1998.

Lenard, Patti Tamara. "The Decline of Trust, the Decline of Democracy?" *Critical Review of International Social and Political Philosophy* 8, no. 3 (2005): 363–78.

———. "Deliberating Sincerely: A Reply to Warren." *Journal of Social Philosophy* 39, no. 4 (2008): 625–38.

———. "Rebuilding Trust in an Era of Widening Inequality." *Journal of Social Philosophy* 41, no. 1 (2010): 73–91.

———. "Shared Public Culture: A Reliable Source of Trust." *Contemporary Political Theory* 6, no. 4 (2007): 385–404.

———. "What Can Multicultural Theory Tell Us About Integrating Muslims in Europe?" *Political Studies Review* 8, no. 3 (2010): 308–21.

Letki, Natalia. "Does Diversity Erode Social Cohesion? Social Capital and Race in British Neighbourhoods." *Political Studies* 56 (2008): 99–126.

Levine, John M., and Richard L. Moreland. "Group Reactions to Loyalty and Disloyalty." In *Group Cohesion, Trust, and Solidarity*, edited by Shane R. Thye and Edward J. Lawler, 203–28. London: Elsevier, 2002.

Levy, Jacob. *Multiculturalism of Fear.* Oxford: Oxford University Press, 2000.

Lewandowski, Joseph D., ed. *Trust and Transitions: Social Capital in a Changing World.* Newcastle: Cambridge Scholars, 2008.

Lijphart, Arend. *Democracy in Plural Societies: A Comparative Exploration.* New Haven: Yale University Press, 1984.

Locke, John. *Second Treatise on Government.* Edited and with an introduction by C. B. Macpherson. Indianapolis: Hackett, 1980 [first published 1690].

Lovell, David W. "Trust and the Politics of Postcommunism." *Communist and Post-Communist Studies* 34, no. 1 (2001): 27–38.

Lowenheim, Oded, and Orit Gazit. "Power and Examination: A Critique of Citizenship Tests." *Security Dialogue* 40, no. 2 (2009): 145–67.

Luttmer, Erzo F. P. "Group Loyalty and the Taste for Redistribution." *Journal of Political Economy* 109, no. 3 (2001).

Luttmer, Erzo F. P., and Monica Singhal. "Culture, Context, and the Taste for Redistribution." *American Economic Journal: Economic Policy* 3, no. 1 (2011): 157–79.

Mackey, Robert. "Arizona Law Curbs Ethnic Studies Classes." *The Lede: A New York Times Blog*, May 13, 2010.

Maloy, Jason S. "Two Concepts of Trust." *Journal of Politics* 71, no. 2 (2009): 492–505.

Manin, Bernard. *The Principles of Representative Government*. Cambridge: Cambridge University Press, 1997.

Mansbridge, Jane J., ed. "Altruistic Trust." In Warren, *Democracy and Trust*, 290–309.

———. *Beyond Self-Interest*. Chicago, University of Chicago Press, 1990.

———. "On the Relation of Altruism and Self-Interest." In Mansbridge, *Beyond Self-Interest*, 133–44.

———. "Should Blacks Represent Blacks and Women Represent Women? A Contingent 'Yes.'" *The Journal of Politics* 61, no. 3 (1999): 628–57.

Marková, Ivana, ed. *Trust and Democratic Transition in Post-Communist Europe*. Oxford: Oxford University Press, 2004.

Markovits, Elizabeth. "The Trouble with Being Earnest: Deliberative Democracy and the Sincerity Norm." *Journal of Political Philosophy* 14, no. 3 (2006): 249–69.

Marschall, Melissa J., and Dietlind Stolle. "Race and the City: Neighborhood Context and the Development of Generalized Trust." *Political Behavior* 26, no. 2 (2004): 125–53.

Mason, Andrew. *Community, Solidarity, and Belonging: Levels of Community and Their Normative Significance* Cambridge: Cambridge University Press, 2000.

McCabe, Kevin A., Mary L. Rigdon, and Vernon L. Smith. "Positive Reciprocity and Intentions in Trust Games." *Journal of Economic Behavior & Organization* 52, no. 2 (2003): 267–75.

McDonnell, Lorraine M., and M. Stephen Weatherford. *State Standards-Setting and Public Deliberation: The Case of California*. CSE Technical Report 506. National Center for Research on Evaluation, Standards, and Student Testing. Graduate School of Education & Information Studies, University of California, Los Angeles. September 1999.

McGeer, Victoria. "Developing Trust." *Philosophical Explorations* 5, no. 1 (2002): 21–38.

McGhee, Derek. *The End of Multiculturalism? Terrorism, Integration, and Human Rights*. Maidenhead: Open University Press, 2008.

McGlynn, Claire. "Integrated Education in Northern Ireland in the Context of Critical Multiculturalism." *Irish Educational Studies* 22, no. 3 (2003): 11–27.

McLaren, Lauren M. "Immigration and Trust in Politics in Britain." *British Journal of Political Science* (forthcoming).

Medrano, Lourdes. "Ethnic Studies Classes Illegal in Arizona Public Schools as of Jan. 1." *Christian Science Monitor*, December 31, 2010.

Miguel, Edward, and Mary Kay Gugerty. "Ethnic Diversity, Social Sanctions, and Public Goods in Kenya." *Journal of Public Economics* 89, nos. 11–12 (2005): 2325–68.

Miles, Alice. "Denial Is Opening the Door to the Extremists." *The London Times*, June 3, 2009.

Mill, John Stuart. "Considerations on Representative Government." In *On Liberty and Other Essays*, edited by John Gray, 205–470. Oxford: Oxford University Press, 1998.

Miller, David. "Immigration: The Case for Limits." In *Contemporary Debates in Applied Ethics*, edited by Andrew Cohen and Christopher Wellman, 193–207. Malden: Blackwell, 2005.

———. *On Nationality*. Oxford: Oxford University Press, 1995.

Modood, Tariq. "Is Multiculturalism Dead?" *Public Policy Research* 15, no. 2 (2008): 84–88.

Modood, Tariq, Anna Triandafyllidou, and Ricard Zapata-Barrero, eds. *Multiculturalism, Muslims, and Citizenship*. London: Routledge, 2006.

Montpetit, Jonathan. "Quebec Martial Arts Team Protests Hijab Ban." *The Toronto Star*, April 15, 2007.

Moore, Margaret. *The Ethics of Nationalism*. Oxford: Oxford University Press, 2001.

———, ed. *National Self-Determination and Secession*. Oxford: Oxford University Press, 1998.

Murighan, J. Keith, Deepak Malhotra, and J. Mark Weber. "Paradoxes of Trust: Empirical and Theoretical Departures from a Traditional Model." In *Trust and Distrust in Organizations*, edited by Roderick M. Kramer and Karen S. Cook, 293–326. New York: Russell Sage Foundation, 2004.

Navarrette, Ruben. "Commentary: Town Makes It Illegal to Fly a Foreign Flag." *CNN*, November 20, 2006. http://articles.cnn.com/2006-11-20/us/navarrette.flag_1_american-flag -mexicans-illegal-immigrants?_s=PM:US.

Newton, Kenneth. "Social and Political Trust." In *Oxford Handbook of Political Behavior*, edited by Russell J. Dalton and Hans-Dieter Klingemann, 342–61. Oxford: Oxford University Press, 2007.

Noël, Alain. "Democratic Deliberation in a Multinational Federation." *Critical Review of International Social and Political Philosophy* 9, no. 3 (2006): 419–44.

"No Stoning, Canada Migrants Told." *BBC News*, January 31, 2007. http://news.bbc.co.uk/2/hi /6316151.stm.

Nye, Joseph S., and Philip D. Zelikow. "Conclusion." In Nye, Zelikow, and King, *Why People Don't Trust Government*, 253–81.

Nye, Joseph S., Philip D. Zelikow, and David C. King, eds. *Why People Don't Trust Government*. Cambridge: Harvard University Press, 1997.

Obiyan, A. Sat. "Political Parties Under the Abubakar Transition Program and Democratic Stability in Nigeria." *Issue: A Journal of Opinion* 27, no. 1 (1999): 41–43.

Offerman, Theo, Joep Sonnemans, and Arthur Schram. "Value Orientations, Expectations, and Voluntary Contributions in Public Goods." *The Economic Journal* 106 (July 1996): 817–45.

O'Flynn, Ian. *Deliberative Democracy and Divided Societies*. New York: Palgrave Macmillan, 2006.

O'Kelly, Ciaran. "Public Institutions, Overlapping Consensus, and Trust." *Critical Review of International Social and Political Philosophy* 9, no. 4 (2006): 559–72.

O'Neill, Onora. *Autonomy and Trust in Bioethics*. Cambridge: Cambridge University Press, 2002.

———. *A Question of Trust: The BBC Reith Lectures 2002*. Cambridge: Cambridge University Press, 2002.

Osaghae, Eghosa E. "Ethnic Minorities and Federalism in Nigeria." *African Affairs* 90, no. 359 (1991): 237–58.

Osler, Audrey. "Testing Citizenship and Allegiance: Policy, Politics, and the Education of Adult Migrants in the UK." *Education, Citizenship, and Social Justice* 4 (2009): 63–79.

Ostrom, Elinor. "Collective Actions and the Evolution of Social Norms." *Journal of Economic Perspectives* 14, no. 3 (2000): 137–58.

———. *Governing the Commons: The Evolution of Institutions for Collective Action*. Cambridge: Cambridge University Press, 1990.

Parry, Geraint. "Trust, Distrust, and Consensus." *British Journal of Political Science* 6, no. 2 (1976): 129–42.

Patterson, Orlando. "Liberty Against the Democratic State: On the Historical and Contemporary Sources of American Distrust." In Warren, *Democracy and Trust*, 151–207.

Pennant, Rachel. "Diversity, Trust, and Community Participation in England." *Home Office: Research, Development, and Statistics Directorate*, 2005. http://www.blink.org .uk/docs/ho_findings_diversity_trust.pdf (2005).

Pettit, Philip. "The Cunning of Trust." *Philosophy & Public Affairs* 24, no. 3 (1995): 202–25.

———. *Republicanism: A Theory of Freedom and Government*. Oxford: Oxford University Press, 1997.

Phillips, Anne. *Multiculturalism Without Culture*. Princeton: Princeton University Press, 2006.

———. *Which Equalities Matter?* Cambridge: Polity, 1999.

Phillips, Anne, and Moira Dustin. "UK Initiatives on Forced Marriage: Regulation, Dialogue, and Exit." *Political Studies* 52, no. 3 (2004): 531–51.

Pitkin, Hannah Fenichel. *The Concept of Representation.* Berkeley and Los Angeles: University of California Press, 1967.

Poole, Oliver. "Arnie the Governor Has a Tough Role to Play." *The Daily Telegraph,* October 9, 2003.

Putnam, Robert D. "E Pluribus Unum: Diversity and Community in the Twenty-First Century. The 2006 Johan Skytte Prize Lecture." *Scandinavian Political Studies* 30, no. 2 (2007): 137–74.

———. *Making Democracy Work: Civic Traditions in Modern Italy.* Princeton: Princeton University Press, 1993.

Quong, Jonathan. "Cultural Exemptions, Expensive Tastes, and Equal Opportunities." *Journal of Applied Philosophy* 23, no. 1 (2006): 53–71.

Rabushka, Alvin, and Kenneth A. Shepsle. *Politics in Plural Societies: A Theory of Democratic Instability.* Ohio: Merrill, 1972.

Rawls, John. *Political Liberalism.* New York: Columbia University Press, 1993.

Reitz, Jeffrey G., Raymond Breton, Karen K. Dion, and Kenneth L. Dion. *Multiculturalism and Social Cohesion: Potentials and Challenges of Diversity.* New York: Springer, 2009.

Reynolds, Andrew, ed. *The Architecture of Democracy: Constitutional Design, Conflict Management, and Democracy.* Oxford: Oxford University Press, 2002.

Rosanvallon, Pierre. *Counter-Democracy: Politics in an Age of Distrust.* Cambridge: Cambridge University Press, 2008.

Rose, Richard. "Postcommunism and the Problem of Trust." *Journal of Democracy* 5, no. 3 (1994): 18–30.

Ross, Catherine E., John Mirowsky, and Shana Pribesh. "Powerlessness and the Amplification of Threat: Neighborhood Disadvantage, Disorder, and Mistrust." *American Sociological Review* 66 (2001): 568–91.

Sanders, Lynn M. "Against Deliberation." *Political Theory* 25, no. 3 (1997): 347–76.

Santa-Cruz, Nicole. "Arizona Bill Targeting Ethnic Studies Signed into Law." *Los Angeles Times,* May 12, 2010.

Saunders, Harold. *A Public Peace Process: Sustained Dialogue to Transform Racial and Ethnic Conflicts.* New York: St. Martin's Press, 1999.

Saward, Michael. *The Representative Claim.* Oxford: Oxford University Press, 2010.

Scheffler, Samuel. "Immigration and the Significance of Culture." *Philosophy and Public Affairs* 35, no. 2 (2007): 93–125.

Schweitzer, Maurice, John C. Hershey, and Eric T. Bradlow. "Promises and Lies: Restoring Violated Trust." *Organizational Behavior and Human Decision Processes* 101, no. 1 (2006): 1–19.

Shachar, Ayelet. "Privatizing Diversity: A Cautionary Tale from Religious Arbitration in Family Law." *Theoretical Inquiries in Law* 9, no. 2 (2008). http://www.bepress.com/til /default/vol9/iss2/art11/.

Shang, Jen, and Rachel Croson. "A Field Experiment in Charitable Contribution: The Impact of Social Information on the Voluntary Provision of Public Goods." *The Economic Journal* 119, no. 540 (2009): 1422–39.

Shapiro, Ian, Susan C. Stokes, Elizabeth Jean Wood, and Alexander S. Kirshner, eds. *Political Representation.* Cambridge: Cambridge University Press, 2010.

Shorten, Andrew. "Cultural Exemptions, Equality, and Basic Interests." *Ethnicities* 10, no. 1 (2010): 100–126.

Skinner, Quentin. "The Paradoxes of Political Liberty." In *Equal Freedom,* edited by Stephen Darwall, 227–50. Ann Arbor: University of Michigan Press, 1995.

———. "The Republican Ideal of Political Liberty." In *Machiavelli and Republicanism,* edited by Gisela Bock, Quentin Skinner, and Maurizio Viroli, 293–309. Cambridge: Cambridge University Press, 1990.

Smith, Graham. *Deliberative Democracy and the Environment.* London: Routledge, 2003.
———. *Democratic Innovations: Designing Institutions for Citizen Participation.* Cambridge: Cambridge University Press, 2009.
Sniderman, Paul M., and Louk Hagendoorn. *When Ways of Life Collide.* Princeton: Princeton University Press, 2007.
Soroka, Stuart N., John F. Helliwell, and Richard Johnston. "Measuring and Modelling Trust." In Kay, *Social Capital, Diversity, and the Welfare State,* 95–132.
Soroka, Stuart N., Richard Johnston, and Keith Banting. "Ethnicity, Trust, and the Welfare State." In *Cultural Diversity Versus Economic Solidarity,* edited by Philippe Van Parijs, 33–58. Brussels: De Boeck, 2004.
Statistics Canada. "Ethnic Diversity Survey: Portrait of a Multicultural Society." 2003.
Stolle, Dietlind. "The Sources of Social Capital." In Hooghe and Stolle, *Generating Social Capital,* 19–43.
"Strike Multiculturalism from the National Vocabulary." *Globe and Mail,* October 8, 2010.
Suberu, Rotimi, and Larry Diamond. "Institutional Design, Ethnic Conflict Management, and Democracy in Nigeria." In Reynolds, *The Architecture of Democracy,* 400–428.
Tolbert, Caroline J., and Rodney E. Hero. "Dealing with Diversity: Racial/Ethnic Context and Social Policy Change." *Political Research Quarterly* 54, no. 3 (2001): 571–604.
Trew, Karen. "Catholic-Protestant Contact in Northern Ireland." In *Contact and Conflict in Intergroup Encounters,* edited by Miles Hewstone and Rupert Brown, 93–106. Oxford: Basil Blackwell, 1986.
Tworzecki, Hubert. "A Disaffected New Democracy? Identities, Institutions, and Civic Engagement in Post-Communist Poland." *Communist and Post-Communist Studies* 41, no. 1 (2008): 47–62.
Tyler, Tom. "Trust and Democratic Governance." In *Trust and Governance,* edited by Valerie Braithwaite and Margaret Levi, 269–94. New York: Russell Sage Foundation, 2003.
Tyler, Tom, and Peter Degoey. "Trust in Organizational Authorities: The Influence of Motive Attributes on Willingness to Accept Decisions." In *Trust in Organizations: Frontiers of Theory and Research,* edited by Roderick M. Kramer and Tom R. Tyler, 331–55. London: Sage Publications, 1996.
Urbinati, Nadia. *Representative Democracy: Principles and Genealogy.* Chicago: University of Chicago Press, 2006.
Urbinati, Nadia, and Mark E. Warren. "The Concept of Representation in Contemporary Democratic Theory." *Annual Review of Political Science* 11 (2008): 387–412.
Uslaner, Eric. *The Moral Foundations of Trust.* Cambridge: Cambridge University Press, 2003.
———. "Segregation, Mistrust, and Minorities." *Ethnicities* 10, no. 4 (2010): 415–34.
Uslaner, Eric M., and Mitchell Brown. "Inequality, Trust, and Civic Engagement." *American Politics Research* 33, no. 6 (2005): 868–94.
Valadez, Jorge. *Deliberative Democracy, Political Legitimacy, and Self-Determination in Multicultural Societies.* Boulder: Westview Press, 2001.
Vertovec, Steven. "Towards Post-Multiculturalism? Changing Communities, Conditions, and Contexts of Diversity." *International Social Science Journal* 61, no. 199 (2010): 83–95.
Vertovec, Steven, and Susanne Wessendorf. "Assessing the Backlash Against Multiculturalism in Europe." In *The Multiculturalism Backlash: European Discourses, Policies, and Practices,* edited by Steven Vertovec and Susanne Wessendorf, 1–31. London: Routledge, 2010.
Walker, Dionne. "Muslim Woman Jailed over Head Scarf in Georgia." *The Huffington Post,* December 17, 2008. http://www.huffingtonpost.com/2008/12/17/muslim-woman-jailed -over-_n_151858.html.
Warren, Mark E. "Deliberative Democracy and Authority." *American Political Science Review* 90, no. 1 (1996): 46–60.

———. "Democracy and Deceit: Regulating Appearances of Corruption." *American Journal of Political Science* 50, no. 1 (2006): 160–74.

———, ed. *Democracy and Trust*. Cambridge: Cambridge University Press, 1999.

———. "Democratic Theory and Trust." In Warren, *Democracy and Trust*, 310–45.

———. "Introduction." In Warren, *Democracy and Trust*, 1–21.

———. "Political Corruption as Duplicitous Exclusion." *PS: Political Science & Politics* 39, no. 4 (2006): 803–7.

———. "What Does Corruption Mean in a Democracy?" *American Journal of Political Science* 48, no. 2 (2004): 328–43.

———. "What Should and Should Not Be Said: Deliberating Sensitive Issues." *Journal of Social Philosophy* 37, no. 2 (2006): 163–81.

———. "What Should We Expect from More Democracy?: Radically Democratic Responses to Politics." *Political Theory* 24, no. 2 (1996): 241–70.

Weinstock, Daniel. "Building Trust in Divided Societies." *Journal of Political Philosophy* 7, no. 3 (1999): 287–307.

———. "Four Kinds of (Post)Nation Building." In *The Fate of the Nation-State*, edited by Michel Seymour, 51–68. Montreal: McGill-Queen's University Press, 2004.

———. "The Problem of Civic Education in Multicultural Societies." In *The Politics of Belonging: Nationalism, Liberalism, and Pluralism*, edited by Alain Dieckhoff, 106–24. Lanham, Md.: Lexington, 2004.

———. "Towards a Normative Theory of Federalism." *International Social Science Journal* 53, no. 167 (2002): 75–83.

Werner, Suzanne. "The Precarious Nature of Peace: Resolving the Issues, Enforcing the Settlement, and Renegotiating the Terms." *American Journal of Political Science* 43, no. 3 (1999): 912–34.

Wikan, Uni. "Deadly Distrust: Honor Killings and Swedish Multiculturalism." In Hardin, *Distrust*, 192–204.

Williams, Bernard. *Truth and Truthfulness: An Essay in Genealogy*. Princeton: Princeton University Press, 2004.

Williams, Melissa. *Voice, Trust, and Memory: Marginalized Groups and the Failings of Liberal Representation*. Princeton: Princeton University Press, 1998.

Williams, Michelle Hale. "Can Leopards Change Their Spots? Between Xenophobia and Trans-Ethnic Populism Among West European Far Right Parties." *Nationalism and Ethnic Politics* 16, no. 1 (2010): 111–34.

Worth, Robert F. "Iraq's New President Names Shiite Leader as Prime Minister." *New York Times*, April 7, 2005.

Young, Iris Marion. *Inclusion and Democracy*. Oxford: Oxford University Press, 2000.

Zimmerman, Lynn. "The English-Only Movement." In *Language of the Land: Policy, Politics, Identity*, edited by Katherine Schuster and David Witkosky, 115–30. Charlotte: Information Age, 2007.

Zureik, Elia, Fouad Moughrabi, and Vincent F. Sacco. "Perception of Legal Inequality in Deeply Divided Societies: The Case of Israel." *International Journal of Middle East Studies* 25, no. 3 (1993): 423–42.

Index